Sites of Transformation

Performance + Design is a series of monographs and essay collections that explore understandings of performance design and scenography, examining the potential of the visual, spatial, material and environmental to shape performative encounters and to offer sites for imaginative exchange. This series focuses on design both for and as performance in a variety of contexts, including theatre, art installations, museum displays, mega-events, site-specific and community-based performance, street theatre, design of public space, festivals, protests and state-sanctioned spectacle.

Performance + Design takes as its starting point the growth of scenography and the expansion from theatre or stage design to a wider notion of scenography as a spatial practice. As such, it recognizes the recent accompanying interest from a number of converging scholarly disciplines (theatre, performance, art, architecture, design) and examines twenty-first-century practices of performance design in the context of debates about postdramatic theatre, aesthetic representation, visual and material culture, spectatorship, participation and co-authorship.

Series Editors
Stephen Di Benedetto, Joslin McKinney and Scott Palmer

Contemporary Scenography: Practices and Aesthetics in German Theatre, Arts and Design
Edited by Birgit Wiens
978-1-3500-6447-8

The History and Theory of Environmental Scenography: Second Edition
Arnold Aronson
978-1-4742-8396-0

Immersion and Participation in Punchdrunk's Theatrical Worlds
Carina E. I. Westling
978-1-3501-0195-1

The Model as Performance: Staging Space in Theatre and Architecture
Thea Brejzek and Lawrence Wallen
978-1-350-09590-8

Scenography Expanded: An Introduction to Contemporary Performance Design
Edited by Joslin McKinney and Scott Palmer
978-1-4742-4439-8

Sound Effect: The Theatre We Hear
Ross Brown
978-1-3500-4590-3

Consuming Scenography: The Shopping Mall as a Theatrical Experience
Nebojša Tabački
978-1-3501-1089-2

Digital Scenography: 30 Years of Experimentation and Innovation in Performance and Interactive Media
Neill O'Dwyer
978-1-3501-0731-1

Forthcoming Titles
Contemporary Performance Lighting: Experience, Creativity and Meaning
Edited by Katherine Graham, Scott Palmer and Kelli Zezulka
978-1-3501-9516-5

Sites of Transformation

Applied and Socially Engaged Scenography in Rural Landscapes

LOUISE ANN WILSON

methuen | drama
LONDON • NEW YORK • OXFORD • NEW DELHI • SYDNEY

METHUEN DRAMA
Bloomsbury Publishing Plc
50 Bedford Square, London, WC1B 3DP, UK
1385 Broadway, New York, NY 10018, USA
29 Earlsfort Terrace, Dublin 2, Ireland

BLOOMSBURY, METHUEN DRAMA and the Methuen Drama logo are trademarks of Bloomsbury Publishing Plc

First published in Great Britain 2022
Paperback edition published 2023

Copyright © Louise Ann Wilson, 2022, 2023

Louise Ann Wilson has asserted her right under the Copyright, Designs and Patents Act, 1988, to be identified as author of this work.

For legal purposes the Acknowledgements on p. xi constitute an extension of this copyright page.

Cover design: Ben Anslow
Cover image © Bethany Clarke / Artevents

All rights reserved. No part of this publication may be reproduced or transmitted in any form or by any means, electronic or mechanical, including photocopying, recording, or any information storage or retrieval system, without prior permission in writing from the publishers.

Bloomsbury Publishing Plc does not have any control over, or responsibility for, any third-party websites referred to or in this book. All internet addresses given in this book were correct at the time of going to press. The author and publisher regret any inconvenience caused if addresses have changed or sites have ceased to exist, but can accept no responsibility for any such changes.

A catalogue record for this book is available from the British Library.

Library of Congress Cataloging-in-Publication Data
Names: Wilson, Louise Ann, 1970- author.
Title: Sites of transformation : applied and socially engaged scenography in rural landscapes / Louise Ann Wilson.
Description: London; New York : Methuen Drama, 2022. |
Series: Performance + design | Includes bibliographical references and index. |
Summary: "In this book practitioner and scholar Louise Ann Wilson examines the expanding field of socially engaged scenography and promotes the development of therapeutic scenography as an applied art form. Offering an account of her own practice combined with case studies drawing on artworks from Early Romanticism and the Land Art movement of the 1960s, Elena Brotherus (Finland), Tabitha Moses (UK) and Marina Abramovic's autobiographical walking-work The Lovers: The Great Wall Walk (1988, China), this is the first book on the emerging area of site-specific and therapeutic scenography. The book analyses how Wilson's interdisciplinary, site-specific walking-performances are created in rural landscapes and seek to emplace and transform a participant's experience of challenging life-events for which traditional rites of passage or ceremonies do not exist. The book explores the therapeutic effect of Wilson's practice, which becomes an instrument for personal and social change and can be understood as a form of applied performance practice. Case studies drawn from her own practice include Fissure (2011), The Gathering (2014), Warnscale (2015), Mulliontide (2016) and Women's Walks to Remember (2018). Each is illustrated and is supported by evidential material demonstrating the effects of the practice and research. Using this series of case studies, Wilson investigates how 'transformation' is achieved through an interdisciplinarily, three-tiered methodological process and the application of the concept of the feminine sublime, which she develops into six scenographic-led principles. These principles were informed by theories and aesthetics relating to landscape, pilgrimage, Early Romanticism, and a close study of the approach of Dorothy Wordsworth and her female contemporaries to landscape"– Provided by publisher.
Identifiers: LCCN 2021027687 (print) | LCCN 2021027688 (ebook) | ISBN 9781350104440 (hardback) | ISBN 9781350104457 (epub) | ISBN 9781350104464 (ebook)
Subjects: LCSH: Site-specific theater. | Theaters–Stage-setting and scenery. | Performance art–Psychological aspects. | Landscapes–Psychological aspects. | Wilson, Louise Ann, 1970–Themes, motives.
Classification: LCC PN2081.S58 W55 2022 (print) | LCC PN2081.S58 (ebook) | DDC 792.02/2–dc23
LC record available at https://lccn.loc.gov/2021027687
LC ebook record available at https://lccn.loc.gov/2021027688

ISBN:	HB:	978-1-3501-0444-0
	PB:	978-1-3502-8275-9
	ePDF:	978-1-3501-0446-4
	eBook:	978-1-3501-0445-7

Series: Performance and Design

Typeset by Integra Software Services Pvt. Ltd.

To find out more about our authors and books visit www.bloomsbury.com and sign up for our newsletters.

Contents

List of figures viii

Acknowledgements xi

Introduction: Setting the scene – *Sites of Transformation* 1

1   Scenography with purpose – seven scenographic principles 17

2   Walking-performance – emplacing a life-event: *Fissure* 45

3   Creating a scene – centring the visual: *Ghost Bird* 79

4   Site and materials – centring the metaphor: *The Gathering* 103

5   Mapping-walks – centring the subject: *Warnscale* 129

6   Giving a voice – centring people and place: *Mulliontide* 159

7   Applied scenography – multiple applications:
    Dorothy's Room and *Women's Walks to Remember* 181

Appendices 205

References 211

Index 221

List of figures

1.1 *Still Life* by Nigel Stewart and Louise Ann Wilson. Figure of The Woman running on the sands, Far Arnside, Morecambe Bay, Lancashire 27

1.2 *Mapping the Edge* by wilson+wilson 30

2.1 *Fissure*. Chris Clark (neurophysicist) talking to the creative team about his tractographic mapping work, UCL, London 57

2.2 *Fissure*. Transdisciplinary research. Neurosurgery at the London Hospital, London 57

2.3 *Fissure*. Transdisciplinary research. Louise Ann Wilson with Mike Kelly (geophysicist), Michael Brada (neuro-oncologist), Chris Clark (neurophysicist) and Duncan Morrison (caver) on site, Yorkshire Dales 58

2.4 *Fissure*. Day Two – Phase 4: 'Disintegration – Loss of Function – The Fall', Robin Procter's Scar, Yorkshire Dales 72

2.5 *Fissure*. Participants ascending Ingleborough Fell on Day Three – Phase 6: 'Resurgence / Resurrection', Yorkshire Dales 76

3.1 *Ghost Bird*. Pregnant Woman in Langden Castle, Trough of Bowland, Lancashire 90

3.2 *Ghost Bird*. Pointing Man, upper Langden Valley, Trough of Bowland, Lancashire 92

3.3 *Ghost Bird*. Naked Woman in shooting butt, Weasel Clough, upper Langden Valley, Trough of Bowland, Lancashire 93

LIST OF FIGURES

4.1 *The Gathering*. Site research at Hafod y Llan Farm, Snowdonia – Welsh Mountain ewes being sorted and marked for pregnancy (single, twins, empty) 110

4.2 *The Gathering*. Storyboard of Tramway Walker and Shepherds traversing the lower amphitheatre at Clogwyn, Hafod y Llan Farm, Snowdonia 115

4.3 *The Gathering*. The Woman at Cwm Llan slate quarry, Hafod y Llan Farm, Snowdonia 120

4.4 *The Gathering*. The 'Skinning of the Lamb' installation in the lambing barn, Hafod y Llan Farm, Snowdon 126

5.1 *Warnscale*. Participant with the walking guide/art book on site in the Warnscale Fells, Cumbria 131

5.2 *Warnscale*. Strand 1: Site/landscape-specific research, Warnscale Fells, Cumbria – dying and falling trees; this location became 'Landmark/Station 13 – Dying Wood (*regeneration*)' 137

5.3 *Warnscale*. Strand 2: Life-event/subject-specific research in fertility clinics – egg collection waiting and recovery room, CARE Fertility, Manchester 138

5.4 *Warnscale*. Strand 3: People/participant-specific research, Warnscale Fells, Cumbria – mapping-walk participant stepping into Black Beck Tarn; this location became 'Landmark/Station 5 – Tarn (*waiting*)' 139

5.5 *Warnscale*. Mapping-walk map drawn by participant JF 140

5.6 *Warnscale*. Participant using geology magnifying glass for close-up looking, Warnscale Fells, Cumbria 145

5.7 *Warnscale*. View/review from the window of Warnscale Head bothy over the valley bottom to Buttermere Lake, Warnscale Fells, Cumbria 147

5.8 *Warnscale*. Book page from 'Landmark/Station 8: Summit Tarn (*vitrify*)' 152

6.1 *Mulliontide*. Wendy Williamson greeting participants at 'Station 4: Kissing Gate – Meres Cliff', Mullion, Cornwall 172

6.2 *Mulliontide*. Fisherman Johnny Pascoe speaking to participants at 'Station 13: The Fishing Boat 'Laurie Jean' – Slipway' in Mullion Cove harbour, Cornwall 174

6.3 *Mulliontide*. Gail Lyons, Russ Stanland and Charlotte Douglas of the St Mellanus Singers singing and laying a wreath of white roses at 'Station 10: Closed Path – Mullion Cove', Cornwall 175

6.4 *Mulliontide*. Participant emerging from the tunnel of 'Station 14: Rock and Tide – Cave', Mullion Cove, Cornwall 178

7.1 *Walks to Remember*. Louise Ann Wilson surrogate walking 'Harold Potter's Mardale Head Walk: "When I kick the bucket, I'll have my ashes scattered at Mardale Head"' 184

7.2 *Walks to Remember*. Harold Potter and Louise Ann Wilson talking via Skype 185

7.3 *Women's Walks to Remember*. 'Margaret Crayston's Upper Eskside Walk: "As a child I walked this valley every day"' 195

7.4 *Women's Walks to Remember*. Jill Peel drawing her memory-map 'Black Combe Circuit Walk: "I envy you going for a walk"' 198

Acknowledgements

Heartfelt thanks to the following...

Those involved in the writing of this book: series editors Scott Palmer, Steven Di Benedetto and especially Joslin McKinney; Lara Bateman, Mark Dudgeon and Ella Wilson at Methuen Drama; Deborah Maloney and Joanne Rippin at Integra; Deirdre Heddon for writing the cover copy; my PhD supervisors, Geraldine Harris and Andrew Quick of Lancaster Institute for the Contemporary Arts, Lancaster University; David Honeybone and David Meikle (both of you have gone above and beyond).

Those involved in the making of the work discussed in this book: the Louise Ann Wilson Company board past and present; commissioners, producers, funders and the significant number of people who have provided support-in-kind; and the people and organizations connected to a site who have said 'yes', not changed their minds and let me get on with it!

Wils Wilson, together we created some extra-special work and I thank you for that and our friendship. Thank you also to the wilson+wilson company board, collaborators and supporters.

The scientists, sociologists, clinics, hospitals, libraries, sites and institutions that have supported my research, including those who have agreed to me drawing, sound recording or filming in strange and at times rather extreme moments(!), and to those among you who have contributed to and/or performed in a work.

The writers, composers, choreographers, makers, builders, technicians, editors, digital-whizzes, printers, layout artists, performers, dancers, singers, musicians, cavers and mountain leaders with whom I have collaborated over the years: you are many, talented and all awesome. A particular thank you to choreographer Nigel Stewart, writer Elizabeth Burns (1957–2015), film editor Janan Yakula and sound artist Lisa Whistlecroft.

All who have engaged as contributors and participants: mappers, walkers, remembers, makers and performers. Thank you for your generosity, sense of purpose and belief.

Those who have participated in a performance, for your willingness to put on walking boots and brave the elements, and to those who have participated from afar.

Introduction

Setting the scene –
Sites of Transformation

Louise's narrative invites us to look and reflect. I sat and looked at the uncurling fern; studied the grains of wood on a footbridge, reflected on the water passing underneath (time passing, life passing). As the path crossed geological boundaries I thought of life's transitions, and the burdens I carried. [...] Thank you and the many women who articulated their feelings. Your words opened my eyes and heart.

(JEFF COWTON, CURATOR, WORDSWORTH GRASMERE
IN RESPONSE TO *WARNSCALE*)

Sites of Transformation is concerned with socially engaged and applied scenography that takes the form of site-specific walking-performance in rural landscapes. To explore this 'expanded' field of scenography, the book case-studies the body of scenographic-led walking-performances I have created in the UK over the last ten years, in which rural landscapes have become sites of transformation. These walking-performances have been created on mountains, across moorland, through subterranean caves, along coastlines and over beaches. They have enabled participants to reflect upon, re-image, reimagine and transform their relationship to challenging, marginalizing or 'missing' life-events. Subjects have included terminal illness and bereavement, in/fertility and biological childlessness-by-circumstance, belonging, loss and repair (personal and to the land), (im)mobility and memory. In this process I have used scenography to emplace an underlying subject matter into rural landscapes, and in so doing have evolved a distinctive type of socially engaged and applied art and performance practice that seeks tangible, therapeutic and transformative real-world outcomes. These real-world outcomes have been experienced by people who have engaged with the walking-performances as an 'audience' member, and by people who are directly affected by the underlying subject matter and the way that the performance influences and informs the understanding, attitudes, and feelings of others. Further outcomes have been seen in the way the walking-performances have informed and influenced wider social dialogues and change. To use a phrase coined by theatre and scenography scholar Christopher Baugh, this is 'scenography with purpose' (Baugh 2012: 36).

In the context of socially engaged and applied scenography created in rural landscapes, a *site of transformation* is where three distinct strands of transdisciplinary research come together:

- *site/landscape-specific* research in rural landscape in which a walking-performance is created and performed – physically or through memory.

- *life-event-specific* research into the subject matter underpinning the walking-performance that, using a scenography, is emplaced into a rural landscape giving context, purpose and meaning to the site.

- *people/participant-specific* research with the people affected by the underlying subject matter and who engage (often through walking) with the creative process and/or the walking-performance, giving the site meaning that is personal and specific to each person.

Using scenographic processes these three strands are later combined to create walking-performances that emplace the life-event into the landscape – giving that landscape (and the performance) context, purpose and meaning. These performances are experienced by participating 'audiences' as they walk through the scenographic landscape. I have found that the more specific each strand of research is, the more effective is the *site of transformation*. Alongside these three strands, I have identified a number of features in my practice that also contribute to achieving a *site of transformation*. I have distilled these features into seven scenographic principles that offer practical ideas and a theoretical framework for creating site-specific walking-performances in rural landscapes. These principles are underpinned by the concept of the feminine 'material' sublime – a concept that I regard as being inherently scenographic – and which is informed by Dorothy Wordsworth's (1771–1855) intense looking and therapeutic use of landscape, walking and dwelling, and her female contemporaries' approach to landscape; for example, poet Charlotte Smith's (1749–1806) socially-engaged use of autobiography and the solitary female figure to reveal and value marginalised voices and lives, and writer Ann Radcliffe's (1764–1823) harnessing of the landscape as a 'theatre' of constantly changing images and perspectives to enable change – personal and social.

Central to this book is my conviction that when it embraces site, life-event and participant, and is underpinned by the feminine 'material' sublime, scenography becomes a catalyst for personal, social and cultural change. It is in this intersection where 'scenography with purpose' (Baugh 2012: 36) does its work, where participants can 'think in ways different to those determined by dominant concepts' and discourses, and where relationships to real-world situations can be changed (Lotker and Gough 2013: 50). The book explores the reasons why, as a visual, sensory, embodied and materially oriented art form, scenography is particularly suited to function in this way, and my scenographic application of:

- visual, compositional, spatial, choreographic and dramaturgical tools to design and emplace each performance in the landscape;
- transdisciplinary creative and research processes to engage collaborators and contributors from fields of practice that are both within and beyond performance;
- storyboards, drawing and map-making within the creative process and the performance;
- walking and other modes of transport as tools to mobilize, engage and immerse participants.

The act of walking is integrated into and embedded in the structure and dramaturgy of each performance, making it a key component to my scenography. Walking does two things. Firstly, walking moves participants through a landscape, takes them off the beaten track into remote sites, and immerses them in the environment and scenography. Secondly, it serves a symbolic and metaphoric function that works in relation to the life-event that is being explored. Through walking and immersion, participants experience the physical, material and environmental forces of the landscape – and the emplaced scenography – in an embodied and multisensory way. Walking is thus designed to encourage and enhance deep engagement with the *site of transformation* and encourage new ways of understanding, thinking and feeling about a life-event. As Rebecca Solnit reminds us in *Wanderlust: A History of Walking*, the act of walking 'exerts body and imagination' and moves the walker 'beyond [their] own knowledge into new possibilities' (2001:101). Across my practice I have engaged participants in solitary, side-by-side, companionable, processional and surrogate walking, and have used walking as a metaphoric and scenographic tool that promotes reflection, observation, creativity, conversation and communitas. Walking – or mobilizing participants on foot – allows them to communicate with others (or themselves) in new ways. My work has also drawn inspiration and symbolic meanings from the form, structure and place-specific practices (rituals, actions and objects) found in walking practices such as pilgrimages like the Camino De Compostela in Spain, St Cuthbert's Way in the UK and liturgical festivals such as the Easter Trideum.

In my practice I combine these walking methodologies with the mobilization of performances and my transformative aims. This means my practice intersects with the field of walking art and can be understood through the concepts of 'therapeutic landscapes' and 'therapeutic mobilities', which evolved out of the former. These interconnected concepts recognise the therapeutic, restorative and transformative potential of the act of walking in landscape. Originating in the field of health geography (Gesler 1992, 1996) therapeutic landscapes are landscapes that through 'place-specific' practices 'become associated with health and healing' (Doughty 2013: 140) and 'the act of moving from one place to another' further promotes a sense of wellbeing (Gatrell 2013: 98). The effect of participants engaging in walking, actions and visual and sensory immersion to experience the performance-scape and the 'supportive socialities and group dynamics' (Doughty 2013:14) that develop amongst participants as they move, are explored in this book.

Processes of pilgrimage and ritualized walking are found in works such as Marina Abramovic's *The Lovers: The Great Wall Walk* (1988), a pilgrimage walk along the Great Wall of China that ritually marked the ending of her relationship with her life partner and collaborator Ulay, and Carl Lavery's *Mourning Walk* (2006), a pilgrimage in memory of his late father, are both works that show how artists engage with walking as an 'integral material to their art' (Heddon and Turner 2012: 225). Creating walking works in response to life-event and autobiographic situations is also integral to work such as Clare Patey's *Empathy Museum: A Mile in My Shoes* (2016), Rhiannon Armstrong's *Public Selfcare System* (2016), Claire Collison's *An Intimate Tour of Breasts* (2016) and Rosana Cade's *Walking: Holding* (2011). To create *Mindwalks* (2017–18), the artist and writer Kate Green walked in sites which were significant to the architect Tony Collier – garden, mountain and coast. He could no longer access these physically due to the immobilizing effects of Motor Neurone Disease. Spending time in each landscape, Green used filmed imagery that captured her own feelings for the site and Collier's memories. Responding to the walking artist Hermann de Vries, who said, 'I walk therefore I am', Collier contested:

I CANNOT WALK BUT I AM – I WALK IN MY MIND: My feet washed by the sea, I leap rock to rock, climbing steep steps, I walk the cliff top.
(Collier and Green 2018, catalogue from *Mindwalks* exhibition)

In a weave of landscape and memory, Green then created a series of immersive installations, one for each landscape, that projected her filmed imagery onto domestic objects – a bed, a curtained window, a painted wall, a Japanese-style screen. These were then underscored with poetry written and spoken by Collier that 'expressed the site' as he remembered and 'walked it in his mind' (Green 2017–18). These works use walking as a means to invite participants to view the world from another person's perspective of illness, surgery or marginalization or 'experience first-hand what it is to walk in someone else's shoes – or hands' (Cade 2011). In its concern with stepping beyond physical limits, *Mindwalks* has close affinities with *Dorothy's Room* (2018) and *Women's Walks to Remember: 'With memory I was there'* (2018–19), explored in Chapter 7.

Many other contemporary performance makers, visual artists and walking artists have created site-specific works in (and inspired by) rural and mountainous landscapes that engage participants on foot and/or immerse them in a performance-scape. For example, the visually and sonically compelling work of composer Hanna Tuulikki (*Away with the Birds* (2010) and *Women of the Hill* (2015)), the company NVA, which creates large-scale performance installations such as *The Storr: Unfolding Landscapes* (2005), the writer Maria Fusco who, for *Master Rock* (2015) recorded and performed 'inside Cruachan Power Station, sited deep inside one of the highest peaks on the West coast of Scotland', and the film maker Shona Illingworth's *Lesion in the Landscape* (2015). For Illingworth, the 'depopulated island of St Kilda was a metaphor for the experience of amnesia and the historical lesions in the physical and cultural landscape of Saint Kilda' (quoted in Hawkins 2015). In *Black Rock* (2017), the scenographer-researcher David Shearing, who creates immersive scenographic environments that transpose materials and phenomena associated with one site into another, brought gritstone, water and cloud (dry ice) – materials that capture the essence of Mount Snowdon – into a studio theatre space. These materials and the space were then animated using film, voice and choreographed movement to 'capture and translate' rock climber Jonny Dawes' 'death-defying' ascent of Snowdon's vertical Indian Face into a visceral, felt experience for the audience' (Shearing 2019: 36). All these works incorporate the geo-physical and non-physical (stories, voices, myths) materials of the site.

The ensemble dance performance works by the choreographers Rosemary Lee (*Passage for Par*, 2018), performance makers Curious (Helen Paris and

Leslie Hill) (*Out of the Water*, 2012) and walking artist Hamish Fulton (*Group Walk – Penzance Beach*, 2013) were created in response to the physical and material phenomena of a coastal landscape, and used visual composition and choreographed movement and stillness to draw attention to the patterns, sensations and shape of sand, sea and cliff. These projects have echoes of *Still Life* (2008, rev. 2009) and *Jack Scout* (2010), two site-specific walking-performances I created with dance scholar and choreographer Nigel Stewart (Sap Dance) in response to different coastal locations overlooking Morecambe Bay. Both works were created using compositional techniques and rules relating to scenic paintings – line, shape, colour, texture, direction, size, perspective and space; pursued a visual, non-verbal performance language and harnessed the materials and phenomena of the site (weather, tides and sunsets. They also used the human figure, who was placed – still and moving, close-up and distant, solitary and in groups – in the landscape. This approach had the effect of the performances being experienced as living pictures or tableaux vivants that magnified and amplified the material, elemental, sonic and sensory aspects of the site – human and other-than-human.

Choreographer and performance artist Ann Carlson's site-specific dance performance *Picture Jasper Ridge: A Performance Hike* (2011) instructed participants to walk in silence to a series of 'tableaux vivants' or 'living pictures' that used actors to 're-create historic photos [dating to the 1890s] near the actual locations where the photos were taken' (Carlson 2011a). The stillness of the performers served to define and draw attention to movement in the environment, and their silence emphasized the 'sounds of the birds, squirrels, footfalls and breathing', which, remarked Carlson, became an 'unusual sound track' (Carlson 2011b).

In *The Living Mountain*, Nan Shepherd (2011: 84) wrote: 'I have walked out of the body and into the mountain.' Landscape, for Shepherd, was experienced not just through the ocular but also in embodied and multisensory ways achieved through walking, touching and dwelling in the environment. This process made the ordinary world extraordinary and led to a revelatory, deeply felt and transformative experience of the mountain, and through it of herself. 'I am not out of myself', she writes, 'but in myself' (2011: 108). Following in Shepherd's footsteps, Simone Kenyon applied immersive and embodied mountain practices when making *Into the Mountain* (2019). Made over a six-year period and culminating in a choreographed dance and choral ensemble work specific to the Scottish Cairngorms, the performance invited participants to walk 'out of our bodies and into the landscape' to seek out 'multiple perspectives of this mountainous environment' (Kenyon 2019). This embodied participation was achieved through a mix of performed movement and music combined with close-up and distance looking, listening and lying down in the landscape. The technique of becoming immersed in the landscape by experiencing it from an unfamiliar perspective is found in artist Graham Miller's *Track* (2011) and Robert Wilson, Theun Mosk and Boukje Schweigman's *Walking* (2012), both of which invite participants to lie face up on a platform and view the environment – trees and sky – from below. Similarly, in *Woodland* (2016), which forms part of French & Mottershead's *Afterlife* series (2014–18), participants are invited to lie on the woodland floor and, with closed eyes, listen to a soundtrack that describes how a dead body, if left for hours, days, weeks, years and millennia, would decompose and eventually metamorphose and become fossilized rock. These immersive performances all bring a deep, multisensory and transformative awareness of the body and the environment, and with *Woodland*, a sense of mortality. Like the other works mentioned above they also have affinities with the land and environmental work of artists such as Nancy Holt, Michelle Stewart, Ana Mendieta, Andy Goldsworthy and the company Somewhere Nowhere, who, using materials of a site, make interventions in the landscape that are designed to draw the viewers' attention to topographical features and environmental phenomena.

Though many aspects of the practice of these artists and companies intersect with my own, I have not identified work that combines a specific rural landscape, walking and performance in the context of specific life-events. It is perhaps this combination that is particular to my scenography.

Approach to writing the book – a scenographer's account

This book seeks to contribute to the widening field of scenography – known by the term 'expanded scenography' – and is designed to open up discussion and encourage new ways of thinking about scenography as an instrument for individual, social and cultural change. It seeks to demonstrate that the possibilities and applications for socially engaged and applied scenography are multiple, and can respond to a range of life-events and real-world situations within many social, health and well-being contexts. It points towards a field of practice that is not only rich in significance and possibilities but is also diverse in its application. Rooted in scenography and performance design, the book brings insights for practitioners, researchers and students working in these widening fields of practice.

As well as intersecting with site-specific and walking practices, and the associated fields of pilgrimage, the transdisciplinary nature of my practice and research means the book offers insights into fields of study adjacent to contemporary performance studies and beyond. These include autobiographical art and performance, environmental and ecological art, dance and performance, community-centred performance, cultural geography and work located at the art/performance and medical/social/environmental science interface.

Written from the perspective of a practicing scenographer, *Sites of Transformation* seeks to articulate, share and value the knowledge and skills learned through many years of professional practice, and make this knowledge 'accessible to others' (Iball and McKinney 2011: 15). Growing appreciation of knowledge gained through practice-led research means that an increasing number of professional scenographer/researchers are bringing insights from the field of practice into the academy.

Ten years ago, I suggested that scenographers have 'a unique set of creative, technical and collaborative skills' (Palmer and Wilson 2011:74). Now, I would add to that list that scenographers are also skilled in: transdisciplinary research, finding ways of engaging with people across a range of circumstances and situations, spatial and conceptual-thinking, composition and design, visual/multi-sensory scenographic-dramaturgy, and observational and visual/multi-sensory noticing. In this regard, and specifically in the context of my landscape-centred practice, the words of theatre scholar Stephen Di Benedetto about theatre and performance designers/scenographers are resonant:

> Designers are inquisitive and are interested in everything that the world has to offer as a potential inspiration for elements within their work. They are tuned to the visual world and draw from it constantly ... Designers seek out those observations by spending time in nature, looking for textures, patterns, colours, and shape.
>
> (Di Benedetto 2012: 20)

This book makes the case for these scenographer/scenographic skills. It explores the forms they take, the way in which they are rooted in materially specific practices, and how they can be applied to life-event situations and used to create rural walking-performances that become *sites of transformation*.

Background – towards socially engaged and applied scenography

The site-, subject- and person-specific walking-performances considered in this book were created between 2011 and 2021. These works build on and were informed by earlier work. Formative to my approach was my training in Theatre Design at Nottingham Trent University, UK where I learnt to analyse play texts, undertake research, design sets and costume schemes, and use models, storyboards, drawings and plans to present my ideas.[1] While studying, I also devised a body of site-specific performance works in locations that included dungeons, underground tunnels, and caves. Often using myths and poems as a starting point, these works harnessed the physical and dramatic qualities of real-world sites and moved participants on foot in and through the performance space. They also forged an appreciation of how site-specific work could produce visually-dynamic and emotionally-powerful performances that harness the fabric and materials of the site (fixed and transient) and become thick in complex levels of meaning. It also gave me a sense of how deeply and viscerally felt the work becomes when participants are mobilized, intellectually engaged, and sensorially and physically immersed in a three-dimensional experience.

As a professional theatre designer I designed productions in theatre-spaces such as the Manchester Royal Exchange in the UK and non-theatre spaces such as a four-storey derelict salt factory for the Ruhr Triennale in Essen, Germany and the River Vltava in Prague, Czech Republic. Regardless of the type of space, my design work sought to harness its architectural features and dissolve the boundary between audience-participants and stage, or removed the stage altogether.

Of further significance are the site-specific performances I co-created with director Wils Wilson as one half of the wilson+wilson company, including *House* (1998), *Mapping the Edge* (2001), *News from the Seventh Floor* (2003) and *Mulgrave* (2005). wilson+wilson worked outside theatrical hierarchies and theatre buildings, liberating us from structural and spatial limitations and decentring our practice and roles. Stepping out of the theatre building removed the divide between the performance and the audience, and meant we could challenge notions of what theatre could be, the form it might take, where it might happen and how it could engage place and people. These performances took many months and years to create, were in all aspects and elements truly site-specific – not site-responsive, site-sympathetic or site-generic – and would not have existed outside the sites in which they were created and performed. This specificity came about because they were created through in-depth site research and engaged intimately with people who knew the site, past and present. I look more closely at the site-specific and mobility aspects of this work in Chapter 1.

In the period while I was co-creating the work of wilson+wilson, I went through the five-year illness and death of my sister and the grief of her loss. Driven by the need to find a creative (and scientific) way of addressing my grief, this experience eventually led to the walking-performance work entitled

---

[1] Louise studied Theatre Design BA (Hons) at Nottingham Trent University, Nottingham, UK.

Fissure (2011), which is the subject of Chapter 2 of this book. It was this experience and performance work that marked a point of departure and a significant shift in my practice towards making scenography that deals with life-events. My aim is to take the reader inside my creative process to illuminate the work and its potential.

At the time I was developing my ideas for *Fissure*, I identified the way in which a dialogical process could inform my creative process while working on *Still Life and Jack Scout* with Nigel Stewart. The latter arose from four 'Dialogues' with people who had different knowledges of the site. These were:

> an 'Underworld Dialogue' with National Trust wardens and plant ecologists about the site's unique flora and fauna; an 'Overworld Dialogue' with RSPB educators and ornithologists about the behaviour of indigenous species of birds, butterflies and bats on the heath and migratory birds on the beach; an 'Innerworld Dialogue' with children at a nearby school for urban children with special needs; and a 'Waterworld Dialogue' with cross-bay guides and fishermen concerning fishing traditions and the Bay's infamous tides, shipwrecks and drownings. Through these dialogues the creative team used experimental cartography, writing, improvisation and notation, drawing, and photography to register and distil their own experience of the place and to evolve material that was transformed into the final performance.
>
> (Stewart and Wilson 2010b)[2]

This type of dialogical social engagement can be seen in the work of Wildworks, Wrights & Sites and French & Mottershead (the latter worked with forensic anthropologists, ecologists and conservators to create the Afterlife series). Similarly, performance makers Anne-Marie Culhane and Ruth Levene, and the performance companies Curious, and Small Acts (Katie Etheridge and Simon Persighetti) (discussed in Chapter 6) make performances that create temporary communities and put people (of a place) centre stage, an approach also seen in the work of the performance company Quarantine (discussed in Chapter 1).

Sites of Transformation *and other writing*

I have published articles and chapters about my work in *The Performance of Sacred Places* (Wilson 2021), the *Performance Research* journal special edition 'On Mountains' (Wilson 2019), the *Language, Landscape and the*

---

[2] See Stewart and Wilson (2010) and Nigel Stewart's chapter 'Spectacle, World, Environment, Void' (2015) for more discussion of this work and the dialogical process.

Sublime Symposium (on-line publication of papers) (Wilson 2016c) and the *Journal of Fertility Counselling* (Wilson 2015c). These writings look at my feminine 'material' sublime approach to the creation of walking-performance in mountainous rural landscapes in life-event contexts. *Sites of Transformation* is, however, the first publication devoted to my practice and research, and the expanded field of socially engaged and applied scenography in rural landscapes. To show both the foundations on which this area of work builds and where my practice intersects with the work of others, within the book I bring the practice of other artists working across a range of creative disciplines – historical and contemporary – into the frame.

Other insights into my practice and research written by scholars working in the field of contemporary performance can be found in the subchapter 'Scenographic Space and Place. Louise Ann Wilson in Conversation with Scott Palmer' (Palmer and Wilson 2011: 63–74), which looks at my work with wilson+wilson, in particular exploring how our site-specific practice removed barriers between the audience, space, performance and performer, engaged all the senses and was created through a socially engaged process. Josephine Machon's *Immersive Theatres: Intimacy and Immediacy in Contemporary Performance* studies how performance makers – working in and beyond theatre – use the 'power of immersive practice' to submerge participants 'in an alternative medium where all the senses are engaged and manipulated', a process, she writes, that leads to 'a deep involvement' (Machon 2013: 21–2).[3] The chapter 'Immersed in the Environment – Off the Beaten Track' explores wilson+wilson's site-specific immersive practice and the use of rural landscape as an immersive environment in *Jack Scout* and *Fissure* with a focus on how the latter used extended walking and pilgrimage-inspired practices to transport and immerse the participant – literally and metaphorically – into the landscape of the performance (a process which I explore in depth in Chapter 2).

The chapter '"Three Miles an Hour": Pedestrian Travel' in theatre scholar Fiona Wilkie's (2015) study *Performance, Transport and Mobility: Making Passage* explores my use of walking and a pilgrimage structure in *Fissure*. Two publications in the *Performing Landscape* series look at my use of rural landscape as a site for performance: Susan Haedicke's *Performing*

---

[3] Machon's book 'offers a model of practice' (2013: xvi) that encompasses case studies and a practitioner's perspective across many forms, methodologies and scales of work, including that of Blast Theory, Brith Gof, De la Guarda, Shunt, Punchdrunk, DreamThink Speak, Wildworks, Artangel, Lundahl & Seital and the one-to-one intimate performance works of Adrian Howells.

Farmscapes (2021), which studies and analyses the scenographic techniques, including storyboarding, I applied when making *The Gathering / Yr Helfa* (*The Gathering*) (2014) on a sheep farm in Wales; and Jonathan Pitches' (2020) *Performing Mountains*, wherein the chapter 'Mountain Site-Related Performance' studies my scenographic use of mountainous landscapes in *The Gathering* and *Warnscale: A Land Mark Walk Reflecting on In/fertility and Childlessness* (*Warnscale*) (2015–ongoing). Here, Pitches recognizes how my practice is deeply embedded in a site and how this is achieved through in-depth research:

> Louise Ann Wilson's work offers one example, whose immediacy and specificity has been highly valued by critics, compared to more site generic and transferable work. Wilson provides a benchmark of quality in this form, according to *The Guardian*'s Lyn Gardner, as her work is genuinely rooted in its location … turning the landscape and the topography into real players.
>
> (Pitches 2020: 17)

Organization of the book

In Chapter 1 I identify some key trends in the development of scenography over recent decades, and in particular the idea of 'scenography with purpose' (Baugh 2012:36). This contextual study is designed to locate my work within a wider set of practices, give readers a greater understanding of how my practice is conceived and help them navigate the subsequent chapters. This chapter explores the broader ideas underpinning my Seven Scenographic Principles and identifies foundational concepts, ideas and landscape-related aesthetic practices, including the picturesque, the sublime, the frame, the viewing station and the trope of the solitary figure that informed them. I look at the way they are underpinned by the concept of the feminine 'material' sublime, and the part it plays in creating a *site of transformation*, chiefly as a materially-specific, embodied and multisensory way of engaging with and being in a landscape. I also look at the work of the writer and walker Dorothy Wordsworth, how she and her female contemporaries informed the development of the seven principles, and how their creative, observational, therapeutic and transformative mode of engaging with landscape and environmental forces seemed closely allied with my own practice, offering an image- and sensory-based language that I regard as inherently scenographic. The chapter outlines and analyses these principles to explain the processes and objectives of 'scenography with purpose' (2012:36) and offers the reader a conceptual framework.

Each of the following chapters features a case study of a specific walking-performance work of mine. To show the developmental arc of my practice, these works are viewed chronologically, and each is considered through a particular thematic lens. Where a walking-performance is rooted in a personal autobiographical life-event or situation, I give a background account of that event to highlight the social and creative significance and purpose of the scenographic work that emerges from it. I also reference the practice of other artists from across a range of creative disciplines, who have worked with similar subject matters.

Chapter 2 examines *Fissure*, a three-day walking-performance work that marked the major shift in my practice towards 'scenography with purpose' (Baugh 2012:36). The chapter looks at the scenographic process of emplacing illness and grief in a landscape through transdisciplinary processes. It also explores my use of structural, compositional and participatory techniques found in pilgrimage and the rite of passage process – with a focus on the ethnographer Arnold van Gennep's three ritual phases of separation, transition and incorporation. The chapter looks at how my practice is rooted in autobiography – mine as well as that of the participants involved – and how it uses scenography as a means of 'staying with the trouble' (or facing a life-event) and transforming it (Haraway 2016: 1).

Chapter 3 goes deeper into my use of image-based and non-verbal scenography, and looks at why this form of walking-performance is particularly suited to life-event subject matters that are difficult to put into words. I study *Ghost Bird* (2012), a silent walk that used hen harriers and the so-called 'Pendle Witches' as a metaphor for acts of persecution.

Chapters 4 and 5 are connected by subject matter and type of location, but work in very different ways. These chapters study works that were designed to create *sites of transformation* for experiences relating to childlessness-by-circumstance. *The Gathering*, explored in Chapter 4, was a large-scale walking-performance created on Wales' highest mountain where the life and reproductive cycles of the ewes which graze there became a metaphor designed to bring new perspectives to experiences of in/fertility and motherhood. *Warnscale*, explored in Chapter 5, is an intimate self-performed work specific to a mountainous area in The Lake District, Cumbria that uses only the mountain's features and ever-changing environmental forces and other-than-human processes (seasons, weather, plants, animals) as a means to speak to and transform participants' experiences of 'missing' life-events relating to involuntary (biological) childlessness. The chapter looks at my reasons for mediating the performance through a walking guide/artist's book without any emplaced performance or intervention in the landscape, and how and why I designed the book using a series of mapping-walks and multiple layers of imagery, maps and words.

In Chapter 6 my focus moves to show how scenography can be used as a tool to frame and perform the concerns and feelings of a location-specific group of individuals. To do so, I look at *Mulliontide* (2016a), which marked another major shift in my practice in the way that it was created in collaboration with, and performed by, the residents of Mullion in Cornwall – 'real people' –, many of whom had lived and worked there for generations. The chapter shows how, by working responsively and developing bespoke processes and performance tools specific to the place and people, it is possible to put people and place at the heart of the performance in a way that gives individuals and a wider community a voice. Working with the term 'autotopography', coined by art historian Jennifer A. Gonzalez (1995: 133), the chapter looks at how objects and locations, specific to each contributor, became autotopographical tools for voicing and sharing deeply felt and personal experiences and concerns about human and landscape loss. Recognizing that people's lives are often intertwined with a specific site or landscape – and drawing on contributors' personal (biographic) stories and setting them in the landscape (topographic) – the chapter suggests that *Mulliontide* can be understood as autotopographic scenography. It also looks at how *Mulliontide*, by placing residents at its heart, continues to live on, grow and develop through a number of contributors who regularly repeat the walking-performance. To do this, they use a book, *Mulliontide: A Guide for Walkers* (2017), after the event as their guide, while at the same time bringing fresh insights and stories as their lives and the landscape they inhabit continues to change.

Chapter 7 explores how *Mulliontide* led directly to my next two projects: *Dorothy's Room* (2018), an immersive multimedia installation, and the participatory project *Women's Walks to Remember: 'With memory I was there'*, both of which furthered the mapping-walk and storyboarding techniques developed and applied in previous works. Both worked with theme of loss in the context of immobility due to illness, ageing or circumstance and were inspired by care home residents involved in *Mulliontide* and Dorothy Wordsworth's *Rydal Journals* (1831–35), which show her therapeutic use of memory-walking to access longed-for landscapes she could no longer visit by physically walking. The chapter looks at my use of scenographic techniques (indoor mappings, surrogate walking and collecting objects, films and sounds) applied in working one-to-one with participants. It considers how socially engaged and applied scenography can develop and use tools, books, objects, and mapping and drawing techniques in response to a range of social, health and well-being contexts and with marginalized individuals, groups and communities, and how this type of scenography can range in form, scale, duration, methodology, participant demographics and life-event context.

Because each chapter pursues specific themes and lines of enquiry, I do not study a particular performance in its entirety. I have, therefore, included a series of appendices to acknowledge and credit the input of all those I collaborate with when creating a performance. These appendices give a comprehensive overview of those I have worked with, from project managers, film editors, choreographers and costume makers to geologists and bio-medical scientists. In addition, each appendix shows the producers, commissioners, funders and supporters, without whom the work would not have been possible.

Book terminology and features

Readers may find it helpful to bear in mind the following explanation of terminology and features that are applicable throughout. To reflect the immersive, active and engaged quality of the work, I use the term *participant* to describe the people who take part in a performance (as walker, viewer or co-creator). Rather than using the word *audience*, this term allows for the co-creative relationship between the participant and the site, the performance and the performer – who are all sharing the same landscape – that develops in my practice.

I have selected three types of visual and supporting materials designed to reveal the multilayered nature of my fieldwork, creative process and practice: photographs and drawings that show my research process; storyboards and maps that illustrate the design process; and production photographs that show final outcomes. In addition, scenographic descriptive writing alongside extracts from poems and other performance-related texts are used to convey the visual, sonic, kinaesthetic, emotional and physical experience of the work as it was designed, though how it was received and experienced was specific to each participant.

Each case study incorporates feedback and responses. These responses take a variety of forms and are gathered in different ways for different works, outlined at the start of each chapter. Methods include post-performance writing, drawing and mapping, questionnaires, email exchanges, follow-up interviews and conversations with participants, performers, partners, subject experts or researchers, and feedback gathered by a producer or commissioner. As feedback is gathered by several means, how I identify respondents can vary across chapters depending on a number of factors, including who gathered the information, whether respondents' names were made available or anonymized and the sensitivity of the subject matter. Where sensitivity is a factor, initials rather than full names are used (always with permission). Feedback material contributes significantly to each chapter and is used to demonstrate and analyse the effects the work on individual participants as well as more broadly. These include short-, medium- and long-term effects as well as effects that were still emerging at the time they were captured.

My preference is that feedback is not sought immediately following the performance, at which time participants are still immersed in the experience, but once they have left the site and had time to reflect. It is not uncommon for participants to reflect how words that adequately express their experience are hard to find immediately and they need time to emerge from the experience and collect their thoughts. As discussed in Chapter 3, following *Jack Scout* and *Ghost Bird*, participants were invited to respond in abstract words and drawings rather than extended sentences. This was highly successful, and my use of drawing to gather responses became so important that it was embedded in the making process of *Warnscale* and *Women's Walks to Remember*, as discussed in Chapters 5 and 7. It is, however, not always appropriate or desirable to gather collaborator/participant responses as doing so is intrusive – what happens on the mountain stays on the mountain. There are two reasons why I have drawn less on my own reflections on the effect of the performance (on me or those I observe in others). Firstly, my attention is on the work (as a performer, guide, designer, mapper, converser and listener) and, secondly, it is my practice to step back and hold the space, so that participants can become immersed. This means that while I am attentive to participants and the performance, I am not at this time in an analytical or enquiry mode. My enquiry happens through the practice, the creative decisions I make and how participants respond, and it is this process that I have sought to demonstrate in the book.

1

Scenography with purpose – seven scenographic principles

> *Scenography now 'extends well beyond traditional notions of theatre and into a much broader range of human activity' that is addressing 'real world' situations.*
> (ARONSON 2018: XIII).

This chapter looks at the field of expanded scenography and maps the wider set of foundational ideas that underpin and intersect my practice including site-specificity, mobility and land art. It explores the concept of the feminine 'material' sublime and the influence that Dorothy Wordsworth and her contemporaries' approach to landscape had on the development of seven scenographic principles. I also consider the influence of other Western concepts and aesthetics relating to landscape that emerged with Early Romanticism. By outlining these ideas, intersections, influences, and the scenographic principles in Chapter 1, my aim is to give the reader a sense of the concepts and practices underpinning the walking-performances explored in subsequent chapters.

Scenography – an expanded field

Scenography, which literally means that which is 'placed on stage' (Palmer 2011: 86), has long since left the bounds of the theatre stage behind and expanded far beyond the 'accepted understanding' of being 'primarily about the creation of the "*mise-en-scène*" for the staging of a play' (Baugh 2013: 223). Rather, 'scenography has grown and in some ways been transformed into an applied art practice that is finding new ways to engage and interact with audiences' (Baugh 2013: 224) and 'some of the major political, cultural and ecological concerns of our contemporary world' (Baugh 2012: 11). This expansion marks important and significant developments within the field of contemporary performance and scenography, and reflects the 'ever greater questioning of the function and purpose of performance' (Baugh 2013: 223) towards 'scenography with purpose' (Baugh 2012: 36). Responding to work exhibited at the Prague Quadrennial in 2011, Baugh coined the term 'socially engaged scenography' to capture 'the significant, profound and innovative developments in the field of scenography that have occurred over recent years' (2013: xx).[1] He said how:

> the need for such a term, or similar, occurred to me when I wrote the 'Scenography with Purpose: Activism and Intervention' chapter in *The Disappearing Stage: Reflections on the 2011 Prague Quadrennial* (2012).
>
> (Baugh, email to the author, 12 August 2016)

I have adopted Baugh's term 'scenography with purpose' (2012:36) as it captures the aims and ambitions of my practice, and this book provides a study of how my practice sits within and has informed this emerging field. My practice also sits within Baugh's analysis of the way that contemporary scenography 'brings us close to early forms of Western and non-Western theatre and performance [which] served the needs of an occasion of some significance' and:

> served useful cultural functions within the social, religious and political life, and places and spaces of performance (architecture and scenography) were determined by the nature of both the occasion and the relationship that existed between performers and their audiences.
>
> (Baugh 2013: 242)

Scholarly interest in the scope and possibilities of scenography as an expanded field of practice and an 'emergent academic field' was first identified and written about by scholars Joslin McKinney and Phillip Butterworth in *The Cambridge Introduction to Scenography* (2009: xii). In this foundational text, the authors investigate the 'purpose, identity and scope of scenography and its theories and concepts' within and beyond the performance (2009: cover). The book points to the 'new

---

[1] 'The Prague Quadrennial of Performance Design and Space was established in 1967 to bring the best of design for performance, scenography, and theatre architecture to the front line of cultural activities' (Prague Quadrennial 2020).

possibilities' for scenography 'achieved through scenographic strategies that comment on our contemporary condition' (2009: 197), and the co-creative role audiences (or participants) play in the scenographic process through participation and interaction – an important development which is reflected in my principles.

Scenography Expanded: Contemporary Perspectives on Performance Design (2017) built on this introductory text and is the first volume in a series of books looking at the rapid growth across the field of scenography and contemporary performance design both in and beyond theatre. McKinney and Palmer work with the term 'expanded scenography' as a means to distinguish between more 'traditional' aspects of the form (such as pre-existing plays or operas that are performed on a stage or in a purpose built-location) and practice and research at the vanguard of this expansion, which incorporates:

> ceremonial performance, mobile technologies and screen-based performance, site-specific and street performance, architectural scenography, performance architecture and experimental work at the intersection of art and theatre, commercial spectacle, applied theatre practice, activist performance and immersive installation.
>
> (McKinney and Palmer 2017: 1–3)

Scenography Expanded further highlights the therapeutic or transformative potential of scenography recognising how:

> Expanded scenography is at once a tool, a system, a process and a generative organism for understanding the complex environment in which we live.
>
> (Aronson, quoted in McKinney and Palmer 2017: xvi)

For example, in the chapter 'Ecologies of Autism: Vibrant Spaces in Imagining Autism' the scenographer/researcher Melissa Trimingham 'demonstrates how scenography may be "expanded" into therapeutic applications' (Trimingham 2017: 183). To do this she analyses the practice-led research project, *Imagining Autism*, that she, and the scholar of applied performance, Nicola Shaughnessy, conducted in collaboration with children with autism, their parents and teachers and psychologists. In the project scenography in the form of 'space, light, projection, sound, costume and props' became a 'means of exploring and developing communication, social imagination and empathy' (2017: 18) that, writes Trimingham, produced a 'rich and sensory' environment that brought about "transformative mixes" of materiality and mind to those who participated' (2017: 194), adding that the therapeutic and transformative 'potential for applied scenography within real-world contexts has been little understood, identified or exploited within education or artistic practice' (2017:183). Trimingham's words do not only remind us that unbounded and set free from the stage, scenography now 'extends well beyond traditional notions of theatre and into a much broader range of human activity' that is addressing 'real world' situations (Aronson 2018: xiii), but they recognise how the field of socially engaged and applied scenography has immense scope that has yet to be fully realised.

Scenography and the scenographer – practice and research

My decision, ten years ago (discussed in Palmer and Wilson 2011:74), to adopt the term scenographer (alongside that of theatre designer) reflected the role that I, like other scenographer/designers, play in the process of performance-making and. More significantly perhaps, it reflected the way in which I was visioning, producing and creating (designing, directing and dramatising) scenographic-led projects. Furthermore, like Trimingham, whose practice informs academic research, by writing about and interrogating my work in the form of articles, book chapters, and in a practice-led research PhD (Wilson 2016c) at Lancaster University, I began to bring research insights into the academy. Recognition of the centrality of the scenographer both within the performance-making process and a person 'authoring' work has led to a growing appreciation of the scenographic process and of knowledge gained through practice, as Baugh recognized, the research-driven art practice of scenography is engaging with:

> research-driven art practice of scenography is engaging with twenty-first century issues of the environment, global warming, ecology, vanishing resources, political inadequacy and corruption, and the effects of globalisation without first waiting upon the dramatist to write the play.
>
> (Baugh 2013: 224)

'Scenography's centrality to theatre-making' is claimed and argued for by the scholar Rachel Hann in *Beyond Scenography* (her term for expanded scenography):

> With notions of dramaturgy and choreography now being considered formative to theatre-making, scenography, too, must make a claim for its centrality if it is to take its place as an equal partner within this triad.
>
> (Hann 2018: 8)

SCENOGRAPHY WITH PURPOSE – SEVEN SCENOGRAPHIC PRINCIPLES

Indeed, scenographers have, I suggest, not only claimed their position in the – scenography, dramaturgy, choreography – creative triad but now take the lead in the making of and using scenographic-led processes that have harnessed the art form as a creative, political and social tool not only in, but beyond theatre, where they apply it in real-world contexts.

One of the first publications to 'examine in depth the work of a contemporary stage designer' is Jocelyn Herbert's *A Theatre Workbook* (1993) in which Herbert explores her design process her process and use of storyboards, costume designs and model boxes as creative, thinking and presentational tools and production (1993: cover). Another foundational publication that offers insights gained through decades of practice is Pamela Howard's (2002) *What is Scenography?* A practising scenographer, Howard takes the reader inside her creative process and uses examples of scale models, storyboards, costume designs, plans and maps to show spatial organization and the relationship of the space to the audience. It was Howard's 'holistic method of visual theatre making' that, in anglophone countries, came to be defined as scenography – a term that recognized how the role of design extended far beyond the creation of the *mise-en-scène* of a performance or a mere backdrop in front of which a play text was performed (2002: xx). As Howard identifies:

> Scenography is not simply concerned with creating and presenting images to an audience; it is concerned with audience reception and engagement, it is sensory as well as an intellectual experience, emotional as well as rational.
>
> (Howard 2002: 4)

Theatre and Performance Designer: A Reader in Scenography (2010), a collection of essays, edited by performance makers and scholars Jane Collins and Andrew Nisbett, that centres around visual composition, space and place, incorporates insights and visual materials from the sketchbooks of contemporary theatre designers, including Rae Smith, who, as I discuss in Chapter 4, uses drawing as a creative, imaginative and thinking tool.

Collectively, these publications value and study the theatre designer's (or scenographer's) process and the expansion of scenography as a practice. They identify the centrality of scenography and the scenographer in the visioning of work, and set the scene for future scenographers and researchers to value knowledge founded in practice. This valuing has led many professional scenographer-researchers to articulate their work through a scholarly lens, and in so doing provide an understanding of what scenography can do and achieve. The wide range of practice and research undertaken in the field (by which I mean out there 'in the world' or 'at the coal face' and with collaborators and participants) reflects how scenography and scenographic processes take place within, and beyond, theatre and performance contexts, and are varied in form, intention and output, making scenography rich in significance, application and purpose. The 'conjoining' of 'scenography with academic research and scholarly inquiry' is described by Baugh as the 'most significant expansion and most radical revisioning of practice' that has taken place 'over the last decades' (in McKinney and Palmer: 2017: 35). As Estelle Barrett points out:

> Creative arts research is often motivated by emotional, personal and subjective concerns, it operates not only on the basis of explicit and exact knowledge, but also on that of tacit and experiential knowledge.
>
> (Barrett 2007: 3)

Across disciplines, tacit and experiential knowledge that can only be found through the process of doing is now given the recognition and value is deserves. It is in the field – when scenography meets participant and an exchange between the two takes place – that the 'work' comes to life, and it is in this moment of being that 'new knowledge or knowing emerge' (2007: 3) This knowledge and knowing – as much of it as can be captured or expressed – can then be reported back, analysed, shared and disseminated.

The significance of the shift towards 'knowledge and insights' achieved through practice is seen in the way that *Scenography Expanded* incorporates writing both by leading scholars working in the field of scenography, including Arnold Aronson, Maaiker Bleeker, Ethel Brooks, Jane Collins, Kathleen Irwin, Thea Brejzek, Marcela Oteiza and Stephen Di Benedetto, and by professional scenographers working across a range of forms, including architecture, site-specific performance, theatre and film. These scholar-practitioners include Christopher Baugh, Dorita Hannah, David Shearing, Nebojsa Tabacki and Melissa Trimingham, whose insights are founded in the field – through creating, making, collaborating, thinking, trying, doing and engaging with audiences. They, like other scenographers whose work straddles practice and academia, are at the vanguard of the art form, pushing it, working it and applying it in sites, people, contexts and situations.

The way that scenography is increasingly finding ways of engaging with major issues and concerns 'of our contemporary world' (Baugh 2012: 11) is recognized by the dramaturg Sodja Lotker and theatre scholar Richard Gough, who state that 'scenography is not a setting that illustrates our actions anymore – it is a body (a discipline, a method, a foundation) in its own right':

> What is important is that scenographies are environments that not only determine the context of performative actions, but that inspire us to act.
>
> (Lotker and Gough 2013: 3–4)

Practitioner-scholars working in landscape and/or social contexts whose practice and research 'inspires us to act' include Tanja Beer, who contributes to the field of ecoscenography – 'a movement that integrates ecological principles into all stages of scenographic thinking and production' (Lotker and Gough 2013: 4; Beer 2021). Leading this movement, Beer creates ecologically orientated projects such as *The Living Stage* 'that combines stage design, permaculture and community engagement to create a recyclable, biodegradable and edible performance space' (Beer 2021). By putting the 'stuff that is not human centre stage' Minty Donald's site-specific scenography focuses on 'the other-than-human in theatre/performance' (Donald 2021a). Over the last six years, her practice and research has focused on the 'performance of/with rivers and other watercourses, such as canals and drainage systems' (2021a), and engages with 'experts from disciplines outside the arts, for instance geographers, geologists, hydrologists, engineers, planners and architects' (Donald 2021b). With the performance makers Quarantine, scenographer/designer Simon Banham creates socially engaged work that the company describes as 'scenography of the everyday', placing 'people who are rarely seen on stage' centre stage (Quarantine 2020a). To stage *Summer. Autumn. Winter. Spring.* (2014–16), 'a quartet of work ... spanning the human lifecycle', the company invited people 'of all ages from babies upwards' from the places in which the work was staged to perform what they describe as 'a piece of mass portraiture' (Quarantine 2020b). Staged over the duration of a day, the work included live performance, installation and film. The project was later distilled into the publication *Summer. Autumn. Winter. Spring. Staging Life and Death* (Banham, Brady, Hunter and O'Shea 2019) that documents the process of making and staging this work, with insights, philosophy and conversations on the themes of life, death and time.

Intersections – site-specificity, mobility and land art

There are three key fields of practice with which my work intersects: site-specificity, mobility (walking) and land art.

Site-specific performance practices

The performance works I created with wilson+wilson were specifically generated for the site – a house, a city, an area of woodland by the sea, a department store – in which they were created and performed. In all aspects and elements they were site-specific – not 'site-responsive', 'site-sympathetic' or 'site-generic' (Wrights & Sites 2001). A genuinely site-specific performance, though, is hard-won. It is achieved through rigorous exploration of the site and is inextricably linked to the place in which it is made; it ceases to exist outside of that place. In work that is truly site-specific, the site is a fundamental and active component of the performance – this is not merely work that is staged outside the theatre or uses a place or envirnoment as a backdrop.

The term *site-specific* theatre grew out of the term *environmental theatre*, coined by the theatre director and scholar Richard Schechner in the late 1960s in response to what he identified as the turn away from 'the orthodox theatre' that, wrote Schechner, 'dominates world theatre today' (Schechner 1971: 379) – where staging is typically frontal, contained within a single frame and viewed from a fixed or static position by an audience seated in an auditorium – towards 'environmental theatre':

> I called the theatre environmental theatre because its first scenic principle is to *create and use whole spaces*–literally spheres of spaces–which contain, or envelope, or reach out into all the areas where the audience is or the performers move. *All the spaces in a theatre are actively involved in all aspects of the performance.*
>
> (Schechner 1971: 379–80)

Detailed in his essay '6 Axioms for Environmental Theatre' (1968) Schechner developed the term 'environmental theatre' in recognition of how, whilst distinct and unique to each, the theatre work of 'many persons from Grotowski, Ronconi, and Barba [Odin Teatret], to the Living Theatre, the Open Theatre, the Bread and Puppet Theatre, and the Performance Group [founded by Schechner in the United States] expanded the relationship between the theatre space and the audience' (1971: 379). This expansion set this work apart from:

> the 'orthodox' theatre – theatre derived from Renaissance and Enlightenment models and scenically characterized by (1) segregation of audience from performers, (2) fixed and regular seating of audience, (3) construction of scenery situated in one part of the theatre only.
>
> (Schechner 1971: 379)

As Arnold Aronson reminds us:

> Proscenium, end, thrust, alley and arena stages, are all frontal in that a spectator observing a performance rarely has to look more that forty-five degrees to the right of left in order to view the whole production and to take in the entire visual and spatial field. [...] as long as there is a single frame and the spectator remains outside it, the performance is frontal.

If, however, the spectator is somehow incorporated within the frame, surrounded by the frame, or surrounded by several distinct frames [...], the performance becomes environmental.

(Aronson [1981] 2018: 8)

Instead, in a process described by Schechner as 'transactional', in environmental theatre, audiences become not only 'scene-watchers' but 'scene-makers (1968: 48). Working in both indoor and outdoor spaces, where design 'made direct use of existing spaces' or transformed found spaces (Schechner 1971: 380), 'All the space is used for performance and audiences', fixed seating is given up allowing for multiple frames, viewpoints, and perspectives, and many and varied focal points (or scenes or happenings) are in play simultaneously (Schechner 1968: 49). 'Audiences are invited to participate' and it becomes 'difficult to distinguish audience from performers' (44). All the senses are engaged, and performative actions 'evoke an empathetic reaction' in audiences (45).

Another feature of environmental theatre is the way 'all production elements speak their own language', are not 'submerged' one into the other but considered to be of equal importance (59). The equal importance placed on 'production elements' such as 'scenery, costume, lighting, sound' and of moving and still imagery (45), means they (design and scenography) 'no longer "support" a performance' ... but are 'at certain times ... more important than the performers' (45). In contrast, text (and the playwright's vision) is no longer considered to be of higher status than other elements, nor is it regarded as the only, right or necessary starting point for a production. Rather, there may be 'no text at all', or text is seen as a material that 'acts as a map with many possible routes' that can be montaged, rearranged, extrapolated, or eliminated – a process that brings multiple voices, perspectives, and subject matters to bear (60).

By the mid-1980s, the term *environmental* became superseded with the term *site-specific* which was widely, and indiscriminately applied to a wide range of sited theatre and performance work that was not physically or conceptually embedded in the space, and did not actively engage participants in '*all aspects of the performance*' (Schechner 1971: 380). The 'dilution and devolution of his original concept' was, as Aronson points out, addressed by Schechner in his revised edition of the book *Environmental Theatre* ([1973] 1994) where he determined that:

To stage a performance 'environmentally' means more than simply to move it off the proscenium or out of the arena. An environmental performance is one in which all the elements or parts making up the performance are recognized as alive.

(Schechner quoted in Aronson [1981] 2018: 173–4)

In her survey of site-specific performance companies in the UK between 2000 and 2001, performance scholar Fiona Wilkie recognises that:

> the term site-specific only really began to have currency in theatrical rather than sculptural terms in the mid- to late-1980s, with companies such as the influential Welsh based Brith Gof popularising the form.
>
> (Wilkie 2002: 141)

With wilson+wilson, this specificity came about because each work was created through extended and in-depth site research engaging the place and the people of that place who knew it intimately, past and present. The process of making *House* led us to liken our site-specific methodology to that of an archaeological dig. The rich layers of material that we gradually discovered, through a process we described as excavatory, revealed forgotten lives, histories and stories held within the site.

Working in 'real-world' locations, wilson+wilson actively involved the people and communities who lived and worked there. For example, making *Mapping the Edge* (a retelling of the Medea myth 'staged' in Sheffield), we engaged with tea-dancers, a former Second World War Women's Auxiliary Air Force (WAAF) officer, an RAF veteran, knife-makers, boxers, bus and tram drivers, and singers in the Yemeni community. We gathered stories and images of their lives and histories and wove them into the fabric of the performance – installations, scenes, sites, routes, scripts, characters and costumes. We worked with archivists in local museums and libraries, and found the lost, forgotten and untold histories of many buildings and sites – some of which became locations the final performance travelled to. To make the final performance of *Mapping the Edge* like the other performances we created, the material we gathered was:

> developed through the filters of design, writing, composition and dramaturgy to evolve cross-disciplinary, site-specific performances that were 'born out of', and 'bespoke' to the people, buildings, towns, cities and landscapes in which, and about which, they were created.
>
> (Wilson in Palmer and Wilson 2011: 75)

A feature of our work was the way in which it had multiple timeframes, interwoven narratives and collapsed the real and the imagined, the factual and the invented. The merging of site and performance is helpfully reflected on by theatre scholar and practicioner Cathy Turner, who makes a distinction between 'what is "of" the site and what is brought "to" it' – elements, she writes, that sometimes 'disintegrate within the performance process and event: place and work maybe co-creative' (Turner 2004: 374).

In *Still Life*, mentioned in the Introduction, the figure of The Woman 'running on the water' for one participant triggered 'recollections of the historical narratives of children dying in the sands and a feeling that [The Woman] represented their mother looking for them'.[2]

FIGURE 1.1 Still Life *by Nigel Stewart and Louise Ann Wilson. Figure of The Woman running on the sands, Far Arnside, Morecambe Bay, Lancashire. Performer: Louise Ann Wilson. Photographer: Nicola Tarr.*

This particular narrative was not explicit in the performance, but was an interpretation unique to this participant. Creating a 'palimpsest' that 'evoked and activated' multiple meanings recognizes how, in site-specific performance, 'neither site nor performance is fixed or graspable, yet both seemed to be glimpsed in the passing' (Turner 2004: 374, 377). Another scenographer who works with site-specific palimpsests is Gerry Pilgrim. She describes how her site-specific performance works *Spa* (2003) and *Hotel* (2000) brought deserted and semi-derelict buildings 'back to life' through a process that layered 'real stories with imagined history' (Pilgrim quoted in Turner 2004: 374).

This layering of site and performance echoes Mike Pearson's archaeological approach to making site-specific performances, explored in *Site-Specific*

---

[2] *Still Life* participant feedback, 2008.

Performance (2010), for which he offers a 'stratigraphy model' that divides into two components – transitory (performance) and fixed (site)[3]:

> Of the transitory component – performance – these might include *text*, *physical action*, *soundtrack* and *scenography*, the latter to include all scenic installation, lighting, amplification, pre-recorded media, technological and technical aspects … The fixed component – site – the layers might include architecture, microclimate, manifestations and patinas of occupancy past and present, aura and atmospheres … All that constitutes its *depth*: archaeological, cultural, psycho-geographical. In performance some are ever present and immediately operative.
>
> (Pearson 2010: 167, 169)

This dual model means that site-specific performance 'can overlay different varieties of narrative – factual and fictive, historical and contemporary, creative and analytical, documentary and dramatic – within a given location', a process that serves to 'reveal the place' (2010: 169). Cliff McLucas, joint artistic director of Brith Gof with Mike Pearson, came to think of this relationship between the site and the performance as that of a 'host' (the site that pre-exists the work) and the 'ghost' (the work/performance):

> The host site is haunted for a time by a ghost that the Theatre makers create. Like all ghosts it is transparent, and the host can be seen through the ghost. Adding to this a third term – the witness, i.e., the audience and we have a kind of Trinity that constitutes the work.
>
> (McLucas, quoted in Turner 2004: 373)

As Collins and Nisbett point out, 'stepping onto the stage changes the status of the viewer from audience to participant' (2010: 9). For wilson+wilson, our 'stages' were everyday and familiar places into and through which participants entered and moved – host, ghost and witness were interwoven, interactive and co-creative.

Site-specific mobility – walking practices

By taking participants out of the theatre building, as we did with wilson+wilson, they became alive to and immersed in the performance not just physically

---

[3] Performance-maker and scholar Mike Pearson's book *Site-Specific Performance* (2010) uses a series of case studies 'staged' in non-theatre locations to offer practical and theoretical insight into the relationship between site, performance and scenario.

but also intellectually, consciously, emotionally and sensorily. A feature of our practice was that we dissolved boundaries between the performance and the participants. For one participant in *House*, this level of immersive engagement brought: 'A new emotional experience that opened parts of my mind and senses that other theatre (media) has never touched before.'[4]

In our performances wilson+wilson moved participants through the site on foot, from room to room in *House*; from boiler room to attic and rooftop via shop floors and lifts in *News from the Seventh Floor*; through coastal woodland and country estate on foot and in golf buggies for *Mulgrave* (2006); across the city of Sheffield on foot, bus and tram in *Mapping the Edge* (2001). Working in this way meant the 'effect of space' became a material element in the experience of the performance' (McKinney and Palmer 2017: 7).

In *Mapping the Edge*, as participants travelled to sites as varied as a Victorian knife-making workshop, a 1960s graffiti-covered underpass, a working boxing club, a post-industrial wasteland bordered by advertising boards and a 1930s ballroom in the basement of City Hall, the city of Sheffield became a massive mobile stage and the distinction between 'performed' and 'non-performed' became blurred; soon it was impossible to distinguish between the performance and the life of the city and its people. Travelling through the ever-changing, multisensory and multidimensional 'living scenes' of the city gave the work a visceral, heightened and filmic quality. Some of these scenes were scenographed and performed by a company of actors: a murder scene taped off and guarded by police officers, a violent street fight, a Yemeni woman carrying her twin children (puppets) and searching for her boxer husband, and a knife-making industrialist who stepped out of the eighteenth century onto a tram. The scenography of other 'scenes' was performed by the city going about its everyday business, which became part of and enhanced the drama: police cars and ambulances travelling at high speed to an incident, a group of punk rockers with Mohican haircuts walking alongside 'our' RAF officer and his WAAF girlfriend, and a bunch of kids shouting over the road to 'our' pregnant mother. As one participant remarked, 'I've never felt drama come so to life!' (*Mapping the Edge* 2001).

Our mobilization of participants and the performance meant that wilson+wilson contributed to the evolution of site-specifc work from 'performance that *inhabits* a place to performance that *moves* through spaces' (Wilkie 2012: 205). Site-specificity, writes the scholar Fiona Wilkie:

> used to imply something grounded and immobile but does no longer. Now, spectators enter into, and walk through both the metaphorical and the physical landscape, making participants *and* the performance, mobile, yet located.

(Wilkie 2012: 204)

---

[4] Hadley Creative Marketing carried out a survey of responses to *House* on behalf of wilson+wilson.

FIGURE 1.2 Mapping the Edge *by wilson+wilson. Performers ascending a tram, Sheffield, Yorkshire. Photographer: Dominic Ibbotson*

Environmental and land art movement

Many of the rural landscape sites in which I have created the site-specifc performances explored in this book are remote, so walking serves both a creative and critical function, a consequence of which is that my practice overlaps the field of walking art. Walking as art – and the intersection of walking and landscape – characterizes the work of Richard Long, for whom: 'The physical involvement of walking creates a receptiveness to the landscape. I walk on the land to be woven into nature' (Tate Gallery 2020b). Similarly, Hamish Fulton in 1973 decided he would 'only make art resulting from the experience of individual walks' when he said 'If I do not walk, I cannot make a work of art', and has summed up this way of thinking in a simple statement of intent: 'no walk, no work' (2020b). The walking practices of both these artists use permanent and ephemeral materials, topography and phenomena of the site, and link their work, like my own, to the environmental and land art or earth art movement.

The term 'site-specific' in the context of theatre and performance evolved out of the environmental and land art movement that began in the late 1960s with artists in New York taking their work out of the gallery and into the landscape, which 'served simultaneously as material for art and as a stage for huge-scale interventions' (Whitworth Gallery 2013). This move was radical and reflected both an interest in bringing art out into the world and, as the Earth

Day observances taking place in America at the time demonstrated, concerns about the impact of human activity on the environment.

I draw some connections between my work and large-scale earthworks such as Michael Heizer's *City: Complex One* (1972–4), Robert Morris' *Observatorium* (1977) and Robert Smithson's *Spiral Jetty* (1970), which bring to mind in their scale and form ancient monuments like the Great Serpent Mound (c. 1070 CE), the Nazca Lines (500 BCE and 500 CE) and Stonehenge (2500 BCE). My practice, though, has closer affinities with land art works that are made using the materials, topography and phenomenon of a specific site in ways that are intimate, ephemeral, time-based and human in scale. Nancy Holt's *Sun Tunnels* (1976), a series of four tunnels sited in the Utah desert, is designed to frame, contain and 'bring the vast space of the desert down to human scale' (Grosenick 2001: 228). The human scale is literally shaped and formed in Ana Mendieta's series of earthworks entitled *Siluetas* (*Silhouettes*) (1973–80), for which she carved and shaped the outline of her own body in earth, water and fire, leaving only a trace of her absent self, as did Andy Goldsworthy in *Black Sand, Morecambe Bay* (1976). In contrast, Goldsworthy's *Hedge Walking* (2014), which captures the effort of moving through a hedge, and Nils Udo's *Waternest* (1995), which places a curled-up figure within a nest of materials of the site, both make the body present – moving and still – within a site. Land artist Michelle Stewart, known for her pioneering use of topography, developed a process of 'drawing with the landscape' using organic and impermanent materials such as earth, wax, seeds and plants. The visually arresting *Niagara Gorge Path Relocated* (1975) unfurled a 460-foot paper scroll (marked with pigment from the site) down the side of a gorge, was designed to 'ghost' where the Niagara Falls had once flowed and in so doing to reveal the past in the present. Drawing attention to the specificity and detail of a site can be seen in Christine Oatman's *Wild Flower Rug* (1977), which references botanical surveying processes that focus on the exact detail of a small square of land. Works such as *Wall Drawn with Snow in Winter and Wool in Summer* (1996) and the *Sheepfold Series* (1996–2002) by Andy Goldsworthy also use materials of the site to draw attention to topographical and man-made features, such as the gradient of a fellside and the shape of a drystone wall, as well as to time passing, daily and seasonal changes, and the movement of animals in a field, as seen in the *Sheep Paintings* series (1990–2000).

In a series of land art works in the Lake District in Cumbria, that centred around trees, the photographer Robert Fraser and writer Harriet Fraser (collectively known as Somewhere Nowhere) created a series of interventions that not only drew attention to but also 'disrupted the accepted view' of the landscape (Fraser and Fraser 2017: 138). *Yellow at the Wasdale Oak* (2016), for which 100 metres of yellow fabric was run down the fellside to the shores of Wastwater below, drew attention to a solitary oak tree intersected by the fabric, while the vivid yellow colour sat in contrast to the slate grey of the scree slope below and unsettled the eye.

These works all use materials to stimulate the eye, disrupt the view and draw attention to specific landscape features. They operate by applying devices common to scenography – colour, contrast, juxtaposition and making strange (defamiliarization) – and also found in my work. Where my practice differs from that of these artists is in my applied use of these devices and materials of, or associated with, the landscape – often as metaphor – in a life-event context. In her response to *The Gathering* writer and critic Lyn Gardner captured this distinction when she wrote:

> This is a piece that makes you look and listen hard – to the unaccompanied voice of a boy singing, to Gillian Clarke's poetic script, to the red woollen tramway that runs down the mountain like a scar. But it also makes you pay attention to what has always been there and will remain long after we are gone: the fall of water, the moss creeping across tumbled stones, the dark, secretive peaks against an endless sky.
>
> *The Gathering* is an intervention in a landscape yet it grows organically from its setting, using what is there – the abandoned dwellings and slate, the waterfalls and rocks – to tell a story of passing time, ancient ways of working, extraordinary fecundity and renewal, but also bitter barrenness. It's lyrical but unsentimental, bloody and brutal. It makes the mountain sing.
>
> (Gardner 2014)

Over many decades of making site-specific performance, I have heard participants express how the experience becomes 'seared to the memory' and 'lives on for some considerable time afterwards' (*House* 1998). They have described how during a performance, a site is seen 'in a totally different light' (*Jack Scout* 2010), and that afterwards it is 'forever altered' and 'never seems the same again' (*Mulgrave* 2006). Another feature is how the performances attract participants who do not ordinarily attend art, theatre or performance events but who feel able to engage because the work happens in places they have a connection to or are familiar with – it is democratizing. These two factors – visceral-effect and engagement – suit performance works that seek to attract subject-specific participants and collaborators, and use that work as a means to alter their view of a rural landscape, and through it, their view of a life-event related situation.

Seven scenographic principles

Dorothy Wordsworth and The Grasmere Journals

Performance scholar Deirdre Heddon's (2012) article 'Turning 40: 40 Turns' locates the walking practices of women within a historical and contemporary context. It was a footnote in this article that referred to Dorothy Wordsworth's

(1771–1855) ascent of Scafell Pike (England's highest mountain) on 7 October 1818 that captured my attention and led me to research her walking practice and journal writing. As Heddon points out, 'Dorothy Wordsworth was, like other "walking women", largely absent from the "canon" of writing on walking, which is male orientated' (Heddon 2012: 70).[5] I was not aware at that point of the significant influence Dorothy's creative and physical approach to, and therapeutic use of, landscape and walking would have on my own practice.

Accompanied by her friend, the poet Mary Barker, Barker's maid, a hired porter and a Borrowdale 'statesman' shepherd to act as guide, she later wrote a vivid account of her experience and surroundings:

> On the summit of the Pike which we gained after much toil though without difficulty, there was not a breath of air to stir even the papers containing our refreshment, as they lay spread out upon a rock. The stillness seemed to be not of this world: – we paused, and kept silence to listen; and no sound could be heard. We were far above the reach of the cataracts of Scaw Fell; and not an insect was there to hum in the air … We now beheld the whole mass of Great Gavel … the Den of Wastdale at our feet – a gulf immeasurable: Ennerdale and its mountains; and the Sea beyond! … round the top of Scawfell-PIKE not a blade of grass is to be seen. Cushions or tufts of moss, parched and brown, appear between the huge blocks and stones that lie in heaps … like skeletons or bones of the earth not needed at the creation, and there left to be covered with never-dying lichens, which the clouds and dews nourish; and adorn with colours of vivid and exquisite beauty. Flowers, the most brilliant feathers, and even gems, scarcely surpass in colouring some of those masses of stone, which no human eye beholds, except the shepherd or traveller be led thither by curiosity: and how seldom must this happen!
>
> (Wordsworth quoted in De Sélincourt 1933: 367)

This extract of Dorothy's account demonstrates a highly scenographic, site-specific approach to – or 'mode' of – engaging with the landscape that

---

[5] In 1822 Dorothy Wordsworth's Scafell account was published by William Wordsworth in *A Description of the Scenery of the Lakes*, where it appeared to be William's own work. Until recently this appropriation of her writing meant her influence, like that of Charlotte Smith and Ann Radcliffe, on the development of Western landscape aesthetics has been under-recognized. For further writing on Dorothy Wordsworth's (and her female contemporaries') influence on landscape writing and their legacy see (Wilson 2019). In this article I reclaim and recover their significance (as a lost canon of writers) and point to a lineage between them and environment-, walking- and landscape-artists including Nancy Holt, Michelle Stewart, Alice Aycock and Ana Mendieta, Nan Shepherd, Alice Oswald, Kathleen Jamie and Helen Mort, Elena Brotherus, Simone Kenyon, Alison Lloyd and Ingrid Pollard.

is alive to its materiality. It is a mode, I propose, that can be understood through the concept of the feminine 'material' sublime. This can be seen in several ways. Her acknowledgment of the physical effort of the ascent and its bodily effects (which as a seasoned walker she takes in her stride). Her sensory – phenomenological – awareness of the atmosphere. Her topographically-located knowledge of the 'boundless' view and how she shifts her attention to features and objects close at hand. Her use of discerning observation and a combination of everyday and metaphorical language to describe what she sees and feels. Her evocation of human, geological and mythical time but also her desire to be in the present moment and with companions. Her appreciation of the shepherd guide – a 'Wise Man of the Mountains' (1933: 367) – and his knowledge of the route, weather, clouds and terrain.

Feminine 'material' sublime / masculine 'transcendent' sublime

The concept of the feminine 'material' sublime is not concerned with gender, rather it is term that encapsulates a mode or sensibility. This sensibility manifests as a way of engaging with the landscape and environmental forces that is located, embodied, multi-sensory, socially engaged and has transformative outcomes.

The feminine 'material' sublime sits in contrast to the masculine 'transcendent' sublime, a concept that came to dominate European discourses on landscape in the Early Romantic period. This concept works with the idea that a transformative experience or a 'higher spiritual or intellectual level' is achieved by 'leaping-off' or 'escaping from the confines of the [everyday] material "world"' and losing the self in a transcendent – mind elevating – metaphysical dimension (Pipkin 1998: 599). Unframed, uncomposed and limitless, a masculine 'transcendent' sublime experience was considered so awe-inspiring that it defied representation, language or definition that could 'measure up to the scale of the experience' (Andrews 1999: 142). 'Transcendent' sublime experiences such as these became associated with landscapes that typically featured grand and un-scalable mountains, wind-swept passes, gorges with waterfalls disappearing into the dark-depths below, unbounded vistas of sky with rolling thunder clouds and deep fathomless oceans. They also became associated with a masculine aesthetic mode that was open to men but closed to women.

The reasons for this gendering and exclusion can be traced to philosopher Edmund Burke (1729–1797), who, in his highly influential treatise *A Philosophical Enquiry into the Origin of Our Ideas of the Sublime and Beautiful* (1757), categorized objects and the 'psychological effects they produced' as either sublime (masculine) or beautiful (feminine):

> Beautiful objects were defined by qualities such as smallness, smoothness, roundness and delicacy and promoted feelings of wellbeing, relaxation and love, whilst sublime objects were defined by qualities such as vastness, darkness, obscurity, infinity and promoted feelings of admiration, astonishment, pain and terror.
>
> (Bainbridge 2008: 176)

Challengers to Burke, such as the poet, essayist and critic Anna Laetitia Barbauld (1743–1825), in her essay 'On the Pleasures Derived from Objects of Terror' (published in 1773) argued that women were just as capable as men of accessing the soul-elevating and mind-awakening 'transcendent' sublime, and the writer and activist Mary Wollstonecraft (1759–1797) 'raged against the ways in which the sublime was often explicitly, and nearly always implicitly, gendered as male' (Battersby 2007: 8). Wollstonecraft, like other writers, refused to accept the feminine behaviours that the concept imposed on women and the limited roles and identities that the masculine 'transcendent' sublime afforded them. Wishing instead to 'assume the role of speaking subject rather than accepting that of object', women sought to shift the boundaries of what they could think, say, do and write (Chadwick 2002: 13). Underpinning these shifting boundaries and forms was an alternative, materially specific, sublime that sat in contrast to the dominant masculine 'transcendent sublime'.

Further research into Dorothy Wordsworth's walking practice took me to her *Grasmere Journals*. It is these writings that directly informed the development of my seven scenographic principles. They also feature in *Warnscale* where, as explored in Chapter 4 of this book, journal extracts were used in the making of that walking-performance, and as a framing device designed to immerse participants in the landscape.

Written between 1800 and 1803 while she was living with her brother William at Dove Cottage in Grasmere in the Lake District, the journals log her everyday life, and are full of vivid descriptions of people, landscapes, sights, sound and noise, tactile sensation and kinetic bodily feeling. They show an awareness of changes in temperature, weather, season, emotion and mood. They are dynamic, non-static and overflowing with different kinds of motion: her own motion as she moves in and through the landscape – skidding on ice, crawling on all fours, lying in fields, woods and trenches, swinging on gates, scrambling up valleys in search of fungi or a waterfall, and the motion of the landscape as it shifts and changes around her – as clouds gather and streak the sky, drenching rain falls, flowers spring forth, trees stir in the wind or fall in a storm, the moon waxes, crows fly overhead and the darkness of night falls.

Research also took me to several of Dorothy Wordsworth's female contemporaries, especially those concerned with landscape and walking such as Ann Radcliffe and Charlotte Smith. Harnessing traditional forms such as journal, letter and poetic writing as well as progressive and experimental forms such as novel, travel and nature writing these writers worked with landscape as a means by which to give a voice to everyday, common-place and 'lived' experiences that otherwise were largely unrecorded or marginalized from mainstream discourses.

Writing in the late 1700s Ann Radcliffe pioneered semi-fictional and non-fictional landscape and travel writing (including an account of the Lake District discussed in Chapter 5) which she used to affect cultural thinking and social change. She was 'regarded as one of the most influential novelists of her generation' (Miles 1995: 2) and was 'well-known in Romantic contexts and remained at the forefront of cultural accounts of the Lakes for many years', providing 'a critical link in the movement towards Romantic ways of thinking about landscape' (Radcliffe 2014: cover). The poet Charlotte Smith pioneered autobiographical writing and used her scientifically informed and intricately detailed description of landscape as a metaphor for 'lived' experiences – her own and those of women that were not usually the subject of literature – the death of children, poverty, marital breakdown and gender inequality.

Together, Smith's, Radcliffe's and Dorothy Wordsworth's feminine 'material' sublime 'mode' of engaging with the landscape sits in contrast to the masculine 'transcendent' sublime. This 'mode' is located-in and present-to the landscape not as a place from which to escape or vanish, but to reappear by facing and imaginatively transforming their feelings or situations.

I now outline each principle by showing how it has emerged from and informs my own practice, where it intersects with the work of Dorothy Wordsworth and her contemporaries, and how other landscape aesthetics contribute.

Principle 1 – site- , life-event- and people-specificity: being located

Principle 1 is about specificity and locatedness. This principle is a literal application of philosopher Donna J. Haraway's term 'being located' to describe how situated and embodied knowledges provide/do not provide 'a view from anywhere' but rather 'a view from somewhere' – that is specific (1988: 581, 590). The principle evolved out of the way in which my practice pursues three strands of transdisciplinary research undertaken on-site and off-site, alone and/or with creative collaborators. These strands are:

> **Strand 1: Site/Landscape-Specific Research** into the rural landscape achieved through fieldwork that involves spending time walking, observing and studying the site, and working with people who have lay or scientific knowledge.

Strand 2: Life-Event/Subject-Specific Research into underlying subject matter achieved by engaging and working with scientists, sociologists, clinicians, and researchers with specialist subject knowledge.

Strand 3: People/Participant-Specific Research into the implications and effects of the life-event/situation achieved by engaging people (individuals, groups, or communities) directly affected by that life-event in the creative process, many of whom become performers and/or participants in the 'final' performance.

Each strand of research captures raw material through drawing, note-taking, map-making, photography, film, and audio recording. Secondary source material in the form of texts, images and objects are also gathered. Later, this material is distilled through the lenses of scenography, writing, music/sound composition and choreography into a walking-performance. These processes have echoes of how Dorothy Wordsworth used her journals to record and describe, in vivid detail, the skills and working lives of local people, for example, labourers working in the fields and shepherds 'salving sheep' (Wordsworth 1991: 87) and people she met when walking the fells – hill guides, vagrants, beggars and widows – whose words she wrote down verbatim. In so doing, she captured and gave value to voices, activities and perspectives that otherwise would have been lost or forgotten, and provided raw material that inspired William Wordsworth's poetry.

Principle 2 – autobiography / autotopography: staying with the trouble

Principle 2 is about first-person points of view. It is about facing and giving a voice to life-event experiences that sit on the edges of mainstream dialogues and often remain unacknowledged – leading to a sense of what philosopher Elspeth Probyn describes as being 'outside belonging' (1996: 8). It is about making-visible experiences that cannot easily be put into words and creating a site – inside belonging – where participants can 'reappear'.

The principle applies Haraway's concept of 'staying with the trouble' (2016: 1), explored more fully in Chapter 2 when I look at *Fissure*, a work that faced illness, death and bereavement. It evolved out of the way my practice is rooted in autobiographical life-events – mine as well as that of the collaborators and participants it involves – and emplaces those lived-experiences into a rural landscape.

Dorothy Wordsworth, Ann Radcliffe and Charlotte Smith used their writing to voice their lived-experiences of life-events including illness, grief, the death of children, poverty, imprisonment, emotional/psychological distress and not being in control of their lives. In so doing they provided a witness for and gave voice to their own and other women's lives. The way in which they noticed the 'commonplace' enabled them to see afresh 'everyday' objects, people and experiences that were ordinarily overlooked, or outside social and cultural discourses. Writing on autobiographical performance, Deirdre Heddon's reflections could have been applied two centuries earlier to the work of these women:

> autobiographical performance was regarded by women as a means to reveal otherwise invisible lives, to resist marginalisation and objectification and to become, instead, speaking subjects with self-agency ... [they] provide a way to talk out, Talkback, talk otherwise. Here, the marginalised subject can literally take centre stage.
>
> (Heddon 2008: 3)

As well as working from autobiographical perspectives Wordsworth, Radcliffe and Smith emplaced lived experiences into landscape. Recognizes how peoples' lives, identifies and sense of self are often understood and expressed through landscapes and objects, this autobiographical/landscape emplacement can be understood through the term 'autotopographic' (Gonzalez 1995: 133).

Principle 3 – landscape materials and environmental forces / metaphor

Principle 3 is about harnessing physical materials and environmental forces and processes of a landscape – geological, topographical, botanical, animal, meteorological and seasonal – as metaphors for a life-event or situation. The principle recognises our powerlessness to control the forces of nature within and around us but notices signs of renewal and transformation.

The principle evolved from my symbolic and metaphoric use of landscape features, environmental forces, people and animals, objects and materials of the sites.

Dorothy Wordsworth's journals show an acute awareness of the fragility of life and the overwhelming forces of 'nature' and how these can cause 'random acts of destruction' (Pipkin 1998: 599). She describes trees being uprooted and thrown over in a storm, hungry skeleton-like deer, and starving children. She acknowledges the physical and emotional effects on people's faces and bodies of time passing, illness and poverty, in close-up detail. She does not shrink from acknowledging the effects of these material forces and processes. Instead, her writing invites:

> a valuing of 'barren, decayed, broken, or encrusted objects that counters imagery presenting Nature as beautiful and fecund ... it accepts parts of

Nature as broken, ambiguous, ruined or barren – not simply Beautiful, not simply powerful.

(Snyder 2001: 144)

Dorothy also wrote about the weather and its physical power, changeability and effects on the body. She describes how it blew her over, drenched her to the skin and had the power to end life. However, she also noticed things thriving and surviving against the odds, despite cold or wind: a delicate flower growing by a single root or a bird singing out of season or rebuilding a broken nest that had taken weeks to build. Rarely does she refer directly to herself; instead, her accounts of nature struggling to survive might be read as metaphors for herself. Often she identifies, and perhaps identified with, solo flowers, such as the solitary columbine:

growing upon the Rocks, here & there a solitary plant – sheltered & shaded by the tufts & bowers of trees it is graceful slender creature, a female seeking retirement & growing freest & most graceful where it is most alone. I observed that the more shaded plants were always the tallest.

(Woof 1991: 103)

Principle 4 – composing and moving through the scene

Principle 4 is about the hybridization of the 'real' with the 'imagined'. It is about drawing a walking-performance out-of and back in-to a rural landscape using a combination of materials from the site, objects, film, sounds, performance, actions, science and text. It is about moving participants through a landscape/performance-scape of constantly changing and unfolding scenes, and using 'viewing stations' from where the optimum of the scene/s is found.

The principle evolved from the way my practice mobilizes landscape, performer and participant and from my use of scenographic devices. These include the use of colour, objects, performers (human and animal), movement, and sound/music to bring focus and draw attention into and across the scene; windows, walls and valley sides frame the scene both literally and in a life-event context. The solitary figure brings human scale and focus to the scene, and through the figure's eyes or situation participants are invited to view the scene.

The term 'viewing station' is borrowed from Thomas West's *A Guide to the Lakes* in which he details the scenery and landscape of the English Lake District and maps the places from where the most 'astonishing' or 'picturesque' views can be found (West [1778] 1802: 93). An early example of a 'viewing station' is the summerhouse at Rydal Hall near Grasmere in Cumbria, built in 1694, from inside of which a 'picturesque' waterfall scene can be viewed. The path to the station winds through deciduous woodland, and on approaching:

> the viewer listens to the noise of the water growing louder [though] his view is blocked [by the summerhouse]. Once inside, and when the door has been closed, the shutters on the large window were thrown back and there, perfectly framed was a view of the tree-shaped falls, the pool in the foreground, and above, in the background, a glimpse of the little rustic stone bridge crossing the upper stream all ideally proportioned to its frame. (Grout 2013)

The anticipatory (sonic, visual and physical) approach to the station, followed by the revelation of the previously hidden scene, provides a dramatic 'reveal'. From within, the dark interior of the 'viewing chamber' acts like an auditorium and the window frames the view in a similar way to a proscenium arch framing a lit stage. The viewer becomes the audience, physically participating in their experience, and the landscape becomes a living, sensory 'scene' constructed using rules of composition and perspective to guide the eye and the gaze.

Ann Radcliffe used the landscape as a mobile 'theatre' of constantly changing images, scenes and topographies experienced on foot, horseback or in a carriage and observed from one viewpoint then another – a viewing/reviewing process designed to transform both the scene and the person experiencing it. Working in this way Radcliffe subverted the Early Romantic trope of the solitary male figure surveying a landscape scene, typified in Caspar David Friedrich's *Wanderer Above the Sea of Fog* (1818), with a female figure who acted as a stand-in for the reader and is designed to empower the reader. In much of her writing Charlotte Smith used the first-person perspective of a solitary female figure who she placed walking through or lying in a landscape. For example, the opening line of her poem 'Beachy Head' – 'On thy stupendous summit, rock sublime!' – establishes the scale of the landscape (Curran 1993: 232). The poem's central figure or character, from whose perspective we are directed to look, soon notices the 'minute detail' and 'fantastic shapes' of the sea creatures whose shells and fossils form the limestone cliff on which she reclines (232). In situ, and without fear of censure, the character then uses the landscape to reveal the hard facts and effects of everyday existence. Doing this, she 'embraces the physical forces of the natural world in order to draw from them an expanded sense of selfhood' (Pipkin 1998: 610–12)

Principle 5 – walking beyond knowledge / beating new tracks

Principle 5 is about beating new tracks – literal and metaphorical. It is about walking 'beyond [...] knowledge into new possibilities' (Solnit 2001: 101), towards: new ways of thinking and feeling, alternative life paths and re-imaged and re-imagined futures.

The principle evolved from the way that walking is embedded in the creative processes, when it becomes a means to explore, research and map a site. It also evolved from the way that solitary, side-by-side, companionship is used as a therapeutic, surrogate and transformative tool and takes on a symbolic function in the context of the life-event being explored.

In the context of her time, Dorothy Wordsworth's walking was radical, and challenged social norms. Her journals show how she walked long distances, day and night, in all seasons, terrains and weather, alone or with others, as a means of seeing, feeling and processing emotions. Her walking was adventurous and exploratory. She literally 'beat new tracks' climbing into undergrowth in search of a specific plant, crawling 'up the little glen' where she 'found a beautiful shell-like purple fungus' (Wordsworth 1991: 103) or leaving the beaten track to search out a waterfall. The act of walking and dwelling also immersed her in the landscape where she was free to think and process her emotions, which became a restorative, regenerative, creative and therapeutic act. Through walking she connected to place and through place she connected to herself. For example, on one occasion, having parted from her brothers William and John, who were walking to Yorkshire, and feeling distressed, she describes how she sits for 'a long time upon a stone at the margin of the lake, and after a flood of tears my heart was easier' (1991: 1). Following this episode, the way she described the look, feel and sound of the environment seemed to be influenced by her mood, and the lake became a mirror to her feelings:

> The lake looked to me I knew not why dull and melancholy, the weltering on the shores seemed a heavy sound. I walked as long as I could amongst the stones on the shore.... Sate down very often, tho' it was cold.
>
> (Wordsworth 1991: 1)

Despite the cold temperature, Dorothy Wordsworth remained outside for more time, not ready to leave until she had processed her emotional turmoil. As well as walking alone, Dorothy walked co-creatively with William Wordsworth who recognized that it was 'She' – through her capacity to look, listen, feel and describe the landscape – who 'gave me eyes, she gave me ears; And humble cares, and delicate fears' (Wordsworth 1851: 183) At other times she walked in order to visit or talk with friends. In *Recollections of the Lake Poets* the poet Thomas De Quincey noted that those she walked with described her as an 'exceedingly sympathetic, always profound walking' companion (De Quincey in Levin 1987: 237).

Principle 6 – close-up and observational looking / alternative viewpoints and perspectives

Principle 6 is about close-up and observational looking leading to new ways of seeing and thinking. It is about seeking alternative viewpoints and perspectives on a landscape and a life-event – literal and metaphorical. It is about becoming physically, sensorially and imaginatively immersed in the site.

The principle evolved out of the way my practice invites participants to undertake close-up, observational and magnified looking and actions that afford alternative viewpoints and perspectives on the landscape and on life-event experiences.

Like Charlotte Smith, Dorothy Wordsworth's close observational studies and descriptive renderings of specific landscapes, seasons and people are highly evocative, intricately observed and underpinned with scientific study – geological, topographical, botanical, meteorological and planetary. At times she must have walked slowly and deliberately, perhaps crouching to seek out and study flowers and plants growing in cracks and crevices or under hedgerows. She also literally changed her physical viewpoint by lying down to look at or listen to trees, light, birds, water and sheep from an alternative perspective 'As I lay down on the grass, I observed the glittering silver line on the ridges of the back of the sheep' (Wordsworth 1991: 93).

Her journals reveal her immense capacity to notice, and record what she sees, hears and feels in descriptive imagery and painterly words that capture and evoke the scene – colour, depth, scale, sound – and the visual and sensory effects of the fast-changing phenomena and environmental forces at work around her, such as wind seen:

> brushing along the surface of the water, & growing more delicate, as it were thinner & of a paler colour till they died away – others spread out like a peacocks tail, & some went right forward this way & that in all directions. ... they made it all alive.
>
> (Wordsworth 1991: 61)

Principle 7 – wonderment and defamiliarization: moments of being

Principle 7 is about aliveness-to and observational looking-at the material and processes of the landscape, environment, and the body. It is about finding wonderment in them, seeing them afresh, and liberating them from their familiar or everyday context and meaning. This principle applies the concepts of 'moments of being' (Woolf [1972] 1978: 81) and 'defamiliarisation' (Lemon 1965: 12). It evolved out of the way my practice notices, reveals and makes visible everyday (ordinary/extraordinary) materials and processes that are usually overlooked, invisible to the naked-eye, hidden or rarely seen in close-up, and defamiliarizes them in a life-event context.

The 'transformative' capacity of Dorothy Wordsworth's and her female contemporaries' approach to landscape comes from an aliveness to their environment and an ability to see and find the feminine 'material' sublime – as a form of 'wonderment' – in the human and other-than-human material of the everyday and the commonplace. The sun glittering on the wool of a sheep, the light moving over water, the movement of the planets or a favourite birch tree:

> yielding to the gusty wind with all its tender twigs, the sun shone upon it & it glanced in the wind like a flying sunshiny shower.
> (Wordsworth 1991: 40).

For Virginia Woolf, 'moments of being' are sudden, revelatory or 'violent shock[s]' that serve to 'punctuate the cotton wool of daily life [which] renders one blind to the particular and the common place' – a state she refers to as 'non-being' ([1972] 1978: 81, 82). For Woolf, like Dorothy Wordsworth, many 'moments of being' occurred while out walking and she often 'found' them in the 'natural' material of her environment, for example in the 'grey-green creases of bark on a tree', the life force of a budding plant, a puddle on a path, the 'ribbed pattern on a shell' or the lined face of an old woman (82–7). Other 'moments of being' were caused by the fleeting effects of phenomena such as moonlight on water, the 'lurid light of a hailstorm' or a 'distinct' sound (84). The effect was that the 'whole world' became a 'work of art', but it also brought Woolf an awareness of her own impotence in the face of forces of 'nature' (84).

Defamiliarization is an artistic technique of seeing 'common things in an unfamiliar or strange way in order to enhance perception of the familiar' (New World Encyclopaedia 2008). The term was first used in 1917 by the Russian literary theorist and formalist Viktor Shklovskii; 'defamiliarization' literally means 'making it strange' (Lemon 1965: 12). Shklovskii explored the different ways in which artistic processes and techniques bring about 'defamiliarization' to stimulate fresh perception. These include 'seeing things out of their normal context'; making things appear 'strange and wonderful'; describing an object as if 'seeing it for the first time' (1965: 13).

Discussing the link between contemporary art and the theatre, Pamela Howard (2002: 207) noted how an object 'when lifted from its normal context and re-presented acquires a new life. It can enable the spectator to see something, as if for the very first time'. Making things appear strange and wonderful through shock and defamiliarization is a scenographic technique that 'can be traced in much pioneering work', such as that of Caspar Neher and Bertolt Brecht, for whom 'the event of making the familiar strange was a device to provoke a more conscious, intellectual and social engagement with what was being presented on stage' (Butterworth and McKinney 2009: 98).

The case studies which follow show how I have developed and applied these principles in a number of performance works. Sometimes one or more of the principles take centre stage, but all of them help to inform and explain the processes and objectives of scenography with purpose.

2

Walking-performance – emplacing a life-event: *Fissure*

> *The physical journey through time and space that is an essential part of pilgrimage can also have metaphorical resonances on many levels. A pilgrimage may be a rite of passage involving transformations of one's inner state and outer status; it may be a quest for a transcendent goal; it may entail a long-desired healing of a physical or spiritual element ailment.*
> (COLEMAN AND ELSNER 1995: 6)

In this chapter I look at how, by emplacing a life-event in a rural landscape, that landscape has the potential to become a *site of transformation* where grief can be articulated, shared, re-imaged and reimagined.

To do this, the chapter explores the performance work *Fissure* (2011), made in response to the illness and death of my sister from a brain tumour, aged 29, and the grief that followed. It was *Fissure* that made me aware of the expressive and transformative potential of scenographic-led walking-performance created in a rural landscape, and demonstrates a major shift in my practice from scenography designed to immerse participants in a site-specific performance to scenography with a purpose, designed to have efficacy in the context of a specific subject matter.

Fissure began as a grief-led impulse to make a private pilgrimage by walking across Yorkshire, a county in northern England, from sea to river source – this walk was intended to give time and space for grieving, alone and with members of my close family. However, once commissioned, that initial idea evolved into a three-day-long public walking-performance – that took the form of a pilgrimage – in the Yorkshire Dales. This location was chosen because my extended family has lived and worked in that area over many generations, and because of its distinctive limestone features – caves, pavements, ravines and underground rivers, many of which I had previously explored with my sister and family.

Fissure took over two years to create. It involved an extended period of creative research that engaged a transdisciplinary methodology and brought together a core creative team (scenographer/designer, writer, composer and choreographer) with place experts (geologist, conservationist and a team of cavers) and neurology and medical experts (neuro-oncologist, neurosurgeon and neurophysicist/imager). Additional advice came from an expert in palliative and end-of-life care with whom I discussed the lack of conversation that exists around grief (something that came to the fore when making *Mulliontide*, noted in Chapter 6). The final work was performed by these experts (three of whom, Michael Brada, Chris Clark and Mike Kelly, spoke directly to participants) and a company of six professional singers and six professional female dancers, a local choir, a band of church bell ringers and handbell ringers.

This chapter explores aspects of *Fissure* that were crucial to the processes of transformation. It looks at both my making methodology and the final performance, and considers how and why the work:

- used an autobiographical lived experience as a starting point, but widened and extended out (beyond a personal therapeutic act) to create a meaningful space for others with a range of experiences relating to grief;
- engaged a scenographic (image-based, non-literal, multisensory and multimodal) language suited to life-event experiences that cannot be expressed in words;
- applied a transdisciplinary methodology that led to a union between multiple art forms, science, landscape and participants;
- was composed in a rural landscape, and used this physically and symbolically through a juxtaposition and collision of landscape, performance, art and neurological science;
- incorporated extended travel, by train and on foot, that physically immersed participants in the performance and took on a metaphorical meaning;
- drew on pilgrimage, in the sense of the performance taking the form of a 'journey (usually of a long distance) … undertaken to a place of particular significance or interest' (*Oxford English Dictionary*), and a three-phase ritual process designed to deepen the role participants played in the performance.

All poem extracts in this chapter were written by Elizabeth Burns (2011) for *Fissure* (Wilson 2011).

To understand better the impact of *Fissure* on participants, I drew on participant responses collated in the weeks following the performance by Audience South West on behalf of the producers Artevents (which commissioned *Fissure* as part of *The Re-Enchantment* (2010–11). I do not have access to participants' names and have indentified this feedback in footnotes. Production credits for *Fissure* are in Appendix A.

Fissure – the need to transform grief (beyond autobiography)

I am often asked whether making *Fissure* was for me a therapeutic or cathartic act. It can be exhausting and exposing to make this sort of autobiographic work (and to talk and write about it for years to come), and I have found it necessary to keep aspects of the experience private, and to keep my sister – the person (and her name) – close. It was a decade after her death that I made *Fissure* and I had, to an extent, learnt to manage an amount of grief. It is important, I think, not to go into a creative process while still in the eye of the storm; rather, some personal processing and acceptance of the life-event in question needs to take place. So, initially, before it became a public work, making *Fissure* might have served a therapeutic purpose for me personally. Ultimately, however, it was not catharsis that I sought; rather, the force driving me to create the work was a desire to express and understand something of the paralysing enormity of grief *and* reach out to others in need of a means by which to transform their own grief into something bearable. In this regard two quotes from artists Lisa Kron and Tim Miller – both of whom perform autobiographical work – that Dierdre Heddon draws on in *Autobiography and Performance* are resonant. 'For Lisa Kron', writes Heddon, '"the goal of autobiographical work should not be to tell stories about yourself but, instead, to use the details of your own life to illuminate or explore something more universal" […] Tim Miller similarly wants to use his individual experience in order to find "a window for" the audience' (Kron and Miller in Heddon 2008: 5). 'If autobiographical performance', adds Heddon, 'is a potentially powerful tool of resistance, intervention and/or reinvention, then it must be so for the spectator as much as for the performer' (2008: 5).

The title *Fissure*, as this poem captures, encompassed multiple physical and symbolic meanings: the longitudinal gap between the two hemispheres of the brain, the metaphorical effects of neurological dysfunction, landscape and geological features, and the grief felt when separated by death from a loved one:

fissure: a break a gap a rift a fracture

fissure: a furrow in the surface of the brain
that which separates the hemispheres
splits the brain in two
once, messages leapt between synapses
now they falter and fall

fissure: an opening made by cracking
the paths of movement blocked

fissure: a splitting or separation
the paths of words choked

fissure: a cleft in rock a chasm in the earth

(Burns 2011)

Following my sister's death, I needed, but could not find, words to express my grief or a way of processing and coming to terms with her illness and death. This unmet need reflected, I suggest, a lack of meaningful or adequate social ritual around death and mourning, particularly for someone who dies at a young age. My response was to make *Fissure*. Driving this was a deeply felt need to face up to, and comprehend, the mechanics of what had happened to my sister: how and why a tumour grows, the illness and symptoms it causes (headaches, seizures, loss of movement and speech), the terminal diagnosis, the death it brought, and the physically and emotionally overwhelming grief that follows. The fact that eighty participants joined *Fissure*, committing three days to the performance, suggested I was not alone in my need for a ritual, or an ongoing process of grieving that mainstream ceremonies don't allow for.

The need to transform, break the silence of grief and find a language for it emerges in the work of many other artists who like me worked in response to personal experiences of bereavement. For example, Jordan Baseman's films *How to Manage Stillness* (2013) and *A Cold Hand on a Cold Day* (2013) were made following the death of Baseman's brother, and Steven Eastwood's documentary film *The Interval and the Instant* (2017) follows four participants through the dying process. Performance maker Ellie Harrison created *The Grief Series* (2011–present) following the death of her brother and other close family members. The series included a variety of performance settings. At its most intimate, in *The Reservation* (2013–14), Harrison met one audience member at a time in a hotel bedroom, where they exchanged stories about grief. This one-to-one work has echoes of dance artist Fabiola Santana's *Home for Grief* (2019) in which she involves participants in the re-creation of inherited but forgotten grief-rituals. On a larger scale, and inspired by the Mexican Day of the Dead, Harrison's *All That Lives* (2020) engages communities in the making of rememberance rituals (2019), whilst in *The Crossing* (2017) she produced a collection of resources that were designed to encourage participants to think about how they might plan a funeral celebration. This work, like Fevered Sleep's *This Grief Thing* (2018–present) and Mats Staub's conversational exchanges in *Death and Birth in My Life* (2018–19), faced and did not shrink from conversations about death and mourning.

Staying with the trouble

For me, making *Fissure* and thereby facing the life-event of my sister's illness and death harnessed and applied Haraway's (2016: 1) notion of 'staying with the trouble'. Trouble is an interesting word, she writes, deriving from a thirteenth-century French verb meaning:

> 'to stir up', 'to make cloudy', 'to disturb.' We – all of us on Terra – live in disturbing times, mixed up times, troubling and turbid times … The task is to make trouble, to stir up a potent response to devastating effect events, as well as to settle troubled waters and rebuild quiet places.
>
> (Haraway 2016: 1)

I set out to use scenography as means of 'staying with the trouble' and in so doing make a 'potent response' to a devastating life-event – but also to create a space, a quiet place that might resonate, be meaningful and have tangible effects and outcomes for others (2016: 1).

I draw a parallel between a life-event subject matter that cannot be fully comprehended or expressed through words alone and the concept of the masculine 'transcendent' sublime which, in terms of landscape aesthetics, is regarded as a 'a state … that cannot be represented, because of its indeterminacy [and] asks for a new language' (Andrews 1999: 148).

The aim of *Fissure* was to find a scenographic language – an image-based, non-literal, multisensory and multimodal language – with which to articulate an experience that could not be expressed in words alone and 'represent that which cannot be represented' to make it visible and speak the unspeakable (1999: 48). What was important, however, was that this language was resonant with others and did not place emphasis on the spoken word, but combined image, poetry, dance, music, sound, science, object and landscape.

The writer John Berger, in his discussion of the inadequacy of words to describe complex ideas and human experiences, notes how images can 'define our experiences more precisely in areas where words are inadequate' (Berger 1972: 33). As this chapter seeks to reveal, scenography as a visually oriented yet multimodal art form is particularly well suited to this purpose.

Looking differently and again

Looking again and differently can be seen in 'Pathologies: A Startling Tour of Our Bodies' by the nature writer Kathleen Jamie ([2008] 2012). Guided by the trained eye of a pathologist, she learnt how to see and understand cancerous cells viewed through a microscope – something she describes as being like 'slipping into a dream':

> I was admitted to another world, where everything was pink. Looking down from a great height upon a pink countryside, a landscape. There was an estuary, with a north bank and a south. In the estuary wing-shaped river islands or sandbanks, as if it was low tide. It was astonishing, a map of the familiar; it was our local river, as seen by a Hawk.
>
> (Jamie 2012: 30)

However, Jamie was unaware that, following a diagnosis of breast cancer, within a year her own biopsy cells would be examined by the same pathologist. Now, she describes how she felt a compulsion, a 'need to look', and through looking 'transform the experience' of the diagnosis, the material of the tumour and her treatment (Collins and Jamie 2013: xx). Because 'I expressed an interest', she writes:

> I was shown my own mammogram images. I sat beside the radiologist in front of her computer screen, as she pointed with her pencil. The image was rather beautiful, a grey-glowing circle, like the full moon seen through binoculars. The tumour was an obvious density. The radiologist and pathologist looked with their eyes, the surgeon with his fingertips.
>
> (Collins and Jamie 2013: v)

This view revealed to Jamie her 'own intimate, inner natural world, the body's weird shapes and forms' ((2012: 13) 2012: 37). Following breast-removal surgery, her need to look continued. Wanting her scar 'off my body and onto the paper' so that she could 'have a proper look at it', she asked the artist Bridget Collins 'if she might draw this curious line of mine. If she might be my eyes' (Collins and Jamie 2013: vii). This patient–doctor–artist collaboration led to an:

> intimate process of looking and seeing as it passes from one person – a cancer patient – looking at herself, from being 'examined' by a surgeon, to being looked at by an artist. In each situation a transformation occurs. The gaze of the patient on her own body and its post-operative scarring is objectified by that of the surgeon assessing the success of his work. But then the creative eye of the artist takes over and what was regarded as a mark of disease and of violation takes on an extraordinary flowering, and becomes a thing of beauty.
>
> (Collins and Jamie 2013: vii)

As well as looking at the line of Jamie's scar, Collins went into the landscape to gather more material. She drew fissured rocks and skylines before returning to her studio to transform her findings – scar, body and land – through creative processes into art objects:

> I admire the cool, precise looking of the pathologist and the surgeon, and I also admire the transforming, creative imagination of the artist.
>
> (Collins and Jamie 2013: vii)

This combination of three different points of view – the patient and her scar, the doctors and her body, and the artist and the landscape – is reminicent of my own need to look at my sister's illness and death, and has echos of the transdisciplinary exchanges that happened between me, the neuroscientists, (physicist, oncologist and surgeon) and the creative team (writer, choreographer and composer). It was these exchanges – and the different ways of looking at a brain tumour that each entails – that provided the raw material, which – after it was filtered through the imaginations of the creative and scientific teams – was transformed into *Fissure* and transformed yet again in each participant's imagination.

Transdisciplinary methodology for socially engaged and applied scenography

> Transdisciplinarity concerns that which is at once between the disciplines, across the different disciplines, and beyond all discipline. Its goal is the understanding of the present world.
>
> (Nicolescu 2002: 44)

Because of its appreciation of the human condition in all its complexity and diversity, and a concern to understand and find 'real world creative solutions' to 'pressing problems' (Bernstein 2015: 2) transciplinarity is a resonant methodological model for scenography that deals with lived experiences, and seeks to find creative ways by which to transform them.

Adopting a transdisciplinary approach to the making of *Fissure* offered me a holistic approach that allowed for a 'fusion of ideas, knowledge, methods, values belonging to several disciplines or fields of study' (Jeder 2014: 128) and made visible the unexpected connections in thinking, concerns and terminology found across and between disciplines. Transdisciplinarity is a method of enquiry suited to the way scenography as an art form makes connections that are not ordinarily drawn between seemingly unconnected elements: objects, places, ideas, images, people, actions, phenomena and processes (human and other-than-human, internal and external, or surface and subsurface).

In *Fissure* these connections can be seen in the way the performance drew together walking, landscape and earth science; neurofunction and dysfunction; death and bereavement; and liturgical and ritual forms. To achieve this collision the performance pursued two strands of site-specific and subject-specific research that engaged collaborators from the arts and medical, earth and social sciences to bring different voices, perspectives and skills to the table.

Autobiography (personal experience) – leading to dance and sung poetry

Seeking a visually led and multisensory language for *Fissure*, I assembled a creative team whose disciplines and practice, while working non-literally and non-narratively, were able to convey the bond between sisters, the physical effects of a brain tumour, the moment of death and the feelings of grief.

My search for the creative team took me to the environmental choreographer Nigel Stewart, whose choreography for *The Saturated Moment* (Sap Dance 2006), performed as a solo by the dancer Dominique Bulgin, was immediately compelling and resonant of the bodily effects of a tumour. Bulgin's gestural quality, her body falling through space, her dislocated, twisted and contorted limbs with a force of their own, and the emotional, yet contained, velocity of the choreography that also became stilled were visually resonant with the physical effects of a brain tumour: movement breaking down and fissuring, and the distorted movement and shaping of limbs. This movement, based on Laban movement analysis, choreutics and motif, effort and shape notation, looked liked and expressed my sister's illness in startling images and without words. They were also resonant of the gestural hand vocabulary my sister and I used to communicate.

To create the choreography for *Fissure*, Stewart applied a methodology that responded to a number of different sources. These included the neuroscientific and medical research and the physical landscape, for example, the action and experience of moving through a narrow cave tunnel in the pitch dark of Long Churn Cave, Burns' poetry and my descriptions of the physical effects of my sister's illness. This material was later developed into choreographic phrases and, working with the dancers, was adapted to fit the particular physical features (and dramaturgical context) of the locations where it was performed. The form and aesthetic quality of the movement at each site were dependent on what that scene conveyed within the overall dramaturgy.

Searching for a writer to create a poetic layer of language led me to Elizabeth Burns, whose poetry is rich in visual and sensory yet pared-back language and often concerned with relationships. Her work includes writing in which she imagines the death of a sister, suggesting an empathy with the relationship that was foundational to *Fissure*. For example, in the poem 'I Dream of the Death of My Sister', she writes, 'Grief eats me. / I can't speak of it. // ... my life is changed now, / something so precious is lost' (Burns 1999: 11). It was because of these poems – their subject and form – that I felt Burns was the writer for the project.

Subsequently, over many months, I shared with Burns personal memories of my sister, describing the stages of her illness, the effort and exhaustion of treatment, her last breath and my request to the undertakers to take care wrapping her body and to 'carry her gently' away.[1] I talked of how, because the tumour affected speech and movement, simple gestures became a form of non-verbal communication and the act of holding hands, or holding on, had deep significance – a motif that found its way into the writing and choreography.

Burns distilled and condensed a huge amount of complex information into a series of poems that found the heart of the subject matter. Her achievement was to weave that material with images and words distilled from other sources – neuroscience, oncology, surgery and the physical landscape. This process led to a series of poems using a three-day and six-phase sequential structure that moved through stages of my sister's illness, treatment and death, and the aftermath of grief. Then, along with other creative and scientific elements, the poems were emplaced and performed in the landscape – many at locations

---

[1] This decription and phrase informed the poem 'Carry Her Gently into the Darkness' (Burns 2011).

that had also informed the poems. This emplacement process brought them together with the other elements of the scenography – dance, singing, objects, materials. I use the word *emplace* rather than *place* to reflect the site-specific and embedded qualities of the interventions I make. Each scenic/scenographic intervention is always about much more than placing or installing a performance in a site; rather, the performance is born from the site and references the site in multiple ways through materials, content, routes and dramaturgy.

Site-specific and subject-specific research

The two types of transdisciplinary research that *Fissure* pursued were distinct yet interwoven. The first strand was site-specific research carried out during field trips and investigative walks above and below ground in the Yorkshire Dales. Experts included the geophysicist Mike Kelly, conservationist Colin Newlands and a team of cavers. The second type was subject-specific research, taking the form of lectures given by neuroscientists and observational work and information exchanges off site in clinics and hospitals in London as well as on site in Yorkshire. Experts included the neuro-oncologist Michael Brada, who had led the treatment of my sister throughout her illness, her neurosurgeon Andy McEvoy and the neurophysicist Chris Clark. Later some of these experts spoke directly to participants, bringing their viewpoint into the frame, and became performers.

Both these strands collected raw material that was later evolved through a scenographic–dramaturgical process into *Fissure*. The research provided imagery, sound, data, materials and text that informed the performance in a complex variety of ways, including the route and choice of key locations for interventions *and* content, the composition and design of each scene, and the poetic and scientific text delivered live by singers and scientists and layered into sound installations.

Site/landscape-specific research – walking, caving and mapping

Looking for sites, locations and routes, I walked the landscapes for months (alone and with the artistic team), following Ordnance Survey and geological maps in the search for visually and metaphorically distinctive terrain that might reflect the underlying subject matter. Seeking ways that the route might also be representative or suggestive of illness, cancer treatment and grief, I took note of where the walking was gentle and steady, and where it became physically challenging and took time and effort.

I traversed limestone pavements – their distinctive fissures caused by rainwater that had seeped into, opened up and dissolved the rock. I noticed the striking visual analogy between the glints (block of limestone) and grykes (fissures between blocks) of these limestone pavements and the gyri and sulcus (furrows) that form the surface of the brain. Later this process of water through rock became resonant with the neurophysicist's use of water to map the brain.

Using surveys of the cave networks, I tracked the flow of water off Ingleborough Fell and found the places where it disappears underground and those where, having met harder rock, it was forced to resurge (resurrect) to the surface. This looking and mapping was underpinned by the architecture of the brain, neurofunction and dysfunction, the devastating physical effects of a brain tumour, and feelings relating to grief.

Walking with Mike Kelly, I saw how geology maps were translated into physical landscape. He explained how 'caves are formed by water seeping and flowing through the bedding planes and vertical joints of the rock'.[2] With Colin Newlands I saw how communities of wildflowers grew in the glints and grykes of the rock and returned 'resurrected' in the ground of a blasted quarry. With local cavers, I explored the hidden underground worlds of Long Churn and Ingleborough Cave. Gradually, these research walks revealed how the landscape was formed from the bones and skulls of sea creatures and, as explained by Kelly, were 'carved and moulded', 'blasted and exploded' by 'powerful geological forces'.[3]

Walking, I collected materials and objects (red wool left on barbed wire and thorn bushes by sheep, red rope used during caving, sheep's skulls and eggshell-thin bird skulls, pheasant and inky-black crows' feathers, geology knives), and the sounds of rock being excavated and crushed were recorded in a nearby working limestone quarry. Later, composer Jocelyn Pook manipulated these sounds, combining them with sound effects collected during neurosurgery, and emplaced them 'on-site' into the physical landscape and installations.

Life-event/subject-specific research – neuro-physics, -oncology and -surgery

My need to comprehend what had happened to my sister led me back to the neuro-oncologist Michael Brada. It was Michael who had led my sister's treatment and told my family that her condition was terminal and when there was no more treatment available. Open to the idea of making a performance

---

[2] Later, these phrases were spoken by Kelly in the live performance.
[3] Later, these phrases spoken by Kelly in the live performance were incorporated into the poem 'A Landscape Carved and Moulded' (Burns 2011).

that explored this subject matter, over many months Michael and I met regularly. He explained my sister's treatment to me, and how and why a brain tumour grows 'when cells lose a mechanism that tells them to stop growing':

> Cells multiply, divide or survive longer than they should and develop properties that they travel and become 'as mould in bread', the bread is still there, the mould doesn't destroy it, but the mould goes into the bread disturbing function and causing loss of movement or speech.
>
> (Brada in Wilson 2011)[4]

The notes I made during these conversations and my sister's detailed treatment records, combined with studies I made of the architectural structure and neurological function of the brain (and dysfunction caused by a brain tumour) all informed the content and structure of *Fissure*.

My need to comprehend also led me to the neurophysicist Chris Clark who, at his laboratory in London, showed me (and later the rest of the creative team) the neuroimaging maps of tumours he creates for surgeons to follow during surgery. These vivid images show how 'streamlines' (lines of fluid that differ when the flow is not steady or becomes blocked) within the human brain become disrupted by a tumour; Chris equates this to a boulder blocking and choking underground river passageways, preventing the water moving through them. He explained how, in a person with a tumour, these blockages lead to cognitive, physical and sensory dysfunction (falling, loss of speech and movement). He also explained how his maps are used in neurosurgery and show what he described as 'regions of interest' to avoid during surgery to prevent damage to good brain matter (in Wilson 2011a).[5]

In London, invited by Andy McEvoy to observe him and his surgical team at work, I wrote detailed notes, drew sketches, took photographs and made sound recordings (none of this material revealed the patient's identity and it was all gathered with written permission). My purpose in making and recording these observations was to understand and see the process of surgery and the material and words used. I also collected raw material that would later be translated into the design and scenography for *Fissure*. I witnessed the cutting and shaving of hair, the marking and cutting of flesh, and the drilling and sawing of the skull. I saw the pulsing white matter of the brain and the locating of tumour cells using tractographic maps to guide the surgeon to the cancerous cells and away from healthy cells. I observed the careful removal of ravaged tumour cells using surgical instruments and the setting aside of this

---

[4] Later, this text was spoken by Brada in the live performance.
[5] Later, Clark spoke these phrases in the live performance and they informed the content of the poem 'Now Begins the Lengthy Crawl' (Burn 2011)

FIGURE 2.1 Fissure. *Chris Clark (neurophysicist) talking to the creative team about his tractographic mapping work, UCL, London. Photographer: Louise Ann Wilson*

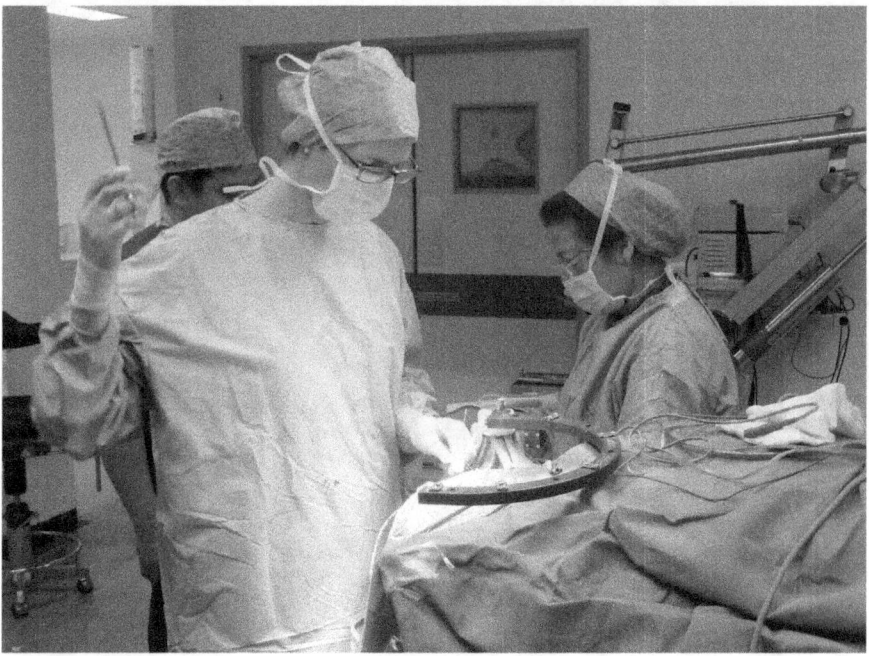

FIGURE 2.2 Fissure. *Transdisciplinary research. Neurosurgery at the London Hospital, London. Photographer: Louise Ann Wilson*

material for biopsy; the use of needles and red silk thread to sew, or 'suture', the tissue and flesh back together; and the surgeon asking for a 'Suture please ... Stitch please ... Cut please'.[6] Then I watched how screws were used to fix the skull-bone back in place.

My meetings with Michael Brada and Chris Clark continued on site in Yorkshire, where the neurological research, the landscape research and all the experts and creative term came together.

During one of these field trips, Mike Kelly explained how the landscape had been changed by tectonic movement, water action, quarrying and the tsunami-like destruction of repeated glacial cycles. Mike Brada, though, looking at the landscape through the eyes of an oncologist, said that nothing in the blasted landscape was representative of the devastating effects of a brain tumour on the human body. The land, he said, *can* survive and repair, whereas a person cannot – their life will end.

FIGURE 2.3 Fissure. *Transdisciplinary research. Louise Ann Wilson with Mike Kelly (geophysicist), Michael Brada (neuro-oncologist), Chris Clark (neurophysicist) and Duncan Morrison (caver) on site, Yorkshire Dales. Photographer: Di Robson, Artevents, all rights reserved*

---

[6] These phrases later were later incorporated into the poem 'Astrocytoma ... The Heavy Weight of Diagnosis' (Burns 2011).

I was privileged in the making of *Fissure* because those involved in creating and performing the work (artists, scientists, dancers, singers) generously 'drew upon, interacted with and responded to autobiographical material relating to' my personal story, and together we found ways of transforming that material into a symbollic form by emplacing it into the landscape (Heddon 2008: 8). The underworld myths and liturgical form that underpinned *Fissure*, combined with its multimodal form of delivery and symbolic use of landscape, elevated my personal experience out of the everyday and into the mythic. Crucially, however, I did not want the performance to be explicitly or literally about me and/or my sister – we were not the subject. Rather, my aim was to use scenography to create a work that was expansive, metaphorical, symbolic and mythic enough to be experienced and felt by participants as if the 'story' were, or could be, their own.

Scenographic dramaturgy: three-day and six-phase structure

An event that had a significant influence on the decision to make *Fissure* a three-day-long walking-performance was the death, mourning, resurrection process and symbolism of the Easter Trideum or Vigil, a Western Christian religious festival that moves from darkness to resurrection. The influence of liturgy and the Easter Vigil on *Fissure* also led to the decision to incorporate choral singing, and poems were later set to music by the composer Jocelyn Pook and performed by six professional singer/musicians using voices and portable instruments, including handbells.

During the Easter festival, death is represented by the extinguishing of candles to leave darkness, grief is represented by the movement of the service into a subterranean space (a tomb), and life and resurrection are represented by the lighting of candles.

One Easter Vigil at Ripon Cathedral had a particularly profound effect on me. Following the extinguishing of candles and darkness on Maundy Thursday, a small carved figure of Christ on the Cross is wrapped and placed in the cathedral's underground crypt, reached via stairways and labyrinthine passages – this action resonated with my sister's body being wrapped and removed following death. Over the next few days, I returned repeatedly to sit and wait with 'the body' until Easter Sunday, when candles were lit, bells were rung and 'the body' was 'resurrected' from the tomb.

Another resonant underworld myth was that of Ariadne's Thread – a red thread spun by Ariadne to help guide Theseus out of the Minotaur's labyrinth. Both this myth and the Easter Trideum suggested locations (caves and underground passages), materials and actions that connected to other research and fed into the scenography – red-coloured thread, wool and rope, the ringing of bells and the lighting and extinguishing of candles. Though not an exact mapping, the Trideum offered a three-day structure that became embedded in the dramaturgy of the performance and was seen in how it moved from above ground (open fell) to below ground (subterranean cave) to above ground again (mountain top). This physical process was designed to echo the themes of life and death, grieving, and resurrection (beyond the material) that are embedded in the Easter story.

- Friday 20 May 2011 – Day One mapped on to how the Trideum foretells the death, grief and resurrection to come.

- Saturday 21 May – Day Two mapped on to how the Trideum moves from light into darkness and silence, symbolizing loss of neurological function and death.

- Sunday 22 May – Day Three mapped on to how the Trideum works with images of resurrection, the ringing of bells and lighting of candles at dawn.

Within each day, a series of 'scenes' explored the progress of my sister's illness, treatment and death, and the grief that followed. I divided these scenes into six distinct phases, each underpinned by neurological knowledge, conversations with my sister's surgeon and oncologists, and personal memories of her illness and death and the aftermath of grief.

Day One. Phase 1: 'Flying High – Death Enters Life – 24-Hour Neurosurgery' reflected how my sister was flying high in her life and career before suddenly, overnight, undergoing neurosurgery to remove a brain tumour.

In this phase participants were introduced to the overarching themes, images, objects and motifs of the performance. This involved a team of six dancers in pairs to represent sisters, a singer who represented death, objects (bread, red rope, skulls) and the metaphorical use of the landscape. For example, having watched the dancers repeatedly fall and get up again, and listening to Death sing 'One Day You'll Fall. And Won't Get Up Again' (Burns 2011), participants walked across the open fell to an abandoned limestone quarry where sounds and words of neurosurgery and stones being crushed rose from below, combined with the singing of the poem 'Cut Apart the Body of the Land':

> cut apart the body of the land
> pluck out the precious limestone
> blast apart the body of the land

cut apart the body of her sister
pluck out the silent tumour
blast apart the body of a/the woman

the eggshell of her skull cracked open.

(Burns 2011)

Day Two. Phase 2: 'Terminal Diagnosis & Medical Interventions' reflected the diagnosis and treatment (radiotherapy and chemotherapy). Phase 3: 'Gift of Time' reflected on how groundbreaking medical treatment gave my sister more time, free for a while from anxiety and exhausting treatment. Phase 4: 'Disintegration – Loss of Function – The Fall' reflected on the return of the tumour, and the physical effects such as loss of movement and speech. Phase 5: 'Death & The Underworld' reflected my sister's death and my family's grief. In this phase, the death and darkness of the Trideum (vigil) were reflected when participants entered the subterranean dark of the cave.

Day Three. Phase 6: 'Resurgence / Resurrection' reflected on resurrection, renewal and living without my sister's physical presence. An example of how this phase related to the Trideum can be seen when participants gathered at dawn in St James' Church in the small Yorkshire village of Clapham. Candles were lit, one by one. Handbells rang, while a choir sang the poem 'After the Long Night':

After the long night
the beginnings of dawn
after the cave-dark
the daylight.

After the silence
the ringing of bells
after the heavy weight of grief
the lightness of her.

(Burns 2011)

Leaving the church, as participants walked up a huge ravine, handbells rang out and dancers reappeared from below ground, returning to the surface at places where the rivers resurge from underground passages when the bedrock becomes impassible. Released from the cave dark, which was representative of the Easter tomb and the processes of resurrection, the dancers joined the participants in their ascent of Ingleborough Fell.

From passenger to walker and pilgrim

Anthropologist Arnold van Gennep (1960: 1) divided rites of passage ceremonies into three distinct ritual phases: separation, transition and incorporation. He called the rites of separation from a previous world 'pre-liminal rites, those executed during the transitional stage liminal (or threshold) rites, and the ceremonies of incorporation into the new world post-liminal rites' (1960: 1). A liminal phase is 'characterized by being on a boundary or threshold, esp. by being transitional or intermediate between two states, situations' (*Oxford English Dictionary*).

In analysing *Fissure*, these phases illuminate how the performance engaged participants in a process akin to a ritual or pilgrimage, removing them from their everyday surroundings and immersing them in a carefully constructed and multilayered event that requires physical, cognitive and emotional engagement. For one participant the performance was experienced like a 'hike in the Yorkshire Dales [that] became a pilgrimage through death and bereavement.'[7]

The ritual process of *Fissure* began with participants' journeys from home to the site. The process then immersed participants in the site and the performance, during which time they 'waver between two worlds' (the world of the everyday and the world of *Fissure*) (van Gennep 1960: 18). Finally, the ritual process worked to draw participants out of the site and the performance, and depart for home.

Journey to the Dales – pre-liminal/separation

Fissure brought together participants from both within and outside of the UK. The majority did not know each other, and no one knew where they would be travelling to or what they would experience over the three days of the performance. Later, one participant remarked:

> No one knew what to expect but all had surrendered, for three days, to 'the all of it'. So, what we had in common that May afternoon was being there.[8]

For many, 'arrival' at the performance 'site' followed a long journey from home that removed them from their everyday lives. The preparation, travel and submission to the three-day performance made by *Fissure* participants was reminiscent of how a pilgrimage is 'made up of organised travel …

---

[7] *Fissure* participant feedback, 2011.
[8] *Fissure* participant feedback, 2011.

construction of temporary communities and the sacrifice of time and effort' (Coleman and Elsner 1995: 205). In a process that relates to van Gennep's (1995: 199) pre-liminal rites, typically pilgrims leave behind the daily demands, conventions and social structures of their everyday lives, including their social status and identity, and enter a special time and place 'set apart' where a temporary 'social' death occurs.

In *Fissure*, at Settle train station, where the performance began, participants boarded a train chartered for the event that took them to Ribblehead station, a journey of twelve miles. Through the progression of this journey, participants crossed over into the world of *Fissure*. To immerse them in the landscape of the performance (literally and metaphorically), during that journey musicians played and sang a poem of the landscape they were entering:

Three peaks high above the railway
Pen-y-Ghent, Ingleborough, Whernside
Scars and moors and fells and the three peaks high above the railway:
Whernside Ingleborough Pen-y-Ghent

(Burns 2011)

The words were designed to draw attention outwards to the landscape through which participants would walk over the next three days; as one participant remarked, the song turned 'familiar and not so familiar place names into soaring poetry'.[9] Working with the rhythm and motion of the train, the landscape song gradually wove into the poem 'The Height of the Hills' about two sisters who, like the 'sun and moon / earth and sky' are 'balanced / two halves of one whole' but are separated (fissured apart) through death (Burns 2011). Together these songs set the scene for what was to come. They also established how *Fissure* would invite participants to notice, look and listen intently, and how, while being rooted in the materiality of the landscape, the landscape would become heightened and made strange by scenographic techniques of estrangement and juxtaposition using a collision of landscape, science and performance across many forms.

Following the train journey, a series of scenes on the station platform and in the quarry further established the performance. One participant remarked: 'We leave for the evening, awakened to the themes of loss and loneliness and to the human scale of the story we have come to witness'.[10]

---

[9] *Fissure* participant feedback, 2011.
[10] *Fissure* participant feedback, 2011.

Journey through the Dales – liminal/transition

As participants became immersed in the 'world' of the performance, they entered the transitional phase of *Fissure*. Anthropologist Victor Turner (1982: 44) used the term 'anti-structure' to describe this temporary state of liminality. In the liminal phase of a ritual process, as explored by anthropologist Edith Turner (2012: 35, 50), participants find themselves '"in the zone" or "in the flow" experiencing a merging of action and awareness' where 'life is expanded and full of meaning [and] we are in a different dimension of human experience'. In *Fissure*, being 'in the zone' related to the time when participants were immersed in all elements of the performance, physical and symbolic, and were open to its scenographic meaning and effects. Participants walked each day in the same group and experienced the landscape and the interventions together, everyone ate together, and some stayed in the same place overnight. During this time, a temporary community was created and people moved from being strangers to participants and then to pilgrims, walking or travelling together in communitas. As they progressed and in between scenes, participants shared conversations and personal stories among and with each other, reflecting the 'strong sense of solidarity and bonding that develops among people experiencing a ritual, rite of passage, or other transitional [liminal] state together' ('communitas' definition in the *Oxford English Dictionary*). As one participant later reflected, 'companionship, solidarity and community was [sic] being developed through the walking'.[11] Remarking on this unplannable aspect of the performance, one participant later said 'how unexpected and particularly enjoyable [were] the number of interesting and inspiring conversations I had with fellow participants'.[12] For another, 'the sustaining atmosphere and the development of being in a group' were an important part of the experience of *Fissure*.[13]

The way *Fissure* mobilized participants in the manner of a pilgrimage can be understood through the conceptual frameworks of therapeutic landscapes and therapeutic mobilities. These concepts recognize the therapeutic, restorative and transformative potential of the act of walking. Cultural geographer Karolina Doughty describes how:

> Walking together is found to have a significant impact on social interaction and together embodied mobilities and supportive socialities transform the

---

[11] *Fissure* participant feedback, 2011.
[12] *Fissure* participant feedback, 2011.
[13] *Fissure* participant feedback, 2011.

countryside walkscape into a mobile therapeutic landscape and a site for shared therapeutic body work.

(Doughty 2013: 140)

Doughty recognizes that this sort of 'shared movement can produce supportive social spaces that are experienced as restorative' (2013: 140). The walkscape of *Fissure* and the 'shared body work' it required were further orchestrated and contextualized by the scenography (140). The work of health geographer Anthony Gatrell is helpful in developing this scenographic walkscape process. He outlines three key 'emplaced' steps to well-being: 'Be active – engage in physical activity; Connect – develop social connections with people; Take notice – be aware of one's surrounding' (Gatrell 2013: 100). He then develops these steps into three principal factors he suggests are found in therapeutic mobilities:

- *activity*, that walking is restorative and can be '*affective*' (the walker is affected by the landscape through which they walk) and '*effective* in maintaining health and wellbeing'
- *sociability*, that the solitary walker often experiences walking as a 'spiritual act' and the communal walker as 'energizing'
- *context*, that walking is 'shaped by the context within which it takes place' and that in turn walking shapes 'contexts'.

(Gatrell 2013: 100–12)

Fissure's engagement of walking and talking as a creative, therapeutic, conversational and performative tool related to Gatrell's three principles and the transformative use of the landscape and activity (walking, actions, visual and sensory immersion), the social effects of communal or solitary walking and the context of the underlying subject matter.

Journey out of the Dales – post-liminal/incorporation

As *Fissure* ended, each participant was given a tiny, fragile, pink-white cockleshell in a small box. This gift marked the beginning of the 'post-liminal/ incorporation' ritual phase (van Gennep 1960: 11). These shells, which consist of two halves, were gathered from the sands of Morecambe Bay, where the rivers that shaped the limestone landscape participants had walked through for three days meet the sea. As the landscape is formed of the bones and shells of sea creatures that over millennia metamorphosed into limestone rock, the cockleshell is a symbol of *Fissure*: the Yorkshire landscape, two sisters, two halves of a brain, fragility, metamorphosis and transformation. Imbued with resonances of the landscapes, narratives, sights, sounds, conversations, and feelings experienced during the performance, the giving and receiving of the shell had echoes of how:

> On their return, pilgrims frequently bring back a token of the place, both as proof of that journey has been completed and as a physical manifestation of the charisma of a sacred centre.
>
> (Coleman and Elsner 1995: 6)

Such 'objects of pilgrimage' act as signifiers and memory prompts that help the pilgrim 'to reconstruct the sacred journey in the imagination' (1995: 6). Many years later, I know of *Fissure* participants for whom the cockleshell remains a precious object – a keepsake that is kept safe and treasured – that takes them back to the physical (external) and emotional (internal) landscapes they walked, communally and alone, during the three days in Yorkshire. Following the performance several participants lingered, wanting to talk or be quiet and still, and many left having made new friends. For most, long journeys home gave space for reflection and time to adjust (to transition out of the liminal space *Fissure* had taken them into) before returning to their every day lives. Some later said they left changed, with alternative perspectives on living, dying and the grieving processes they had experienced.

Orchestrating the landscape and emplacing scenes

During the three days of *Fissure*, eighty participants travelled first by train, which brought them into the heart of the Dales, and then on foot over a twenty-mile route that circumnavigated, descended beneath and finally ascended Ingleborough, a mountain that is visible for miles around. The process of orchestrating the performance into the landscape builds on the very meaning of *scenography*. The word is derived from two components: the 'skeno' or 'skene' refers to space or scene and 'graphia' to the act of writing or drawing, so literally it means 'drawing *in* or *with* the scene' (Palmer 2011: 52). Writing in *Poetics* (350 BCE), the philosopher Aristotle described how the term 'skēnographia' was first used by Sophocles when he introduced scene painting into his theatre performance of Aeschylus' *The Oresteia*. These 'scenes' were drawn (painted) on to two-dimensional 'skēnē' and worked in tandem with the three-dimensional architecture of the theatre to create the environment or *mise-en-scène* of the play.

Scenography – '*drawing* in or with *the scene*'

As they walked, following a carefully planned route, participants moved through a multidimensional scenic environment of ever-changing topographies. The landscape became a vast mobile 'stage' – a 'living' multidimensional canvas on which a series of interconnected and juxtaposed scenes were mapped and drawn *out of* (by which I mean site-specifically inspired by and born out of the landscape) and drawn back *into* (by which I mean emplaced). Each scene was located in a site chosen for its physical, visual and metaphorical resonance, and came into view as participants walked step by step and mile by mile. I did not want the landscape to be a backdrop, but a dynamic environment. It was a other-than-human performer, and limestone pavements, caves, sinkholes, cairns, meadows, boulder fields and the mountain became part of the scenography.

The scenes emplaced in these sites consisted of one or a combination of elements, including dance, music, sound installation, sung poetry, land art, a geological interlude, a neuroscience lecture, oncological facts and reflection. These interventions were designed to place neurological scientific and medical facts into a scenographic frame as a counterpoint to the abstract and poetic.

Performers were deliberately placed alongside an existing feature that, in the context of the performance, took on a new or different meaning and added to the scenographic effect. This related to how, as a pilgrimage moves from one site to the next – each chosen for its distinctive features (a split boulder, a watery cave, a fork in the road, a summit-top cairn) – sites gain cumulative significance and meaning that intensifies as the story progresses. Gradually, through the collision of landscape, performance, art and neurological science, the scenography became increasingly layered and complex – adding to the dramaturgical trajectory of the whole performance.

As the performance progressed, each scene added more meaning to those that came before and after. This process reflected how the 'meaning of an image is changed according to what one sees immediately beside it or what comes immediately after it' (Berger 1972: 29). Scenes did not draw direct or literal comparison between the human anatomy and the physical landscape, but I used a series of juxtapositions. So, for example, the fissures of a limestone pavement related visually to the folded surface 'gyri' of the brain's surface, but it was not suggested that these two elements were the same things. Similarly, a blasted quarry related to the surgical removal of a brain tumour, but they were not collapsed together; rather, a defamiliarizing and uncanny connection was made between the two.

Objects, materials and design interventions

In a space as expansive as the Yorkshire Dales, where everything in the landscape was part of the scenography, it was necessary to draw participants' attention to where a scene was staged and direct them where to look. All design interventions brought additional layers of meaning to the scenography and were designed to draw attention to an aspect or feature of the landscape – fissures, pools, ravines, cuttings, darkness – and make the feature strange or heighten its impact by lifting it from the everyday.

The interventions were made using materials, objects or sound collected on site or related to the neurological research. Many designs were made with red materials, which stand out against the colours and tones of the landscape: the red wool I found on site, red ropes used by cave divers to guide them back out of a cave, the red threads used for 'sutures' (stiches) by a neurosurgeon, the colour of Ariadne's thread.

Because the route for *Fissure* extended over many miles of remote and physically challenging landscape, I made the installation interventions small scale, portable, visually clear and quick to emplace. Similarly, costumes were practical, lightweight and portable – walking boots that could be danced in, layers of clothing that allowed movement, and a colour palette based on the lichen on the rocks and a group of angels in the stained-glass window of St James' Church in Clapham, where the performance began at dawn on the morning of the third day.

Collision of landscape, performance, art and neurological science

In this section I show how the performance was emplaced in the landscape by analysing a selected number of scenes that took place on Day Two of *Fissure*. As it had ended the night before, this day began at Ribble Head Quarry, a dramatic site chosen for its epic – human-made – scale and form, and as a metaphor for the opening of the skull in neurosurgery and the removal of tumour cells from the brain.

It was early morning, not long after sunrise, and Michael Brada, the oncologist, met participants on the outer edge of the quarry. Next to him a sign read 'Danger of Falling' and behind him the quarried ground dropped vertically away. This was the start of Phase 2: 'Terminal Diagnosis & Medical Interventions'. Here, he described how a tumour doesn't grow in one mass but infiltrates the white matter of the brain like 'mould growing inside bread'. He explained how neurosurgery can remove some of the tumour's bulk but cannot remove it all (and significant invasion risks damage to 'good' matter). He said that in my sister's case, treatment could be given, but that in the end the diagnosis was terminal. Below him, in the huge hollowed-out space of the blasted quarry, a dancer repeatedly took a loaf of bread from an enormous pile of loaves, broke it into two halves then placed each separate half on two more growing mounds of fissured bread. The bread, and the dancer's actions, referenced the breaking of communion bread, the multiplying cancer cells and growing tumour, the fissuring of neurological function (headaches, seizures, loss of speech and movement) and the fissuring of the person.

Following a short walk, the next scene took place in a barn, where Chris Clark, the neurophysicist, showed participants the tractographic maps of 'streamlines' in the brain blocked by a tumour that are used in neurosurgery.

Participants then walked across fells to Long Churn Cave, an underground river and fissured cave passage formed by water seeping and flowing through the bedding planes and vertical joints of the rock. The passage was visible from the surface and was chosen because it is possible to see a dancer below the surface crawl, swim and squeeze through the physically challenging and exhausting subterranean water-filled passageways and sumps. This site became a metaphor for the dark and claustrophobic cylindrical tube of a magnetic resonance imaging (MRI) scanner used by Clark to image the brain and give radiotherapy treatment.

In *Fissure*, participants witnessed one dancer as she moved above ground, tracing and following the underground progress of a second dancer as she crawled and swam through the water-filled passage of the cave network below. The movement of the second dancer caused the water to make a glooping sound as it washed and banged against the cave walls – a sound that was reminiscent of an MRI scanner. Surfacing, the exhausted dancer dragged herself out of the watery tunnel, and together now both dancers performed a duet of wide-ranging, dynamic and interconnected movement – before she crawled back underground and into the watery depths. As she disappeared from sight, a choir emerged from another passageway and sang the poem 'Now Begins the Lengthy Crawl' (Burns 2011). The words of this poem named and described the cave system through which the dancer below moved, woven with terminology used to describe the brain structure, the effects of a tumour and my sister's treatment (as written down for me by Michael Brada). This intersection meant all elements of the scene – scientific, medical, situational, poetic and choreographic – were site and subject-specific:

now begins the lengthy crawl
a struggle   a rough crawl
    grade II astrocytoma
narrow rift   acute bend
    glioma

torturous upstream crawl
>   *daily, 33 times*
abandoned passage
>   *26 January – 12 March 1998*
entrance has been blocked
>   *Temozolomide*
[…]
monotonous crawling
>   *5 days every 28 days*
again the way forward is impassable
>   *12 monthly cycles*
a complex of crawls
>   *August 1998 – August 1999*
beyond this the fissure is completely choked
the terminal sump
a black void beckons
there is no sign of any way on

(Burns 2011)

Geophysicist Mike Kelly then emerged from a passageway beneath which participants were standing and explained how the distinctive fissures of a limestone pavement are caused by rainwater that has seeped into, opened up and dissolved the rock (his intervention and discussion of how water forms this landscape relates back to Clark talking about his use of fluid to map the position of a tumour in a brain). The dancer who remained above ground, in search of the one below, moved over an extensive area of limestone pavement, leaping the glints (blocks of limestone) and grykes (fissures between the blocks). Participants followed, jumping and striding over the pavement too. There is a striking visual analogy between the glints and grykes of these limestone pavements and the gyri and sulcus (furrows) that form the surface of the brain. The landscape becomes strange and defamiliarized, and readable in multiple and complex ways. At a bend in the river, multiple dancers in pairs climbed and helped each other scramble out of multiple underground cave passages. In a physical expression of repeated cycles of treatment, they relentlessly and exhaustingly climbed out and up a steep bank before falling backwards, down and in again.

Later that day, Michael Brada waited for participants, sheltering from the wind beneath a drystone wall. Participants had just descended from Thwaite Cairns, a series of summit cairns chosen because of their striking sculptural appearance and position, following an extended walk through flower meadows that marked Phase 3: 'Gift of Time'. The stonewall represented the end of freedom, treatment and recovery. From now on, the illness would progress. This undramatic location marked the end of medical intervention and hope. For the second time this day, Michael Brada spoke directly to participants and explained:

> tumour cells are on some kind of path of evolution. For some reason they accumulate, or there is a change in the genetic make-up, and they become faster and behave in more aggressive ways. This change is almost inevitable … this however is a person, a sister, a daughter, a friend that we are talking about and their illness will devastate them and those left behind.
>
> (Brada in Wilson 2011a)

Participants then climbed a high wooden stile into Norber Erratics, a field of massive boulders transported from their origins by glaciers and split/fissured in half by weather and gravity – chosen because of their scale, geological origins and visual resonance with the two hemispheres of the brain and the metaphor of a fissuring body. This site marks the beginning of Phase 4: 'Disintegration – Loss of Function – The Fall'. One massive erratic was marked with a thin line of bright red sheep's wool pushed into a fissure that ran through the centre of the boulder. From within the boulder, a sound track manipulated and combined the sounds of neurosurgery recorded in the operating theatre with scraping, gouging, scouring sounds recorded at the working quarry. This track was designed to ghost the massive and powerful glacial movement that carried and deposited these rocks in this site. Moving over the boulder, a dancer leapt, balanced, climbed and held on, but her movement was beginning to become disconnected and fissured:

> inside her brain a break a gap
> a rift a fracture tracts broken
> paths blocked a cleft in rock
>
> fall synapses
> cleft chasm broken
> *fissure fissure fissure*
>
> (Burns 2011)

At Robin Procter's Scar, a high cliff-face caused by a geological faultline and chosen because of its scale, rough texture and connection to the faulting body explored in this scene, a red rope was used to bind together the trunk of a split hawthorn tree that had grown out of a boulder fallen from the cliff-face above.

FIGURE 2.4 Fissure. *Day Two – Phase 4: 'Disintegration – Loss of Function – The Fall', Robin Procter's Scar, Yorkshire Dales. Dancer: Jennifer Essex. Choreographer: Nigel Stewart. Photographer: Bethany Clarke/Artevents, all rights reserved*

On an adjacent boulder a dancer used her fingertips to hold her contorted, semi-mobile body horizontally on the face of the rock. The effort of this is immense: her body was bent back, her movement had fissured away and the challenge of holding herself there was seen in the whiteness of her knuckles and her inability to move. All she could do was hold on.

The dancer's choreographed body, the boulder, the split tree, the red rope and the cliff-face all contributed to the visual representation of the effort and difficulty of illness. One participant described how they 'could feel the extremes of the physical consequences of dealing with the illness in the body, that tension, that stress'.[14]

Following a mile-long walk along a narrow path contained on either side by a stone wall, participants arrived at Endcombe Tunnel. This location marked the start of Phase 5: 'Death & The Underworld'. The tunnel consisted of two passageways running under the fell into Clapham village, and was chosen for its echoing darkness and uncertain length, and as a spatial metaphor for passing from life into death through a tunnel. Inside the tunnel the recorded sound of slow, shallow breathing was heard seeping from tiny speakers

---

[14] *Fissure* participant feedback, 2011.

hidden in the walls. Halfway through the dark tunnel, the silhouetted figure of Death appeared, framed by daylight beyond and behind him. As participants passed, he sang the poem 'Her Birth Her Breath':

her birth
    her breath, her breath, her breath
her life on earth.
    her breath, her breath, her breath
then death arrives and takes away
    her breath, her breath, her breath

(Burns 2011)

As participants emerged from the tunnel, the bells of St James' Church tolled twenty-nine times, the age my sister was when she died. From here, the route took them through a woodland to Ingleborough Cave, a subterranean cave system with labyrinthine passages, underground rivers, pools, caverns and stalactites and stalagmites, chosen because of its association with the underworld and resonance with death and the darkness of grief. Inside, the subterranean depths of the cave echoed with the singing of the poem 'Take This Thread', the words of which were passed, like synapses passing messages in the brain, from singer to singer through the cave:

[...] *This thread will disappear*
inside the earth

the way a river disappears in limestone.

This thread will travel
where you cannot follow

only rock and water
no grass   no sky
no trees   no stars
no moon   no sun
only rock and water

The river of her life has disappeared.
She walks in fields of the underworld
through white gardens made of limestone

(Burns 2011)

One of each pair of dancers – representing the younger sister – followed a red rope into the darkness before she disappeared into death, out of sight and beyond reach, leaving the older sister behind. In silence, participants left the cave to wait overnight for dawn.

The impact of *Fissure*

In response to the juxtapositions of landscape, science and art, one participant spoke of 'the mix of lectures, song, music, dance and landscape – interweaving, interlinking, making connections ... I know those places very well but now will see them all very differently'.[15] Another described how they 'had never thought of the similarities between the brain and landscape before – that was a fascinating connection'.[16] A third remarked on how the 'integration of geological features and the body [was] made real through the intervention of the experts'.[17]

Meaning that was specific and significant to each participant also accumulated as the performance progressed. Indeed, the carefully composed scenographic dramaturgy of *Fissure,* while framing and guiding meaning, left space for participants 'to assign meaning' in the context of their own personal experiences of illness, death and bereavement (Bennett 1990: 44). This process of co-construction reflected how:

> Pilgrimage sites have no meaning in themselves [but are] articulated through the use of space, movement, image and object. A pilgrim brings their own meaning and interpretation to the pilgrimage site which acts as an 'empty vessel' into which is poured hopes, prayers and aspirations.
>
> (Coleman and Elsner 1995: 209–10)

Many participants took part because of personal, and for some recent, experiences of illness and bereavement. After the event, one said:

> I have been excitedly attempting to describe to my friends something you really had to be there for ... I know we all brought our own experiences of love and grief – for me my ex-partner died of cancer a year ago; it would have been her birthday last weekend and I couldn't have imagined a better way to celebrate that anniversary.[18]

---

[15] *Fissure* participant feedback, 2011.
[16] *Fissure* participant feedback, 2011.
[17] *Fissure* participant feedback, 2011.
[18] *Fissure* participant feedback, 2011.

While walking the *physical* landscape, participants were simultaneously walking *interior* landscapes relating to personal loss. The process of externalization enabled meaning to be made that took one participant to 'places they never thought possible'. This suggests that *Fissure* created a site in which people could reflect upon the effects of death, illness and bereavement in a way that could be considered transformative:

> *Fissure* has haunted me. As we walked across this place, I found myself shaken by its vastness and velocity ... My sense of scale of the landscape completely shifted when I began to learn more about the mapping and function, or rather dysfunction, of the brain. This was punctuated by bells, song, wind, cries, conversation, exchange, memories ... And loss. How loss can seep into every part of you and the landscape ... How walking through this 'place' can lead you somewhere, ever so different from where you began ... arriving somewhere you never thought possible.[19]

Feedback, though, revealed that participants needed time and space for meaning to be created during and after the event. In her work on embodied scenography, McKinney discusses how the process of grasping meaning does not occur through working intellectually, but elsewhere in the body. 'It is only after the performance', she writes:

> that I start to pick out particular feelings and responses. During a performance we are not necessarily aware of attending to the individual components of scenographic spectacle.
>
> (McKinney 2013: 69–70)

In *Fissure*, the physical journey, the landscape and the effort of walking all gained symbolic and metaphorical resonances. For example, on Day Three, during the final ascent of Ingleborough Fell, a site chosen because of the connection between mountains and sacred or pilgrimage sites, one participant remarked that they:

> loved the way the piece tested my body's limits and on that climb on day three I could not help wondering what it must be like to be so ill that your body is tested to the limit and to the end.[20]

---

[19] *Fissure* participant feedback, 2011.
[20] *Fissure* participant feedback, 2011.

FIGURE 2.5 Fissure. *Participants ascending Ingleborough Fell on Day Three – Phase 6: 'Resurgence / Resurrection', Yorkshire Dales. Photographer: Bethany Clarke/Artevents, all rights reserved*

On the day, however, the wind rose to gale force, the performance was rerouted off the mountain before it reached the summit, and an alternative ending was staged in the village hall. The intervention of weather in this way brought another layer of metaphor.

Following the event, many participants reported that the complex combination of walking, landscape, science, communitas, dance and poetry that the scenography for *Fissure* contained helped their own processes of grieving. For one, it gave 'permission to think about myself and to feel my own profound sadness':

> This would have been too intense if it had been a conventional play – the space provided by the music, the pauses and the walking across the three days was an invaluable part of the experience and allowed me to reflect on and digest it. The beauty was nurturing, the company stimulating and supportive, the music and dance powerful, the use of the landscape and architecture fascinating – and beyond words. I'm a person who usually expresses myself in a strictly factual style.[21]

---

[21] *Fissure* participant feedback, 2011.

This participant also commented that *Fissure* 'unleashed different ways of expressing [their] experience ... beyond words'.[22] Along with the other responses, this feedback confirmed my belief in the efficacy of scenography created in a rural landscape to transform experiences of illness, death and grief.

---

[22] *Fissure* participant feedback, 2011.

3

Creating a scene – centring the visual: *Ghost Bird*

Scenography as a visual and multi-sensory artform uses a 'multiplicity of images – visual and aural' and comes into its own in situations when words alone are not enough to describe a complex lived-experience.

(MARRANCA 1976: X)

In this chapter I explore my deepening move towards what Bonnie Marranca (1976: x) termed a 'theatre of images' and my use of non-narrative, non-verbal and visually orientated scenography to convey complex ideas and deal with challenging subject matter. The chapter looks at how I worked to create a walking-performance that was dramaturgically coherent, but stripped out text, spoken word and a linear, sequential or narrative line, and worked with stillness and silence. This was designed to draw participants in and encourage detailed looking, listening and contemplation of the performance and the environment in which it was located.

The chapter looks at a search for an effective visual scenographic language with which to 'create a scene' in two senses of the phrase. The first is to 'create a scene' in the sense of 'establishing the background, setting, or context for a play, story, account' in the form of a staged picture or scenes in the landscape. The second is to 'create a scene' in the sense of 'the action of creating or causing a scene ... with a public display of emotion or strong feelings' ('create a scene' defined in the *Oxford English Dictionary*).

To do this, I use *Ghost Bird* (2012), a silent walking-performance and live-art installation that communicated primarily in images, as a case study. This work pursued and furthered the use of visual scenography, metaphor and materials of the site that I began working with when creating *Fissure, Still Life* and *Jack Scout*. The chapter articulates how, and why, the scenography for this walking-performance:

- used multiple visual and symbolic metaphors – landscape, environment, human and animal – designed to draw attention to the plight of the hen harrier and the persecution of the 'Lancashire Witches';
- composed scenes using materials and environmental forces associated with the site and the human body by working abstractly and pictorially;
- stripped out spoken and written word, text and narrative, guided participants without a person or character leading the way and invited them to engage in silence without speaking or being spoken to;
- gathered participant responses through visual/non-verbal methods.

Ghost Bird's incorporation of walking, dance, performance and live-art intervention reflects how scenography has affinities with and sits on an ever-shifting continuum between art forms, including site-specific performance, performance art, environmental dance, environmental art and land art – often moving between forms during a single performance.

Ghost Bird was performed in, and specific to, the Langden Valley in the Trough of Bowland, Lancashire, an upland landscape internationally important for its heather moorland, blanket bog and rare birds. It was made as a response to the plight of the hen harrier in the north of England. 'Once prevalent in northern England, hen harriers have been persecuted by gamekeepers and their existence is threatened' (Jude Laine, Royal Society for the Protection of Birds (RSPB), for *Ghost Bird*).[1] The performance drew parallels between the treatment of hen harriers and the persecution of Lancashire women accused of witchcraft in the seventeenth century. The title of the performance celebrates the bird's beauty while drawing attention to its fragile existence, and holds a double meaning. It refers to the grey feathers of the male hen harrier that give it a ghost-like appearance when seen in silent flight – looking like an apparition. The title also refers to the increasing absence of the species due to persecution, which is wiping it out, and plays on the idea that a sighting is so rare, it might be a ghost.

---

[1] Landowners and managers, the RSPB and other partners in the Langden Valley and the Forest of Bowland Area of Outstanding Natural Beauty work together to combat the illegal destruction of the hen harrier and persecution of raptors locally, regionally and nationally.

In *Ghost Bird* a series of visual scenes were designed to draw attention to and make visible the injustice, prejudice and persecution of the hen harrier and the Lancashire Witches. Though carefully composed, these scenes were not explicit or literal; rather, they gained meaning cumulatively and gave participants the 'intellectual freedom' to 'make their own story of the story in front of them; to translate image into words' (Lehmann 2006: 99) through a process that Joslin McKinney defines as one of 'co-construction' (2017: 102). Also, *Ghost Bird* did not create scenes that were loud or overt, but used the human body and moorland environment to make living pictures that were still and quiet and that at first glance appeared to be beautiful and poetic, but were, in context, unsettling and challenging. In this way, the performance demonstrated that scenography 'is not as benign as has been previously perceived' but can 'move us [...] disturb us, challenge us and affect us. [...] have power over us [...], command our attention and affect our emotion (Lotker and Gough 2013: 4).

The chapter uses participant feedback to explore the outcomes of this scenographic exploration. Participant responses to *Ghost Bird* were received after the show in words and drawings as well as through feedback forms, email and direct correspondence. Production credits for *Ghost Bird* are in Appendix B.

Lancashire Witches 400

The year 2012 marked the 400th anniversary of the 'Lancashire Witches' trial, which saw twelve people (ten women and two men) from the Pendle area of Lancashire hunted down and accused of causing death by witchcraft. Following a three-day trial at Lancaster Assizes Court, ten of the accused were sentenced to death and hanged. Collectively these people became known as the Pendle or Lancashire Witches. Against a background of poverty and religious persecution, it is widely accepted that the trial was unfair because it was 'based on rumour, idle gossip and false confession' (Lancaster Castle 2020).

When invited by Green Close Studios and Lancaster Arts to create a site-specific performance for the Lancashire Witches 400 project (2012), I wanted to redress the troubling imagery that persists around the Lancashire (or Pendle) Witches. These caricatures serve to dehumanize individuals who were unfairly tried and hanged for crimes they did not commit. Instead, I determined to portray a sense of these people that would make them tangible – not 'witches' or crones but people, women and men, made of flesh and blood.

I chose to look for a site that was off the beaten track, harsh and open to the elements in the Trough of Bowland, the area of exposed moorland between Pendle and Lancaster through which the accused Pendle Witches were forcibly walked before being imprisoned in the dungeons of Lancaster Castle to await trial. Their exact route is unknown, but it was a journey of fifty miles through remote, exposed and physically challenging terrain that consists of heather moorland and peat bog.

Research revealed that the area continues to follow the tradition of grouse shooting. The link between this present-day hunting and the hunting of the Lancashire Witches in this landscape captured my imagination and I turned my attention to the hen harrier known to nest in the upper reaches of the Langden Valley.

Image and visual metaphoric communication

> Metaphor heightens symbolic communication ... purposeful structure allows for meaningful encounters to occur.
>
> (Potash 2020: 14)

The coming together in my imagination of these two stories of persecution – the Lancashire Witches and the hen harrier – suggested to me the possibility of a double and interchangeable metaphor with the landscape as a common factor in both stories.

A metaphor can convey meaning for 'something inherently complex, open-ended, and resistant to compact literal statement' (Hills 2017). The term *metaphor* comes from the Latin *metaphora*, 'carrying over', which in turn comes from the Greek *metaphorá*, 'transfer':

> When we resort to metaphor, a term that routinely stands for one thing or kind is made to stand for another, suitably related thing or kind instead ... The effect is to *transfer* the term in question from its accustomed place in our verbal classificatory scheme to some other unaccustomed place for special temporary expressive purposes.
>
> (Hills 2017)

My creative concerns were: firstly, how a specific landscape could be used as a metaphor for the hen harrier and the Lancashire Witches simultaneously; secondly, how I could use scenography to draw these interconnected metaphors *out of* and back *into* the landscape; and, finally, what the physical and embodied experience of walking through the landscape could bring to the making of that metaphor:

> Use of metaphors in scenography relies on more complex interaction between text and image as means of exploring possible meaning or significance of text. This often demands more time or more conscious effort on the part of the spectator to register the full significance of image in relation to text.
>
> (Butterworth and McKinney 2009: 95)

Specifically, however, *Ghost Bird* was a creative enquiry to find out how I might use non-verbal scenography (with minimal written text) that avoided explicit representation, making it 'suggestive rather than illustrative'. I also wanted to find an abstract and non-literal image-based language capable of holding complex, challenging layers of symbolic meaning, the understanding of which was open to individual interpretation whilst also being 'dependent on shared practical, national, cultural, aesthetic knowledge' (2009: 164). This was an important enquiry because I wanted to develop a practice of effective and affective scenography the impact of which, 'like all symbols [...] relies on shared cultural sensibilities and potent images held in common by the creators of the production and their audience' (2009: 160).

Scenographic looking: search for a site, materials and images

With a concept in place, I now needed to find a specific site. It was the spring of 2012 and the hen harrier's breeding season. Jude Laine, the RSPB officer tasked with monitoring and protecting breeding hen harriers had taken me to a moorland in the Langden Valley. This was one of the few remaining breeding sites for the hen harrier in the UK, and we hoped to sight a male perform its spectacular dance: a series of steep climbs, swooping dives and acrobatic twists and rolls, designed to attract a female. This remote upland landscape was once the English stronghold for the hen harriers; now, however, the breed is close to extinction, with gamekeepers across the UK accused of illegally shooting the birds or destroying their nests, eggs or chicks.

Close to the fell top, in a narrow and steep-sided valley with a meandering stream running through it, Jude and I sat down low among the flattened woody heather, silently searching the expansive sky with the naked eye and through binoculars for signs of a male hen harrier performing a sky dance. Its presence would have marked the possibility of the birds nesting. But our wait was in vain – no birds appeared, and the sky remained empty.

After a number of hours of patient and silent waiting, we stood to leave. Now, looking at the valley from an elevated perspective, I noticed we had been sitting in between two rows of hand-crafted, horseshoe-shaped, elegantly curved drystone walls, nestled low in the peaty ground and camouflaged among the heather. Scattered in the undergrowth around them were brightly coloured spent gun cartridges and grouse feathers. This remote landscape, which on first appearance has a striking beauty with its interconnecting valleys, river and streams, painted with purple heather and contained by an expansive sky, has a less romantic aspect: the stone enclosures were shooting butts used for the commercial shooting of grouse. The butts give cover and camouflage to the 'guns', while the 'beaters' force the birds to break cover and fly upwards in the direction of the guns.

More and more butts came into view, and we went to locate them. There were twenty shooting butts in total, ten in each row. They are painted with white numerals, 10 to 1 down one side of the valley and 1 to 10 up the other side. The number an uncanny echo of how ten of the twelve people accused of witchcraft and taken to Lancaster Castle were eventually hanged. Later, lower down the valley where the Land Rovers pick up and drop off the shooting parties, I found a few champagne corks and was told that it was not uncommon to celebrate a shoot.

Leaving Jude to keep searching the sky for the hen harrier, I made my way through the butts and further up the steep-sided valley to the topmost reaches of the moorland. White-painted marker posts guided my way. At the top, where the boggy peat plateaus out and meets the weathered sky, I noticed white-topped cotton grass waving flag-like in the wind. Looking back, I saw Jude standing stock still, a solitary figure in the landscape, searching the widening sky and pointing over to me. In a moment my thoughts crystallized, and I knew I had found the site and, as this distillation of my fieldnotes shows, the materials, actions and themes with which to compose the visual scenographic language for *Ghost Bird*:

> the absent hen harrier
> empty nests and no eggs
> heather and cotton grass
> peat and bog
> water running into streams
> feathers
> white posts
> the numbers 1–10

shooting butts with curved drystone walls
discarded gun cartridges and champagne corks
remote, tiring and physically challenging terrain and walking
solitary figures – silently watching, waiting and pointing
an expansive sky, clouds, wind and rain – empty of harriers

The abiding image that took shape in my imagination was that of naked human figures, males and female, curled up – foetus-like – nested inside the curved wall of a shooting butt, part sheltered but vulnerable, with naked skin, veins and muscle translucent and exposed to the environment and elements. In my mind were the closely studied bodies seen in the paintings of Lucien Freud, for example *Naked Portrait* (1972–3) and *Standing by Rags* (1998–9), and Jenny Saville, for example *Propped* and *Branded* (1992) and *Fulcrum* (1998). These imagined figures were a metaphor for the witches and the harrier, of birds' eggs and human gestation, and destroyed nests and ended lives – both human and animal.

Consolidating ideas

From bottom to top, the Langden Valley extends for two-and-a-half miles, with a river – the Langden Brook – and a rough-made track running through it. In the upper reaches of the valley, where the shooting butts are located before the path rises steeply to the open fell, there is small shooting barn named Langden Castle used as a base for grouse-shooting parties. At the end of the season, shooting barns in the Trough of Bowland are lined with purple heather gathered from the moor, creating a room in which to celebrate and feast.

Off site, research into the personal, historical and social circumstances of those accused as witches in the seventeenth century revealed the poverty and hardship of their lives and the religious prejudice that ultimately led to their deaths. I visited the pitch-dark underground prison in which the accused were kept at Lancaster Castle, and learnt of the damage caused to body, bones and lungs during death by hanging. A wood carving of the execution depicts four of the women hanged from a rope off a cross beam, their toes peeping from under the skirts of their long dresses, while another three women wait in line to be hanged. These are images I returned to when composing the performance and each scenic intervention.

Sites have an uncanny habit of holding and revealing unexpected histories, and further research revealed that – unknowingly – in choosing to locate the performance here, I had probably selected the route (up Langden Valley, from Pendle to Lancaster Castle) along which the accused Lancashire Witches were marched. Furthermore, Langden Castle (the shooting barn) was used as their overnight prison. These findings made the site and harshly beautiful landscape particularly visceral and resonant, and located the work across time and space. Having obtained permission to use the barn, which outside the hunting season is locked and shuttered with metal window covers, this interior location gave me a site that, while remote, was controllable. Plus, because it was possible to access the valley in a four-by-four vehicle, I could bring voluminous quantities of site-inspired materials and objects (eggs, spent gun cartridges, feathers, peat) from off-site. Inside I found a fireplace, candles and a row of empty coat hooks. Later, during the performance, a single pale-white coat was hung on ten of the hooks. This created an installation that was reminiscent of the wood carved image of bodies hanging and metonymic of the ten people eventually hanged at Lancaster Castle. In an act of prayer and remembrance, a lit candle burned above each coat and brought light into the darkness of the womby/cell-like room.

Making *Ghost Bird*, I continued my site work with the environmental choreographer Nigel Stewart and the geophysicist Mike Kelly with whom I had worked on *Fissure*. During a material-sourcing field trip, Kelly taught us how to read the river and see and hear the energy and eddying flow of the water as it foamed, swirled and coursed off the moorland, through the valley and past the barn. In parallel, the sound artist Lisa Whistlecroft captured the sound of the stream and layered these river recordings with sound recordings of the hen harrier's distinctive call. Stewart derived raw movement material from these river studies, and with the dance artist Julia Griffin developed it into repeatable choreographed sequences. These sequences, performed by Griffin while eight-and-a-half months pregnant, were emplaced in the Langden Castle (barn) installation.

Distillation of research

Ghost Bird took shape as a continual walking-performance that ran non-stop for five hours, with scenes located and spread along the circuitous five-mile route. These scenes were composed using only materials and research of the sites, the underlying subject and the human body. I made the performance continual to echo the walking of the prisoners and as a way of choreographing the viewing of the scenes without needing a person as a guide, and in such way that allowed participants to take their time.

Though it was experienced by participants as a whole, for ease of explanation the work can be divided into three parts:

- A walk with signs to guide participants up the Langden Valley that transitions them into silence.
- An installation in Langden Castle performed by a dancer.
- A series of installations on the moorland performed by life models and 'Pointing People'.

Participants were able to set out on foot any time between 10am and 3pm. Their route followed a rough track along the valley bottom, then rising steeply onto and across open heather and peat moorland to the summit, before dropping back down into the valley via the shooting butts and back to the start.

Non-verbal imagery and silent guides

Over many years of making site-specific performance that has moved from room to room in a house, travelled by bus and tram across a city, journeyed on foot and via golf buggy through miles of woodland, through a department store via goods and customer lifts, over shop floors and into attics and cellars, I have used a number of techniques to guide participants through the performance. wilson+wilson used clear and simple gestures to lead participants from one scene to the next and to direct them where to sit or stand and look. We also used sound, light, action and actors in character to guide this. In *Still Life*, small groups of participants were led by a silent guide (not in character) from cliff-top to sandy shore, over limestone rock and salt-marsh grass. For some sections of the walk, participants found their own way from scene to scene by following footprints left in the sand and trails of objects discovered on site, such as fallen apples, pottery fragments thrown up from eighteenth-century shipwrecks and plastic bottles. For *Jack Scout*, audiences of eighteen at a time were led by two guides (who were costumed and embedded within the performance) through the heath, along the shoreline and over the beach. In *Fissure* and *The Gathering* participants, as one large group and at times in smaller groups, were led by mountain leaders, and a guide waiting at each scene showed them where to stand or move.

For *Ghost Bird*, to ensure participants became immersed without interruption or interference in the world of the performance, I chose not to use a formal guide or walk leader. Instead, I incorporated a range of non-verbal and visual guides within the performance. Informing this decision was a desire to re-create my first field-trip experience when I spent time waiting for the hen harrier to appear and as a consequence became gradually more immersed in the landscape.

Signs, arrows, 'Pointing People' and installations

In *Ghost Bird*, upon arrival at the site, participants were met by a 'front-of-house manager' who shared a map of the route, explaining that the walking-performance would not be led or guided, but that they would follow a series of signs and arrows posted along the route, and that at three locations, silent

'Pointing People' would act as visual guides. Before participants began their walk, they read a sign that gave a basic context to the performance:

> YOU ARE ABOUT TO WALK UP THE LANGDEN VALLEY
>
> THIS JOURNEY HAS HISTORY
>
> THIS VALLEY IS ONE OF THE LAST PLACES IN ENGLAND WHERE THE PERSECUTED HEN HARRIER NESTS
>
> THIS VALLEY FORMS PART OF THE AREA THROUGH WHICH, IN 1612, THE ACCUSED PENDLE WITCHES WERE MARCHED TO LANCASTER CASTLE, WHERE 10 WERE HANGED

The first section of *Ghost Bird* was a two-mile walk along the Langden Valley to the barn, moving through a variety of terrain. This linear walk transitioned participants into silence and drew them into the performance. Their route was marked by a series of signs and arrows placed sequentially along the track, showing them the paths and tracks to follow and later the direction to take on the open moorland. Each sign had four rows of stripped-back information; as the extracts of four signs below demonstrate, this was designed to locate and attune participants to the landscape, contextualize their walking-performance with reference to the plight of the hen harrier and the walk made by the Lancashire Witches, and guide them towards walking in silence:

> MIRY ELLIS
> 1544
> FIRST PRINTED RECORD OF MALE AS NATIVE
> SPEAK NORMALLY
>
> BIRCH BANK
> 1900s
> WIPED OUT IN MAINLAND BRITAIN DUE TO PERSECUTION
> SPEAK QUIETLY
>
> BLACK CLOUGH
> 1969
> 30 BREEDING PAIRS IN BOWLAND
> SPEAK IN WHISPERS
>
> WEASEL CLOUGH
> 2012
> 0 BREEDING PAIRS IN BOWLAND
> SILENCE

The top row on the signs gave the name of the location, as shown on an Ordnance Survey map. These reflect how the landscape is named using words derived from Old Norse that describe it through its physical features and habitat. For example, *clough* is a rift or ravine, *pitt* or *pit* is a hidden cavity, *syke* is a small stream and *lingy* is the word for heather. So Lingy Pitts means a hidden cavity where heather grows, and Weasel Clough is a rift or a ravine inhabited by weasels. I used these words to locate the walk and draw participants' attention to the physical shapes, forms, colour, flora and fauna of the landscape, and to a naming system that would have been in place in 1602 when the valley was walked by the Lancashire Witches. That these words were the names of places in the landscape was made explicit, and the sound and feel of the words were a way of creating atmosphere. How participants pieced these texts together and constructed meaning was left open.

The middle rows of text on the signs gave a date and a historical fact relating to the history of the hen harrier and its presence and persecution in the UK and the Trough of Bowland. These dates began at the start of the walk in the 1400s, when hen harrier numbers were healthy, and went through to the 1900s, when the species was widely persecuted; thereafter numbers recovered before diminishing again to the present day (2012 – the year of the performance), when the number of hen harriers is zero. This establishes a human timeframe and context that stretched back centuries and linked the hen harrier, the Lancashire Witches and the participants across time and space.

The bottom row of text invited participants to reduce their speaking to each other, if they were walking in a group, from speaking normally, as they might when walking with friends, to speaking quietly, then in whispers and eventually silence. Because the first stage of the walk was extended in distance, I did not introduce silent walking from the start, but gradually. Often, when first setting out on a performance, participants talked and shared the occasion and experience with each other, but I wanted to give them permission to stop talking and become immersed in the experience, attentive to the landscape and the performance.

The first of the 'Pointing People' was a woman located outside Langden Castle (the barn). Participants passed through a gate marked with a sign that read:

LANGDEN CASTLE
1960
POPULATION STABLE
650 BREEDING PAIRS IN BRITAIN
SPEAK IN WHISPERS

The sign on the gate made a link between the stability of the breeding hen harrier in the 1960s and the pregnant, soon-to-give-birth woman (a dancer) they were about to witness inside the barn. Langden Castle consists of three areas, with two open-ended spaces either side of an enclosed space. All three were intended to be read in the context of the others as a type of triptych – a form I return to regularly because it brings images together but keeps them separate, in juxtaposition, enabling the viewer to read each element and make visually cognitive connections. In one of the open spaces, hundreds of translucent white duck eggs covered the floor and spilled out of the doorway. The floor of the second open space was covered in a deep carpet of soft white feathers that whipped up in flurries when the wind rushed through. And the central enclosed space was covered with a deep layer of dark-earthy peat.

FIGURE 3.1 Ghost Bird. *Pregnant woman in Langden Castle, Trough of Bowland, Lancashire. Dancer: Julia Griffin. Photographer: Manuel Vason*

As participants approached the barn, the Pointing Woman directed them towards the entrance of the central space. She was costumed in a dappled-brown dress referencing the colours of the female hen harrier's plumage, designed as camouflage for her and her nest in the woody heather.

In the semi-darkness inside the barn – made soft and unstable underfoot by the peat – a peat fire burned red-orange in the hearth. On the other side of the room, ten ghostly-white garments hung on hooks – these stood for the ten hanged Lancashire Witches and were lit with a candle placed in their memory. The darkness of the space also suggested the underground prison the witches were kept in at Lancaster Castle. Slowly, a semi-naked dancer, eight-and-a-half months pregnant, emerged from the peat, her body shifting into shapes that echoed a tortured body and a bird in flight and her pregnant tummy echoing the translucent eggs in the space next door. From within the peat, the womb-like sound of water and the piercing cry of the hen harrier could be heard.

All elements – the words on the sign, the fragile/fertile eggs, soft/plucked feathers and a semi-naked/exposed pregnant woman moving through a floor of thick peat in front of the fire and the white dresses – were designed to work together. This carefully chosen combination provided clues and visual triggers for participants to link up in a way that connected the presence and absence of the people accused of witchcraft as well as the vulnerability and persecution of the hen harrier. Combined, this space layered and brought together all the metaphors of the performance, as highlighted in these participant responses:

> I absolutely loved the [barn] with the eggs all those shades of white, and feathers, and the white wall and dark peaty corners inside with the streaming-water sound and pregnant woman truly inhabiting the space.[2]

> Watching the naked pregnant dancer in the barn made me realise the preciousness of procreation – be it human or in birds/animals ... beautiful and poignant.

The dancer moved imperceptibly slowly through the peat. Her arm gestures reached, folded and turned. Based on the movement of water in the river outside, when slowed down and placed in the context of the hen harrier, this movement suggested a bird in flight or nesting, but her movement contorted too – designed to suggest the effects of pain and hanging on the body.

When the sun came out, daylight beamed into the space in narrow shafts of white light that edged through the shutters covering the window. As the dancer moved into the window space, this momentarily had the effect of making her appear like a flesh-and-blood religious icon. Her tempo increased at times before it slowed and was arrested in extended periods of active stillness. This cycle was repeated non-stop for five hours and was witnessed by participants as they arrived at the barn throughout the day.

After Langden Castle, the valley and the track rise steeply and participants ascended towards open moorland. At the top of the track, a huge mound of

---

[2] Participants' feedback in this chapter does not identify respondents by name or initials and will not therefore be given an individual footnote.

spent gun cartridges, shaped to echo the contours of the fells, was placed to come into view suddenly and with a shock. Brightly coloured, the gun cartridges sang out in contrast to the muted tones of the surrounding fells, and made material the reality of grouse shooting and the numbers of birds shot.

Circumnavigating the mound, a sign invited participants into silence and an arrow guided them off the rough track and on to the open moorland, thick with heather and peaty underfoot.

LINGY PITS BREAST
2010
804 BREEDING PAIRS IN BRITAIN
SILENCE

Signs continued to the top of the moor. At the brow of the hill, set against the expansive, empty sky, the first of two solitary, silent and still Pointing Men came into view. These men were barefoot and costumed in pale grey/white tailored suits designed to echo the ghostly grey-white feather of the male hen harrier, the white posts used for navigation in poor visibility and the white cotton grass that flourishes in this habitat.

FIGURE 3.2 Ghost Bird. *Pointing Man, upper Langden Valley, Trough of Bowland, Lancashire. Performer: Jim Hendley. Photographer: Manuel Vason*

Their suits were designed to make them visible and uncanny – out of place on the moorland. Their bare feet, which sank into the dark, muddy peat, added to their strangeness and were a visual nod towards the poverty-stricken Lancashire Witches who made their way over that fell, perhaps poorly dressed for the terrain and the harsh unforgiving environment.

Behind the Pointing Man, a row of twelve feather-shaped flags ran along the horizon and drew the eye upwards to the massive empty sky devoid of dancing 'ghost birds' – the name used to describe the acrobatic flight of the male harrier. Each flag referenced one of the twelve people accused of witchcraft, and were scaled-up versions of the bird feathers found during my first site visit with Jude. The Pointing Man beckoned participants across boggy ground, bobbing with white-tipped cotton grass, and pointed them down into a narrowing valley framed on either side by the two rows of shooting butts made of drystone wall. Inside each butt, a thin line of heather was placed in the gaps between stones – a reference to the decoration of shooting barns and designed to draw the eye to the curve of the wall and the crafted construction of the butt. It was also a simple intervention that elevated the butt out of 'ordinary time' into a scenographic object. Laid on a rough grey blanket on the peaty ground in each butt, a naked human (ten women and two men) was nestled, curled up, egg or foetus-like and barely protected against the wind, rain and sun of the changing weather.

FIGURE 3.3 Ghost Bird. *Naked woman in shooting butt, Weasel Clough, upper Langden Valley, Trough of Bowland, Lancashire. Performer: Susan Hill. Photographer: Manuel Vason*

My use of the human body, like my use of peat, gun cartridges, feathers and eggs, multiplied to become many: a team of twenty took it in turns so that ten butts (the number of people hanged) were peopled at any one time. As the life models walked across the moor to or from their position in a butt, they wrapped themselves in a grey blanket, an action and image designed to echo the walk across the fell by the Lancashire Witches.

The scenes in the shooting butts were the realization of the image that came into my mind's eye with such clarity during my first field trip to the site. They brought together the history, both past and present, of the site – the grouse shooting, the hen harrier and the walk of the Lancashire Witches. Participants did not expect these images/scenes to be found inside the butts, and for many it was a disturbing, shocking and poignant experience:

> Using the naked bodies in the landscape by association created a special sense of vulnerability of human and bird life in the environment.

> I found the imagery and the experience disturbing, moving and intriguing. The dance in the barn and the naked performers in the 'hides' were deeply poignant and the installations were both beautiful and shocking.

Having walked through the valley of shooting butts, a second Pointing Man directed participants back towards the mountain of spent gun cartridges and a sign that read:

WEASEL CLOUGH
2012
0 NESTING PAIRS FOUND IN BOWLAND
SILENCE

As they walk, they passed signs designed to help them relocate to the physical landscape and emerge from silence.

Weather as scenography – atmosphere and imagining

Over the weekend of *Ghost Bird*, the weather ranged from dry and bright to overcast and showery with dark, glooming clouds and low mist. This weather as scenography added to the atmosphere and evoked the drama and anguish of the Lancashire Witches. On the second day, the sky was grey and the mist lowered before rain and wind set in, which, wrote one participant, meant: 'The landscape was rendered eerie and disquieting – one had a real sense that the Pendle accused [Lancashire Witches] walked through such a landscape'. Similarly, for another, 'although it was atrocious, the weather added to the atmosphere and you could almost picture how the witches would feel crossing the landscape'. A third described how *Ghost Bird*:

> conveyed the atmosphere of what it must have been like to have been brought from Pendle to Lancaster ... the wind and the rain contributed to the overall melancholic atmosphere.

And another said that they 'felt for the life models keenly in that wind, which added to the sensation of fragility'.

Getting in close, empathy and scenography

One of my intentions when choosing not to guide participants through *Ghost Bird* using a walking leader or a character/performer or limit the time they could spend in the performance was to give them time and space to experience the work as if it were a gallery or installation space. Invited to move freely within the mapped and routed parameters, participants became immersed, without interruption, in the environment and landscape of the performance. I also wanted them to view the landscape and the human bodies within the installations in close-up detail: the taut tension of the skin of the pregnant dancer's belly; the uniqueness of each life model's body curled up in a shooting butt; shivering flesh and goosepimpled skin; the downy hairs on a back or arms; veins under pale translucent skin; red hair; a tattoo; freckles; grey hair; folds of flesh or ribs visible through skin. Every one was unique. Every one was startling in the flesh, creating a moment of being and defamiliarization in this context, and seen afresh due to the effect of seeing a naked person 'nesting' in the landscape, and then, looking closer, seeing their bodies were goosebumped in the shivering cold. Using the human body in a hostile landscape, affected by the elements – cold, wind, rain – as a metaphor for both the Lancashire Witches and the hen harrier gave them tangible form and evoked fellow feeling in the participants, who might themselves be challenged by the effects of the walk, the weather, the topography and their empathy with the exposed and naked bodies. One participant later wrote that during *Ghost Bird*, she had 'a sense of being at one with them – the birds, women persecuted as witches', adding 'the presence of vulnerable people in [the landscape] somehow brought the land closer to my heart'.

Signs and silence – no spoken word

My strategy of gradually withdrawing conversation was intended to move participants' attention from themselves and their own concerns towards the landscape – visually, sonically and the sensory effect of walking on their bodies – and then to the plight of the hen harrier.

An element that informed my thinking on the use of silence was how during my first research trip with Jude Laine, we remained silent and still, not drawing attention to ourselves, so as not to disturb or discourage any harrier should it appear. So while choosing not to guide *Ghost Bird*, I knew I wanted participants to experience the performance in silence. The aim of this was to create a time and space for meditation on the plight of the hen harrier and the physically challenging journey made by the Lancashire Witches. It was important that each participant could go at their own pace and take time to walk, look, think and also stop and be still – just as Jude and I had spent time waiting and looking for the hen harrier. I intended this measured pace full of awareness and stillness – a type of mindful walking – to draw people's attention to the landscape and the installations and give them time to reflect and make meaning of each scene.

Participants agreed that the signs drew their attention to the site. One described how they 'slowed you down and lessened conversation as you rose up through the valley'. Others reported that the 'positioning of the signs caused me to stop and notice the close up and far views'. and 'made me look and focus more carefully, made me more aware of wildlife … to open my sense and be more receptive'. For some, this focusing brought about a different kind of walking and looking. One participant, who described how 'ordinarily I'm moving quickly, looking at the big picture and then at my feet', found herself 'scouring the area for birds and other beautiful things much more than I usually do'. Another participant remarked that 'the change to whispering made me more contemplative. As I walked into "silence" I felt even more contemplative'. For another participant who 'did the walk alone', the lessening of conversation meant they 'were able to reflect and absorb, without external chatter'. This is important because sometimes a large number of participants talk as they walk, which can be distracting for other people, so inviting participants to be silent can be beneficial for the group.

Stripping out word, text and narrative

In *Ghost Bird*, text was minimized to a series of signs and instructions placed along the length of the route. The minimal text on these signs was designed to draw attention and attune participants to the physically challenging landscape walked by the Lancashire Witches, and also to introduce partcipants to the plight of the hen harrier by showing how its numbers have declined to the point of near-extinction in recent decades. The texts were deliberately stripped back and non-prescriptive. This stripping-out of words left space for participants to 'access potential meaning' by bringing their own perspectives and contexts through which to 'see' and respond to a performance – and make and produce meaning (Lehmann 2006: 99; McKinney and Palmer 2017: 112).

Participants were given no further information on what they would see, where or when. Designing *Ghost Bird*, I deliberately constructed the performance as a series of scenes and installations that appeared in the landscape unexpectedly and were made from a juxtaposition of materials not ordinarily seen in the same frame. I also wanted everything that participants experienced – planned or unplanned, physical or phenomenological, designed or serendipitous – to add to and inform their experience. The less the production information outlined or explained in advance of participants setting off, the more work participants needed to do to make imaginative and interpretive meaning of what they were seeing. This reflects how the 'logic of visual dramaturgy develops through':

Sequences and correspondences, nodal and condensation points of perception and the constitution of meaning communicated through them (however fragmentary it may be) in visual dramaturgy are defined by optical data.

(Lehmann 2006: 93)

In their discussion on modes of scenographic representation and its metaphoric 'or poetic' qualities, Butterworth and McKinney (2009: 95) acknowledge the time and 'more conscious effort on the part of the spectator' required 'to register the full significance of image in relation to text'. By stripping out the text to the essential minimum required for participants to navigate the sites and to give some context, *Ghost Bird* created imagistic metaphors layered with complex and multiple meanings that accumulated as the performance progressed and required interpretive effort on behalf of the participants. 'This accumulation of meaning and effort happens because images, more so than words, can potentially offer 'multiple meanings or signifiers' (2009: 164). 'This is because images are polysemiotic in nature', meaning they have a 'multiplicity of meanings, or bear many different interpretations' ('polysemous' defined in the *Oxford English Dictionary*), and what follows is that 'images can slide between significations and thus offer a more poetic experience for viewers' (2009: 164). However, because 'There are potentially as many meanings as there are viewers' (2009: 164), *Ghost Bird* sought to guide (without dictating) meaning through its use of visual scene-making that used site-specific materials and phenomena to evoke a sense of human and animal persecution, suffering and endurance – which spans time and generations.

Feedback from participants shows how *Ghost Bird*'s use of metaphor and visual dramaturgy elicited different responses. One person wrote how the performance was 'very beautiful, thought provoking and touching', adding:

> It demanded effort – physical, intellectual and emotional. It offered visual moments that added up and increased in intensity, so the cumulative effect was greater than the (apparent) sum of parts.

For another, the effect of the visual dramaturgy was that they 'enjoyed being in silence and letting the experience speak, without too much analysing or consciously trying to make sense of it'. Another person thought:

> a complete understanding would have meant spelling the meaning out ... It left lots of room for personal input, thought, contemplation. And while I didn't understand all of it, I'd have left less satisfied if I had.

Avoiding a narrative-led scenography meant that *Ghost Bird* left space for participants to make connections and, as one remarked, they 'enjoyed picking up on the clues left'. For another, this piecing together continued after the event: 'It is a rare and valued thing, for me, to find a performance which engages me for so long after the event, and which allows questions to permeate and marinate rather than be completely understood'. These responses show how *Ghost Bird* produced a creative space – a 'scenographic exchange' – between performance and participant (2009: 194). In McKinney's research into 'the nature of communication between scenography and audience', participants were invited to respond to a performance by 'making images of their own which':

> reflected, elaborated and reinterpreted the scenography and demonstrated how the original image of the performance multiplied and mutated. Here, scenography could be seen to be capable of working as an agent of exchange. The audience, stimulated by scenographic constructions, imagined or remembered their own images. The performance and the reflection on it was a construction of multiple reflections and perspectives. Following this line of thinking, audience members can be thought of as co-creators of scenography as far as it is they who find potential stimulation or agreement in or with an image and complete it for themselves through projection and appropriation.
>
> (McKinney 2009: 194)

Participant reflections: visual/non-verbal methods – scenographic exchange

Over a number of years, participants at my performances have described finding words alone an inadequate means of expressing their experiences (from wilson+wilson through to the present day). This meant that feedback has been a reflective act for participants, offering a space for contemplation. Going back to wilson+wilson, participants often sent poems, cards or letters that described and captured the lasting effects of a performance. Many said that they needed time to let the experience run through their minds and gain some distance and perspective before responding meaningfully or constructing a clear meaning. For some, however, this sort of clarity was not possible or desirable. My preference, then, is not to ask for written feedback immediately after a performance, when participants are still absorbed in and moved by their experience. Doing so does not recognize the time and processing space needed before words come.

An alternative way of gathering feedback soon after a performance – one that Nigel Stewart and I first used post *Jack Scout* – is to offer participants drawing materials and invite them to capture and express their experiences using pictures, symbols, colours, impressionistic words (or poems) rather than extended sentences. This non-verbal method enables immediate feedback to be given that is not tidied-up or over-processed by the contributor.

One participant, Hermione Roff, a child and family psychotherapist who came to *Ghost Bird* with a client, wrote about their day in the form of a poem entitled 'Tracing the Ghost Harrier'. The poem reflected on her client's engagement with the performance and that client's post-show drawing of a 'perfect egg shaded in / translucent pink' (Roff 2014):

> I brought a little ghost bird
> Along with me,
> Scrawny, frighted,
> Feathers alert for ruffle.
> Her eyes flickered rapidly
> Left, right, right, left, in
> Startle at so much space, then
> Fell, half lidded, in ready
> Anticipation of death.
> We went past a shed,
> Hundreds of eggs spilling through the open
> Door. In a barn a

Pregnant woman unfurled her wings and
Flailed against a flaming fire. We saw
Mounds of thousands of
Spent cartridges, their colours
Brilliant, red, yellow, green, against the
Wintry heather.
White sails, pinned to
Tall towers,
Franticked their feathers
Against the wind.
Shooting butts concealed
Naked human forms, huddled
Foetal like against the cold.

In all this she
Never said a word.
We met people who
Looked at us and
Spoke to me, but
Not to her, as if she were
There yet not there.

In the end we were asked to
Draw a re-member of our journey.
She took a single piece of
White paper and drew a
Perfect egg shaded in
Translucent pink.
Underneath she wrote
'ME'.

At the time of *Ghost Bird*, Roff's client was aged twenty-two and had 'suffered for many years from quite severe depression. It took a lot of courage for her to agree to come' to *Ghost Bird*. For Roff, the poem gave a feeling of 'the poignancy of life as seen and experienced through this young woman's eyes, the pain of being in the created world, *of* the created world and yet so separate, so detached and yet so thoroughly part of it all'.[22] These responses engendered by the performance and expressed through the drawing, poem

---

[22] Email from Hermione Roff to the author, 18 July 2015.

and Roff's reflections point to how socially engaged and applied scenography, especially when it centres the visual, creates a transformative space that can achieve significant therapeutic and expressive outcomes. They also point to how scenography offers tools that can be used both during and beyond the performance event. As I explore in Chapter 5 when I look at the making of *Warnscale* and Chapter 7 looking at the making of *Women's Walks to Remember*, I use drawing as a tool within the creative process to facilitate exchanges between the scenographer and co-creative participants. These exchanges happen on site in the landscape as well as indoors in a domestic or therapeutic setting, and place scenographic exchange at the heart of the performance-making process. In fact, scenographic exchange becomes the performance work.

4

Site and materials – centring the metaphor: *The Gathering*

> The Gathering *showed me my own pain head-on but disguised as the ewes' fate!!!*
>
> (*THE GATHERING* PARTICIPANT, MZ)

This chapter looks how scenography can explore complex themes associated with fertility and parenthood. It examines *The Gathering / Yr Helfa* (*The Gathering*) (2014), a five-hour-long walking-performance created on a sheep farm located on the highest mountain in Wales, UK, and commissioned by National Theatre Wales. Its purpose was to explore and reveal how human and animal reproductive cycles are seemingly robust, yet are in fact fragile and impermanent. I achieved this by using metaphoric/symbolic imagery designed to evoke multiple meanings. All the images were created using materials from or associated with the site, and were polysemous in that they had multiple and interconnected meanings.

The Gathering took 200 participants on a circuitous, four-mile route that began in a lower valley and ascended into the mountain, before looping back down to the centre of the farm (Hafod y Llan) accompanied by 200 ewes gathered off the lower slopes of the mountain. Once on the farm, participants made a weaving journey around the farm buildings, and the performance continued in sheep pens, stables, barns, trailers, an old farmhouse and fields.

Participants were divided into ten smaller groups of twenty, led by a mountain guide carrying a red-and-white flag with designs based on ear-markings used to indentify the different Hafod y Llan Farm flocks. As they walked, a continuous series of scenes unfolded around and alongside them, performed by the shepherds of Hafod y Llan Farm, a brass band, children from the local primary school and a company of professional actors who played characters in a series of visual, poetic, sung and choreographed scenes. There were six characters. The Old Shepherd was linked to the mountain, the rams, and the cycles of death and renewal. Two Shepherds were linked to seasonal and annual cycles on farm and mountain. The Woman was linked to the life, reproductive and fertility cycles of the ewes and the women of the farm in past generations. The Boy was linked to the lambs, and shared facts and figures about their gestation, birth and how they are taught about the mountain. The Tramway Walker was linked to the industry – the slate quarries and the copper mining – that had at one time dominated the landscape, and left it marked and scarred. Also linked to the industrial and social history of the mountain was The Deiniolen Band, a traditional slate-quarry brass band that played regional hymns, the notes of which at times during the performance were broken down to reference the ewes calling in the fields. The children of the local Beddgelert primary school showed archive photos of the people – shepherds, farming families, miners, quarrymen – who had inhabited Hafod y Llan Farm over many generations. Doing this, the children – a symbol of the next generation – served a role designed to link the farm's past with the present and into the future.

My focus in this chapter is on three distinct and yet interconnected aspects of the performance: the character or figure of The Woman, the ewes and The Tramway Walker. The Woman performed a series of scenes on the mountain and the farm, and the actual ewes were seen and heard live, and were also mediated through film and sound that was incorporated into scenes and installations. The stories of The Woman and the ewes were interwoven and designed to be read in relation to each other. Inspired by the women I found in the farm's archive, The Woman became a metaphor for the ewes, and the ewes became a metaphor for animal and human reproductive and life cycles and stories. Together, they carried the emotional core of the performance, and it was the ewes' annual and reproductive cycles that provided the dramaturgical structure of the whole performance. Some scenes that involved the ewes showed out-of-season activities and processes not ordinarily seen by people outside the farming community, and some made visible internal processes that occur within the body. This process served to defamiliarize and make strange the material and brought a sense of wonderment. The third aspect is the abstract figure of The Tramway Walker, who traversed the landscape following the route of a disused tramway in operation around the 1880s that was used to transport slate out of the quarries and off the mountain. Sections of this route, carpeted in red in a scenographic intervention, were ascended by an aerial dance artist playing The Tramway Walker, adding a visually abstract dimension which drew attention to the marks left on the landscape by historic industrial activity.

In different ways, these three aspects of the performance revealed the scale and topography and the farming and industrial history of the landscape that the ewes inhabit. All were designed to be read in conjunction with each other and in the context of life and reproductive cycles, and all used materials and processes from the site. I wanted participants to view the landscape, and the performance, and to enter more deeply into their purpose and concerns, through the figures of The Tramway Walker, The Woman and the ewes – visually and metaphorically these figures carried the central meaning of the performance. They also demosntrate my applied use of the trope of the solitary figure.

The chapter uses my fieldnotes and extracts from the performance script (unpublished) – these include The Boy's factual/poetic texts written by me (Wilson 2014) and extracts from the poem cycle written by Gillian Clarke (2014).[1] In the performance, these two forms of writing were combined into a script that revealed the ewes' annual, reproductive and life cycles. All the texts were site-specific and informed by the Hafod y Llan Farm shepherds talking and sharing their work with me, and the creative team, which, as well as Clarke, included composer John Hardy and choreographer Nigel Stewart, over many years.

Participant feedback referred to in the chapter was collated by National Theatre Wales in the weeks following the performance – I do not have respondents' names. Production credits for *The Gathering* are in Appendix C.

Background – an attentiveness to things and their effects

When making *Fissure*, a fox-killed lamb captured my imagination – uncanny and beautiful, the dead lamb was laid in a rocky field and, with its eyes open, looked perfectly formed and alive, yet its ribcage and organs were exposed through a blood-red wound in its side. This lamb, and my fascinated reaction to it, showed 'the curious ability of inanimate things to animate, to act, to produce effects dramatic and subtle. Thing-power arises from bodies inorganic as well as organic' (Bennett 2010: 6). The lamb also embodied the fragile and precarious ecology of sheep farming and the closeness of death to life. It is the effects of 'thing power' – of objects and bodies, and how they might be used metaphorically – that as a scenographer I worked with and harnessed when creating *The Gathering*. I developed a scenographically motivated 'attentiveness to things and their effects' by looking, listening and making connections between things (2010: xiv).

---

[1] Clarke was the National Poet of Wales (2008–16). A selection of the poems she wrote for *The Gathering* were later published in *Zoology* (Clarke 2017).

When I set out to find a site where I could use the material processes of a flock of sheep as a metaphor for human and other-than-human life, death and reproductive cycles, I chose Hafod y Llan Farm because it is a site where robustness, fragility and impermanence are all integral. It is an upland farm owned and managed by the National Trust that grazes a flock of 2,000 Welsh Mountain sheep on the foothills and summit of Mount Snowdon.

Extended and observational research

Over the next four years, I undertook site-specific research at the farm that fell into three distinct strands: the ewes and Snowdon flock on the farm and mountain; the people and families who have shepherded over generations, especially the women; and the physical mountain (Snowdon) that has been shaped and marked by farming, slate quarrying and copper mining. Each strand of research showed me the farm through the eyes of those with intimate and expert knowledge of it, and enabled me to gather raw data that informed the routes, location choices and dramaturgical structure of the performance, as well as the material and content of scenes, characters, costumes, writing (poems and factual texts) and choreography.

During this research period, I became immersed in the farm, observed closely and recorded my findings through note-taking, photography, film and sound recording. I also used drawing, which required a deeper level of looking that can lead to a deeper level of seeing, feeling and understanding the thing being looked at – the topography, how it was linked by paths and is marked by farming and industry, and movement through the landscape, distant and close up. Later, both the drawings and the photographs were used as resources and materials when I designed the performance through a storyboard-assemblage process. The film and sounds I captured provided footage that became part of a series of installations.

In the *Snowdon Shepherd: Four Seasons on the Hill Farms of North Wales* (1991) visual artist Keith Bowen used drawing and painting to capture 'month by month how the flocks are bred, grazed, shared and sold' (Morris in Bowen 1991: Foreword). Bowen spent hours studying and sketching the shepherds and sheep before he began to see, feel and understand their movement patterns and actions. Using drawing as a way of seeing, he captured the shapes and patterns of the scene and the colours of the seasons, rock and weather.

Drawing as scenographic creative and methodological tool is common to performance design. I reflect on the role it plays in my practice – a process I have come to refer to as drawing it out:

As a site-specific landscape performance maker drawing enables me to see and feel the landscape to which I am responding; through it I become embedded in a place and more able to notice its detail and form and its still and dynamic qualities.

(Wilson, quoted in Casey and Davies 2015: 75)

For theatre designer Rae Smith, drawing is a creative, imaginative and thinking tool that allows many ideas to be in play at once – on the page and in the mind. Smith writes of how she is 'always drawing, and always quickly: as a reaction, a direct form of communication of ideas within the collective process of making a piece of live art' (Smith in Collins and Nisbet 2010: 377–85):

[I use drawing] as a method of communication, to record, to express imagination, to think about a show in retrospect or to draw something I can't remember. Drawings may occur within the process of making work: in research and development, workshops; the storyboards and costume drafts of the design process; in showing and presenting the designs, during rehearsals and throughout the tech and previews.

(Smith 2021)

Other artists – close observation: see, feel, understand

The time I spent at Hafod y Llan Farm observing and logging the shepherds' activities sits in the context of the work of other artists who have also used visual art, photography, film, poetry and prose, performance and walking practices to document upland sheep farming – bringing land, people and sheep closer. Like *The Gathering*, much of this work shows life and death processes in the flesh, and frames them not as brutal, but as facts of existence that can be full of beauty and wonderment. This work follows in a tradition of writing and films that show the struggles and hardships of farmers and animals living in isolated locations and extreme weather conditions. Examples include the films *Too Long a Winter* (1972), *A Winter Too Many* (1989), *The Dale That Died* (1975) and more recently *Addicted to Sheep* (2015), in which the director Magali Pettier portrays a family's life on their hill farm in Teesdale, County Durham, and writing such as James Rebank's *The Shepherd's Life: A Tale of the Lake District* (2015) and Amanda Owen's *Yorkshire Shepherdess* series (2014, 2016 and 2019). Working collaboratively to create *Gathering: Hill Farming, People, Animals and Landscape*, the photographer Kate Bellis and sculptor Sally Matthews spent time over a fifteen-month period working 'closely with the hill farming community, animals and landscape' at Tarset in Northumberland (VARC 2005). Bellis' photographs captured community and domestic moments, ranging from sheep sales and shearing to a farmer bottle-feeding a lamb, whilst Matthews' life-size sketches show the anatomy *and* energy of the ewes and rams. Collectively, our work documents and 'celebrate[s] a way of life and [a] landscape under threat' (Bellis and Matthews 2005) without shying away from revealing the cycles of life and death and the fragility of existence where the weather (rain, snow, wind, drought) can make or break a season. Farmer David McCracken, who featured in their work, has a deep and intimate knowledge of the land achieved through working and walking it day after day and year after year. In *Farm Walk*, McCracken led a series of walks on his farm in Northumberland, during which he shared the farm as he sees it: 'changes in growth, habit, wildlife, weather, the condition of fences, lying water and the location of animals' (McCracken 2013: 19). One participant described how they 'normally' walk 'very blindly', whereas the farm walk caused them to 'look at what is around' (2013: 19). McCracken's material has echoes with how Arwyn Owen and his team of shepherds at Hafod y Llan Farm showed me, and later the participants, the farm and the animals through their eyes.

Harriet and Robert Fraser's (Somewhere Nowhere) land art work, mentioned in the introduction to this book, forms part of a large body of work they have created that is concerned not only with rural upland landscapes but with the people-of, and living-in, those landscapes – their 'culture, heritage and way of life' (Somewhere Nowhere 2016–17). At the heart of their work is the way it seeks to listens to, and capture, the voices of those who 'know a patch of land intimately' and are alive to it (Fraser and Fraser 2014). In *Landkeepers*, they spent time with 'hill farmers in the Lake District in rain, snow and blazing heat, for shearing, inspecting, showing, selling and the final process, slaughter', from which they produced a series of photographs, poetry and prose (Somewhere Nowhere 2014). Similarly, working for 'just over a year' to 'gather images, recordings and writings' in *Voices from the Land* they 'collated stories and viewpoints of farmers across the Yorkshire Dales: men and women, young and old' into an exhibition of portraits, landscape photographs, interview excerpts and audio clips, displayed alongside artefacts and archival writing of farming life and practices (Somewhere Nowhere 2016–17). Central to Somewhere Nowhere's practice is a desire to share and communicate through image, word and object 'what is involved in nurturing animals and land with those outside the farming community' (2016–17).

In the guided walk/performance, *The Only Place We Ever Knew* (2010), artist and farmer Ffion Jones gave 'audiences a rare glimpse of a Welsh hill farm' from her own located perspective as well as that of her own 'farming family' (Jones 2014: 60), about whom she writes, 'With repeated exposure to this particular terrain we have "feet for the place"– an embodied understanding of the nature of the ground under-foot' (2014: 63). Moving across the land they farm and inhabit, Jones and her family showed participants farming activities, performed 'lay-choreography' (2014: 64), and shared places, stories and memories that were of personal and historic significance, that otherwise would ordinarily 'remain hidden to the average walking visitor' (2014: 60).

Common to the practice of Bellis, McCracken, Somewhere Nowhere, Bowen, Jones and myself is the process of close-up and immersive looking that seeks out detail, pattern and understanding that can only be found through knowing a place intimately. This could be from first hand embodied knowledge or by spending time with those who have that knowledge. Another common factor is a desire to show and share the ordinary/extraordinariness of the upland hill farm. Where my practice, and specifically *The Gathering*, differs is the life-event context in which I placed the mountain, sheep and people at Hafod y Llan Farm.

'Cynefin' – flock, people, mountain

'Cynefin' – the ewes and the Snowdon flock

The early stages of my research coincided with a time when, in my early forties, I was facing the fact that I had possibly left becoming a parent biologically too late. In the hope of resolving this 'missing' life-event, I underwent an unsuccessful cycle of *in vitro* fertilization (IVF). Following this, my options, as outlined by the clinician, were further rounds of IVF with my own eggs or donor eggs, no further treatment or adoption. However, the projected success rate of this second round of IVF had reduced from the previous level of less than 5 per cent to less than 2 per cent. Given the high physical, emotional and financial costs of the treatment, I decided this percentage was too low and chose to have no further treatment – a decision and circumstance that left me feeling empty. So I was forcibly struck, when observing the shepherds scanning the ewes for pregnancy, that they referred to those that were not pregnant as 'empties' before spraying them on the neck with a black mark and 'turning them up to the mountain'. Witnessing the 'empty' ewes had the same shocking and visceral effect on me as seeing the fox-killed lamb, and the experience was 'an actant', by which I mean:

> a source of action that can be either human or non-human; it is that which has efficacy, can *do* things, has sufficient coherence to make a difference, produce effects, alter the course of events.
>
> (Bennett 2010: viii)

In this moment, where the ewes' emptiness collided with my own, I knew I had found the centre of the performance, and decided to put the ewes' stories to metaphorical use by harnessing them as the lens through which to view human life and reproductive cycles.

As my research progressed, I observed the annual cycles of gathering, marking, checking, sorting, injecting, shepherding and shearing. In July I watched the shepherds shear the ewes to remove the coarse 'kempy' fleeces, designed to protect the ewes and the foetuses they carry from driving rain and winter conditions on the mountain, and neatly roll and tuck the fleeces into large balls.

Gradually I began to see the patterns of the ewes' seasonal and reproductive cycle. This cycle, as my fieldnotes record, starts in November, the mating season, when the ewes who are 'seasonal breeders, come into season with the fading light' and are tupped by the rams (the tups). In April the lambing season starts, and the ewes give birth to the next generation. In August the male lambs are taken for slaughter. In September the ewe lambs are sold to other breeders (thirty are retained for breeding) and the older 'draft' ewes, aged five to six years, are taken to market and sold to lowland farms, where they continue to breed.

FIGURE 4.1 The Gathering. *Site research at Hafod y Llan Farm, Snowdonia – Welsh mountain ewes being sorted and marked for pregnancy (single, twins, empty). Photographer: Louise Ann Wilson*

Cycles and cycles of repair and renewal were also resonant and provided raw material that proved particularly significant. For example, there was the unceasing sound of ewes calling to newborn lambs in the springtime, the motherless lambs crying for milk and a field of distraught lambs and mothers calling out for each other after weaning. Particularly striking, however, was the way orphaned lambs were adopted by ewes whose lambs had died. This process of adoption and surrogacy involved the shepherd taking the corpse of a stillborn or dead lamb away from its mother. He inserted a knife into the dead lamb's woollen coat and made a series of cuts at the neck and around the legs before peeling the fleece away from the sinewy but muscular body beneath. I noticed how the tongue of the skinned lamb lolled out of its open mouth, and the strangely beautiful, marble-like lines of blood vessels on the pink-fleshy inside of the freshly skinned fleece. The shepherd then scooped up an orphaned lamb and, in a way reminiscent of a child being pulled into a woollen jumper, fitted the skinned fleece over its back legs, front legs and head. Once dressed, the lamb was placed with the grieving mother ewe; recognizing the smell of her own dead lamb held in the fleece now worn by the new lamb, she began to lick it. Finally, the shepherd gently but firmly guided the lamb to the ewe's milk-filled udders and helped it suckle. Half an hour later, mother and lamb had accepted each other and the adoption was complete. Combined, this research provided the raw material, themes and structural form of the performance and the performance script.

One other cycle that emerged during my research was the intergenerational knowledge and memory of the mountain that is passed from ewe to lamb. 'The lambs are taught the boundaries, the sheep know their place, their boundaries are an invisible line or wall' (Wilson 2014). In the English language this sense of belonging to a place or a habitat and of understanding where on the fell they can roam, graze or shelter is known as *heaf* or *heft*. In Welsh this sense is known as *cynefin*. The shepherds at Hafod y Llan Farm agreed that, like the flocks they tend, they too have *cynefin* – a sense of being 'right' in the environment. This cycle informed the themes of intergenerational belonging, family and bloodlines coming to an end that ran through the performance.

'Cynefin' – the shepherds and women of the farm

The farm archive holds photographs, articles and documents that showed its shepherds and families going back many generations. These photos became a rich source of images, stories, characters, locations, routes and physical materials used in the performance. Of particular interest to me were the farm women. Using this source ensured that the human element of the performance was site-specific. Photographs showed, for example, an older woman blowing a conch to call the farmers in for tea, a woman shepherd sorting sheep, a woman and a young girl standing behind a mound of rolled fleeces outside the now-derelict Hafod y Uchaf (Upper Summer Dwelling), a girl in a white cotton slip dress standing on a rock in the middle of the river as the men dipped the sheep so that the river water could wash away the lanolin in their wool, and rows of men hand-shearing the sheep while the women bundled up the fleeces, just as the shepherds do today. One figure who leapt from the photos was Lily (Lil) Williams. We saw her as a young woman dressed for a party in a striped dress, in the garden of the Old Farm House bottle-feeding lambs, bringing tea to the family in the meadow at haymaking time and, as an older woman, dressed in a black coat waiting by a car.

Lily's son Bleddyn, a member of the William's family who had farmed at Hafod y Llan since 1856, returned to the farm to meet me. This was his first visit since he had collected Lily in 1997 when she was forced to leave the farm after it was sold, never to return. Bleddyn brought with him a private family photo album and told me many more stories that spoke of powerful bonds between the people, the farm and the landscape, and the inevitable passage of time. Walking the farm together, in Le Tŷ Hafod y Llan (the Old Farm House), he showed me photos and described the house as it had been when he lived there. He told me how, on the day he collected Lily, the family ties to the farm and land had broken for good. Bleddyn's stories and the photos of Lily – mixed with those of other farm women in the archive – combined into the figure of The Woman and informed the location of her scenes and the themes underpinning them.

Lily was married to Prys Williams, Bleddyn's father. One photograph showed Prys as a boy, perched on a stool and dressed in his Sunday best – neat jacket and short trousers. This photo inspired the figure of The Boy and his costume design. The figure (or character) of The Old Shepherd was designed (and costumed) to represent a physical embodiment of Prys as an older man (also seen in photos) and of the generations of shepherds that had worked on the farm over many decades and who, like the character, had the mountain in their blood.

'Cynefin' – the physical mountain

Spending time with the shepherds revealed how the mountainous landscape of the farm was formed through geological processes, but had been changed, marked and scarred by human activity such as farming, copper mining and slate quarrying over many generations. The remnants of these industries, such as slag heaps, buildings, tramways, and paths and entrances to copper mines, are easily overlooked. One such scar stretched the length of the valley and revealed the route of the tramway line – including two steep, nearly vertical, inclines where a weighted pulley system was used to lower and raise the slate trucks simultaneously. To warn that these trucks were coming, a man walked ahead of them waving red flags.

Archive photos show historical and political events such as Prime Minister William Gladstone opening the Watkin Path that leads to the summit of Snowdon on 13 September 1892. This event on the mountain was attended by hundreds of people. A band played and, as the plaque on Gladstone Rock reads: 'The multitudes sang Cymeric hymns' (my fieldnotes). Archival research showed these hymns included 'Bryn Calfaria', 'Llanfair' and 'Rhys-y-Groes'. Further research linked these hymns to the Snowdonian tradition of brass bands that formed around the slate quarries, including the Cwm Llan slate quarry at Hafod y Llan Farm. The brass of their instruments is made of a composite of copper and nickel, a material that further linked them to the mountain through the copper mined there. One such band, from the neighbouring valley, was the Deiniolen Band.

Distillation and design process

Once research from each strand was gathered, I considered how to work with, connect and emplace my findings in a way that created a dramaturgically and scenographically coherent performance. Driving this complex design process, in which many layers of material have to be distilled, is the need to communicate the underlying subject matter and themes. This involved a process of scenographic assemblage achieved by storyboarding each scene and dramaturging the effect I wanted that scene to generate. These storyboards were supported by a series of technical drawings and maps showing each location and the route that participants and performers would take, while technical drawing showed the design and position of objects and interventions in greater detail.

Storyboards – scenographic assemblage

Creatively, the storyboarding and mapping processes involved a distillation and reimagining of the raw materials through a process of scenographic assemblages. These assemblages used a combination of elements and were a hybridization of real (live and recorded) farming activities and semi-fictional imaginings that were combined to create a scenographic palimpsest.

Working in this way, having 'drawn' the performance out of the landscape through observational and extended research (by which I mean it was inspired by the site), I then 'draw' scenes back into the landscape using materials and objects of the site. These included woollen fleeces, red carpet, slate, hay, brass instruments, beds, archive photos, sheep- and lamb-related objects, shepherds, sheep and dogs. This process is a literal working out of the meaning of scenography, 'drawing *in* or *with* the scene' (Palmer 2011: 52), and demonstrates how the decentring of performance forms and values, away from traditional building-based and script-oriented models, has tended towards 'the visual image over the written word, collage and montage instead of linear structure' (Balme in Baugh 2013: 224). My reasons for using scenographic assemblage can be understood through Jane Bennett's concept of vibrant matter:

> Assemblages are ad hoc groupings of diverse elements, vibrant materials of all sorts. Assemblages are living, throbbing confederations ... An assemblage is never a stolid block but an open-ended collective, a non-totalizing sum.
>
> (Bennett 2010: 23–4)

However, Bennett's particular take on assemblages is to do with how they reveal the agency of matter, whereas my emphasis, intention and agency as the designer is deliberately to select and place objects together in such a way that generates effect.

Though the overall design left space for meaning to be constructed as the scenes progressed and accumulated, the performance (as my design process reveals) was meticulously composed and had the themes of life and fertility cycles coursing through it. So while the dramaturgy resisted explanation, I made sure 'accurate clues are provided' for participants to 'fill in the gaps' by drawing on their own experiences, imagination and feelings to interpret what they were seeing (Howard 2002: 210).

Practically, the storyboarding process involved me drawing a series of collaged images that are made by literally cutting up my research materials (photographs, sketches and maps) and reassembling them to create a picture for each scene. Rooted in the site, the process wove together the 'real' with the imagined, creating a scenographic hybrid. I also drew a series of maps – equivalent to the ground plans and technical drawings that are produced when designing for the stage. These maps helped me work out where to locate scenes in such a way that incorporated both expansive viewpoints and vistas, wide-open and large-scale features (such as mountain peaks, industrial scars marking a rock face, rivers and waterfalls and farm fields) as well as more intimate and enclosed sites (such as houses, derelict quarry buildings and copper mine shafts, and barns and sheep pens). So that participants always had something or someone to notice, look at, or listen to I also used the maps to ensure interventions were spread along the whole length of route. These maps also helped me plan the dynamic figure-of-eight (non-linear) route that participants would follow into and out of the mountain, and the parallel routes (close-up and distant) that ran alongside the participants which the performers would follow. The final route – taken by the participants – ran the four-mile length of the mountain and around the farm centre, and deliberately moved through terrains that ranged from woodland and open mountain to farmyards and lowland fields. It was made up of a criss-cross of interweaving, dividing and joining tracks that was intersected by other tracks taken by actors (in character), shepherds, sheep, dogs and The Tramway Walker, and was designed to give ever-shifting vantage points on scenes – moving and static – that unfolded around them. This was a deliberate reference to how pilgrims move through varied terrains, often looping back, and gain distance and close-up perspectives on routes and locations that are yet to be visited.

The storyboards and maps, as well as being creative tools, were used to communicate the performance to the large team of people involved in its realization. The process was collaborative, too, because the design for each scene incorporated materials from the writer, composer and choreographer. However, it is the scenography that organizes and brings these components together.

FIGURE 4.2 The Gathering. *Storyboard of Tramway Walker and Shepherds traversing the lower amphitheatre at Clogwyn, Hafod y Llan Farm, Snowdonia. Drawn by Louise Ann Wilson*

The Woman's scenes

The figure of The Woman was both abstracted and used as a narrative device. Compared to The Tramway Walker (see below), she had a more direct relationship to the underlying subject matter and the ewes – she was a singing, choreographed and performative figure. I placed her in a series of 'visual' and 'poetic' scenes sited on the mountain and in the farm in carefully chosen locations – a derelict farmhouse, abandoned quarries, a mound of slate up on the mountain where the ewes roam and the roaring river at Afon y Llan waterfalls. Each scene was self-contained, although designed to connect to what came before and after, so meaning was cumulative. Unlike paintings of a solitary figure, such as Caspar Friedrich's *Wanderer Above the Sea of Fog* (1818) where the viewer looks on to the figure surveying the scene, The Woman was not viewed from afar or from a single or static viewpoint. Rather, I designed the scene in such a way that participants moved around her and gained multiple perspectives on her – from all sides, at a distance, up close, from above and from below. As well as seeing her in the frame, the scenes were designed so that participants would view the landscape from her perspective and in the context of the performance. The aim was for them to see and feel what she was seeing and feeling; this meant she was in some scenes staged more like Friedrich's painting of a small lone figure in *The Monk by the Sea* (1808–10) or Dorothea Tanning's *Self-Portrait* (1944). But because of the context of *The Gathering*, the most direct comparison to my use of the solitary figure is Elina Brotherus' use of this trope in the Annunciation series (2009–13). This body of self-portrait photographic works was created over a four-year period, and it documents Brotherus undergoing repeated cycles of fertility treatment. Classical paintings of the Annunciation by artists such as Fra Angelico (c. 1450) and Vecellio Tiziano (1535) represent 'the announcement, made by the angel Gabriel to the Virgin Mary', that she would conceive a child ('Annunciation' defined in the *Oxford English Dictionary*). Staged in the domestic realm, Brotherus' attempts to become pregnant through medical rather than divine intervention are carefully composed and unflinching in detail. With a scenography of frame, object (symbolic and medical) and light, one image, *Annunciation 7, Day of The Annunciation* (2011), shows her seated at the dining-room table where she self-injects fertility drugs into her swollen, needle-marked and bruised abdomen (Brotherus 2015). In a number of images created with direct reference to Friedrich's *Wanderer Above the Sea of Fog*, Brotherus places herself as a solitary figure in a vast landscape. For example, in *Annunciation 30, Last in My Line* (2012) Brotherus stands looking away from the viewer over a city skyline wearing a bright red coat.

As the title suggests, she is contemplating how her family line (biologically) will end with her, and in *Annunciation 31, The End* (2013) she faces a white, snowy, untrodden landscape. Open to multiple meanings, but viewed in the context of the series, this image creates a sense of vast and bleak but beautiful emptiness and uncharted territories. It suggests a woman unable to overcome forces of nature beyond her own control, but the possibility of a yet-to-be-discovered alternative future.

The writer Ann Radcliffe, discussed in Chapter 1, offers another helpful reference point here. In *Observations During a Tour to the Lakes of Lancashire, Westmoreland, and Cumbria* she described an ascent of Skiddaw, a mountain in the Lake District, UK, she made on horseback. Her multisensory and visually evocative account detailed the effects on her body, psychological state and visual perception of Skiddaw's 'precarious precipices', 'wind gusting, dread-making ravines', 'tremendous chasms', 'roaring torrents', 'gushing spring' and ridges of 'whitish shivered slate' (Radcliffe [1795] 2014: 150). Having reached the summit, Radcliffe described the fresh 'alternative' perspective she gained on the 'vast tracts of low country' laid out 'like a map' beneath her: 'We stood on a pinnacle commanding the dome of the sky. The prospects below, each of which had been before considered separately as a great scene, were now miniature parts of an immense landscape' ([1795] 2014: 151–2). Descending, she observed:

> each mountain below gradually re-assuming its dignity, the two lakes expanding into spacious surfaces, the many little vallies, that sloped upwards from their margins, recovering their variegated tints of cultivation the cattle again appearing in the meadows, and the woody promontories changing from smooth patches of shade into richly tufted summits.
>
> (Radcliffe [1795] 2014: 154)

In her fiction writing Radcliffe used semi-fictional landscapes, created by an imaginative montage drawn from a hybrid of 'travel literature, topographical art and her own invention for the locales in her novels' (E J Clery in Radcliffe [1797] 1981: ix). These fictional landscapes, resonant of the Skiddaw scenery, became a theatre of constantly changing images, scenes and topographies into which her stories were plotted and through which her female characters journeyed. Radcliffe worked with these landscapes to reveal the social 'plight' (or situation) of her female characters, which she transformed by framing the scene (and the situation) from one vantage point and then reframing both from another perspective. For example, in her novel *The Italian* (1797) Radcliffe used the devices of a room and a carriage window to frame a scene, which she then reframed from a different vantage point in a way that diminished mountain peaks, precipices, rivers and ravines that had previously been physically and sensorially overwhelming. This process gave the novel's fictional heroine the 'strength to bear' and 'elevate' herself beyond her circumstance ([1797] 1981: 90). She, in turn, is designed to awaken the reader's imagination to the possibility of change and enable personal and social empowerment. In *The Gathering*, the process of moving through the landscape and viewing and reviewing it from different vantage points and perspective was put to literal and metaphorical use in a way that is comparable to Radcliffe's work.

Thematic 'modes' – filling, emptying, grieving

The Woman's scenes incorporated the ewes and materials associated with them and the mountain – woollen fleeces, slate, water, brass instruments – and she was dressed in clothes that referenced the ewes. One costume was a creamy-white woollen coat with a distinctive coppery colour ruff, like the Welsh mountain sheep, and another was a black woollen coat based on an archive photo of Lily Williams (participants are shown this during the performance) and made resonant through the story of the 'empty' ewes that are given a black mark and 'put back on the mountain' or taken to market to be sold on as 'draft' or 'broken mouth' ewes. This was linked to the story of Lily leaving the farm for good, which in turn connected to how the 'draft' ewes are loaded onto trailers to be transported to market. The black coat, in one reading, was designed as a fairly straightforward translation of a ewe being marked black, but as an object it goes beyond conveying what happens to the ewes and carried with it other ideas of leaving home, being out in the cold, not being pregnant and the ending of family lines. Together, and in different ways, every object and material used in the performance carried a symbolic weight and spoke metaphorically to the human-female/animal life-events: fertility and breeding, pregnancy and loss of pregnancy, birthing and adopting, non-biological mothering.

Each of The Woman's scenes explored different aspects of the reproductive and fertility cycles, both human and animal (the ewes), and worked with a thematic mode that had a symbolic and visual resonance:

- *filling* – fertility, reproduction, birth and cynefin;
- *emptying* – loss of pregnancy, offspring or a parent;
- *grieving* – infertility, ageing, leaving the farm, ending of family bloodlines and cynefin.

These 'modes' informed the location choice and use of materials, poetry and choreographed movement based on the physical actions of shepherds working with the sheep and the fleeces. They included shearing, rolling, tucking and imagery showing lambs in the womb and birthing. In the performance this movement became abstracted.

At Hafod y Uchaf, the derelict remains of a shepherd's summer cottage, the mode was *filling* and reflected fertility, pregnancy and the desire for a child. Here, The Woman wore a cream underslip designed to reference the ewes when they are shorn in July and the shape of the body that is revealed below the wool. She filled the room with rolled-up fleeces of wool until it overflowed, re-creating a scene directly based on an archive photo showing a woman and a young girl sorting a mound of fleeces in this same place before it was abandoned. What was this scene that participants witnessed and what did the fleeces represent? Fertility? Desire for a child? Pregnancy? Is each fleece an ovum? An embryo? A foetus? She sang gently and inwardly, lullaby-like, with words set to a traditional folk song:

The womb's warm room
where the lamb grows in its cradle.

In the blood-lit cave
life becomes lamb,
limbs budding in the warm dark,

multiplying and dividing cells
ova, zygote, embryo, foetus,
developing muscle, bone,

a force unstoppable
as the river
in the mountain's womb.

(Clarke 2014)

At Cwm Llan slate quarry, the modes were multiple: *filling, emptying* and *grieving*. Here, under the summit of Snowdon, the shepherds were placed high up on peaks and promontories encircling the participants and the valley, which echoed with their shouts and whistles. Nestled in the valley bottom, the remains of buildings and slag heaps of Cwm Llan slate quarry were seen. Islands of sharp-edged shards of slate were heaped in flattened mounds, and on the far tip of the central island, the solitary figure of The Woman came into view. Standing in stillness she wore the cream woollen coat with a copper-coloured collar and was surrounded by a small flock of black-marked ewes. She was dwarfed by the expansive sky, the mountainous landscape around her and the distant peak of Snowdon.

FIGURE 4.3 The Gathering. *'The Woman' at Cwm Llan slate quarry, Hafod y Llan Farm, Snowdonia. Performer: Ffion Dafis. Photographer: Lizzie Coombes*

At Afon y Llan (waterfalls), where the mode was *emptying*, The Woman was viewed from afar: participants saw her and the river she stood in from an elevated bird's-eye perspective. In the scene, The Woman's coat, clothes and boots were neatly folded and placed on the riverbank. Stranded on a rock in the middle of the churning water of the Afon Cwm Llan, barefoot, The Woman wore only the pale-coloured slip we first saw her in at the derelict cottage. Her movements, and the fleeces of wool that were placed on the rock around her, unravelled with gravity and the flow of water. The mode of this location echoed the flow of the water and the downward gravity of its force as it emptied off the mountain. What was this scene showing? A miscarriage? A stillbirth? A suicide? Grief? Just audible above the rage of the water, she sang:

Is this birth, or death?

How can I lick this corpse to life,
love's chemistry raging
in my blood, her brain?

I will try, obsessed.
I drink it, smell it.
It is mine, this death in birth.

I thirst for my lamb, still-born, still warm,
lick him clean with a growl of love.

(Clarke 2014)

At Hafod y Llan Farm (the Old Farm House), once lived in by generations of shepherds and their families but now falling into dereliction, the mode was *grieving*. This was inspired by Bleddyn's story of Lily Williams leaving the farm forever, and incorporated his family photographs. Outside the house, archive photographs of it as it once was showed women bottle-feeding lambs by the garden gate, making butter and sitting on a chair in the porch. Inside the house, Bleddyn's photographs show the once-neat living room with chairs, rag rug, polished fireplace and brass candlesticks on the mantelpiece. Now, however, the house and room were empty and the fireplace was broken. Into that empty space were placed fleeces that covered the floor and mounded up into the corners. The Woman, wearing the black woollen coat, stood among them. At her feet was a suitcase containing a heavy black stone taken from the river and placed there by her during the performance of the poem cycle at the quarry, as a symbol of the weight of an empty womb. In a lamenting voice, full of grief, she sang:

'Empty' ewes marked black
bearing their nothing like a stone.
The womb clenches like a heart
against the void as they wait
weighted, for a journey.

Branded barren. Empty.
Hollow on the holy hill,
without foetus, without future.

She must leave the mountain,
the end of her line,
the last cord cut.

(Clarke 2014)

The ewes' scenes

Annual and reproductive cycle – poems and facts

Working to emplace the ewes' cycles, I found it was not possible to organize them into the landscape in a linear timeline: locations that were scenographically suited to one stage or aspect of the cycle did not map out sequentially on site. Instead, I chose to work with the ewes' cycles in two ways. I broke down the full cycle into a non-linear sequence of scenes and interventions emplaced in settings across the whole site, but in a location that was 'right' for that material and chosen for its physical, historic and symbolic resonance. These fragmented 'scenes' accumulated meaning and gradually built into a more complex picture. As one participant remarked, 'various little scenes are connecting up, and making a bigger and bigger picture'.[2] The second way involved me directing a theatricalized and visually heightened performance of the complete poem and factual cycle in one location. This performance incorporated the brass band, the actual shepherds and the professional actors who played the characters of the Old Shepherd, the Two Shepherds, The Woman and The Boy. I sited it in a semi-derelict slate quarry building that sat beneath the summit of Snowdon, where it was possible for all 200 participants to sit in the round. This remote location brought the industrial, sheep and mountain strands of the work together, and was where the ewes passed 'cynefin' to the lambs and the 'empty' ewes were sent.

Two hundred live ewes and 'real' shepherding activities

Scenes located on the mountain and the farm incorporated live ewes and were performed by the shepherds and their dogs. These were deliberately designed to take participants close to the ewes and gave a first-hand, unmediated account of the ewes that sat in contrast to the poetic and the purely visual.

At Hafod y Llan Farm, every September thousands of sheep are gathered off the mountain. This large-scale annual event was not repeatable every day for the three-day duration of the performance; instead, I designed a scaled-down version by sending a group of ten shepherds out onto the mountain at the start of the performance. They gathered 200 sheep off the lower fell and drove them down to the farm, where they were rounded up in a series of pens. Here the shepherds talked directly to participants, showing how they sheared the sheep and rolled their fleeces, checked the ewes' health and fertility by feeling their udders, feet and hinds and counting their teeth, and describing how 'lambs are born with milk teeth', then at:

12 months have two teeth – Dau dant
24 months have four teeth – Pedwar dant

---

[2] *The Gathering* participant feedback, 2014.

28 months have six teeth – Cegllawn or 'Full Mouth'
Last teeth – 'Broken Mouth'

(Wilson 2014)[3]

The shepherds explained how the 'broken mouth' ewes were marked and separated from the flock, loaded onto a trailer and driven off the farm to market.

Two hundred objects and ewes, trumpets and brass, sound and film – ghosting

The ewes were also mediated through objects, sound and film showing out-of-season activities that were incorporated into the scenes and installations. To replace or ghost the full number of sheep, I used a smaller flock of sheep and objects, sounds and metaphors to stand in for them.

As participants arrived at the upper foothills of the farm, where the September gathering of sheep begins, the shepherds, whom they have followed into the mountain, stood above them on high peaks from where they call and whistle to their dogs. These figures encircled the participants, and their calls echoed around the valley. Here, because the majority of the ewes (other than a few the 'real' gathering had missed) had been gathered already, I used a flock of brass instrument players to 'ghost' the sound of the absent sheep. The decision to use a band in this way was a direct reference to the quarry brass band and the band that played on the mountain during Gladstone's opening of the Watkin Path event. The brass band was used throughout the performance, and became a metaphor for the ewes and sheep.

As well as reflecting the sounds of the ewes in the September gathering, the band's playing was inspired by recordings I made at different times of the year. These included the ewes and lambs chorusing and calling in the fields at lambing time, a flock crying out after weaning and a solitary ewe bleating in a lambing field for her lost lamb. Picking up on the sound of the solitary ewe, in the early stages of the performance a single trumpet player stood in the centre of the same field and played a series of 'bleating' notes. These notes were elaborated upon by another trumpeter located further up the valley. This process was repeated all the way up the hillside – witnessed and heard by participants as they walked – until a chain of trumpet calls helped lead them up to the top of the mountain and the site of a derelict slate quarry. Here a band of brass instruments picked up the chain of notes, and then the players slowly descended the slope, bringing the participants with them like

---

[3] The shepherds said these words live (less formally) and the words also formed part of The Boy's factual/poetic texts (this is extracted from those).

sheep being gathered in by the shepherd. Gradually the music was organized and orchestrated into patterns and recognizable tunes that echoed around the bowl-shaped valley. The tunes in turn were the same 'cymeric hymns' that were played at the historic Gladstone Rock ceremony, where William Gladstone addressed a crowd of 2,000 people as he opened the Watkin Path up Snowdon. The final scene of the performance was staged back in the lambing field where, early on, the solo trumpet player had sent the sheep-call out to the mountain. In this final scene, participants were surrounded by a flock of brass players: the flurry of notes they played ghosted the ewes calling their lambs in spring.

On the farm, 200 sheep-related objects were arranged in a pattern on the floor of a yard. Each object stood for one of the 200 ewes sold as 'draft' (old/infertile) at the market in September. Among these objects was a gate, a winter-feeding trough, a red work glove, a milking bottle, a pair of clippers, an ear-cutting knife and a wooden stile. Words chalked on a slate told participants:

> In September, 200
> 'broken mouthed',
> 'draft ewes' that would
> struggle in upland conditions
> are sold at Dolgellau Market
> to lowland farms
> where they continue
> to breed.
>
> (Wilson 2014)[4]

In another yard a sound recording of 200 'draft ewes' was heard echoing from inside a now-empty trailer that had taken the draft ewes to market, and visual footage recorded in previous years of the ewes streaming onto a trailer and being sold formed part of an installation in an old stable. This footage was mixed with that of sheep coursing like a river down the valley, moving in rows and patterns across the mountainside, flowing through a gate or sheep-hole in a wall like salt through an hourglass, flooding into the farm and moving through sorting pens. These many layers of footage were edited into a dreamlike flow of sheep and mountain that was projected on a triptych of fleeces, suspended above a row of beds inhabited by the character of the Old Shepherd. These elements created a scene inspired by Bleddyn's stories and the shepherd's sense of cynefin. In choreographed movements, based on the actions the shepherds use when gathering the sheep from the mountain, the Old Shepherd tumbled between the beds until he rested in one, as if on his deathbed. In another yard the

---

[4] Extracts from The Boy's factual/poetic texts written in installations on the farm.

recorded sound of a 'motherless lamb' crying for its mother was placed inside a row of three woolsacks bulging with wool, like a pregnant ewe.

Triptychs – 'Skinning of the Lamb': lambing barn scene

A lamb's birth and mothering cycles were portrayed in a series of multimedia installations that used the triptych form – a direct and deliberate visual reference to Western Christian paintings which saw a relationship between animal and human reproductive cycles. In art history, paintings of the Nativity and the Annunciation often take the form of a three-panel triptych: 'A picture or carving (or set of three such) in three compartments side by side, the lateral ones being usually subordinate; chiefly used as an altar-piece' ('triptych' defined in the *Oxford English Dictionary*). I used this form to suggest a creative link between Western Christian religious imagery seen in paintings such as these, particularly those painted in stables and farm locations, and the scenes I was making, staged on a real farm and using sheep as the subject.

These interventions and forms were designed to bring participants up close to the fleshy, bloody, interior, visceral and biological material and physical reality of the ewes – the ultrasound scanner used to count foetuses, the black-marked 'empties', the dead lamb stripped of its fleece and the ewe suckling the adopted lamb. I did not want the performance to shrink from these material processes; instead, I wanted it to look closely, be shocked, perhaps, but to see the wonderment in these realities.

The scenography for *The Gathering* worked with the technique of valuing and finding wonderment in the material of the everyday and in interior, overlooked, invisible or rarely seen processes, and making them visible but also strange. This process of defamiliarization was designed to liberate objects, materials and processes from 'ordinary' meaning so that new/different meanings can be discovered in the context of the underlying life-event – and bring about revelatory experiences. For example, the 'Skinning of the Lamb' installation, staged in the lambing barn, was designed as a Nativity scene and used to show the lamb–ewe adoption process and suggest connections to the human process of birthing, stillbirth and adoption.

In the semi-darkness of the barn, a deep layer of sweet-smelling hay covered the floor and the barn murmured with the sound of suckling lambs and swallows recorded here in the spring. At the far end of the barn, three empty woolsacks were suspended from a beam. Beneath each sack was a sheep-shearing bench on which lambing-related objects – feeding bottles, a prolapse ewe spoon, syringes, colostrum feeder, gloves, a knife – were placed, as if on an altar. On the sacks, a film – sectioned into three to create a triptych – showed the shepherd skin a dead lamb, dress a live lamb in the fleece and help it suckle its 'new' mother, who adopted it as her own.

FIGURE 4.4 The Gathering. *The 'Skinning of the Lamb' installation in the lambing barn, Hafod y Llan Farm, Snowdon. Photographer: Lizzie Coombes*

The Lambing Barn scene was open to interpretation, and meaning could be derived or conjured by individual participants, as the following response suggests:

> *The Gathering* continues to invade my everyday with constant flashbacks to our time on that mountain ... Things come into my head all of the time ... the barn. The triptych. The straw. Was it the lamb of God we were witnessing in that footage? Not sure.[5]

As well as showing and making material the bloody, brutal and beautiful wonderment of the adoption process, this Nativity scene re-figured the 'normalised social and cultural identification of women in the role of biological (pregnant, birthing and breast-feeding) mother' that is often portrayed in classical and contemporary art (Throsby 2004: 162–3) and offered the possibility of alternative types of mothering – non-biological and non-gender-specific.

Another triptych-style scene, 'The Scanning of the Ewes', was sited in a small barn called the hydro room where metal scythes, cross-cut saws and sharp-pointed shears hang on the wall. Three peat-cutting shovels were suspended from a cross-beam, and beneath each one, a ram's skull sat on a milking stool. Projected onto the shovels, a triptych of films showed imagery

---

[5] *The Gathering* participant feedback, 2014.

of the grey-pixelated ultrasound image of the foetus inside the ewe morphed with imagery and sound showing the ewes being scanned. The room rang with the sound of the scanning machine's metal doors clanging, the ultrasound camera whirring and the scanning man calling the results. The film then showed how the ewes were marked with coloured spray on the back of the neck, the colour showing the number of lambs each ewe was carrying:

No mark: single foetus
Blue mark: twins
Separate mark: triplets
Black mark: empty

(Wilson 2014)

The Tramway Walker and abstraction

The scenography was to engage visually, historically and metaphorically with the industrial history of the landscape inhabited by the ewes. During the performance, the figure of The Tramway Walker walked the length of the tramway from the valley bottom up to Cwm Llan slate quarry at the top of the valley, and then back again. This figure was dressed in red and carried red flags in either hand. Walking in silence, her route paralleled and wove through and across other moving elements of the performance, including the participants. Her walking drew attention to the contours and shape of the landscape and the criss-cross pattern of paths, tracks and industrial scars. Two sections of the tramway, where there were near-vertical inclines, were carpeted with a run of bright red carpet which made them visible from miles around. To make her stand out against the red carpet, as The Tramway Walker ascended and descended the red scar she changed from a red costume into a white costume.

This installation distilled three aspects of the site's history: the red carpet was a direct reference to how the 'kempy' wool of the ewes was used to make carpets; the red colour of the carpet, flags and costume were a reference to the red flags that were used to warn of the tram coming; and The Tramway Walker's ascent and descent of the tramway incline on a rope and pulley referenced the weight system used to lower and raise the slate trucks. As participants followed The Tramway Walker along one section of the tramway, sounds recorded on the farm such as gates opening and shutting, electric shears and other machinery were played, designed to 'ghost' the memory of the tram.

The figure of The Tramway Walker was deliberately abstract and open to multiple interpretations and metaphorical meanings. As a spectacle it had echoes of site-specific land art designed to bring a first level of visual engagement, signalling to participants that this performance was going to make them look at the landscape differently. The historical references brought a second layer of engagement that embedded this extended scene into the landscape, while the materials used to construct it connected it to both the history and other elements of the performance. The third level of engagement was metaphorical. Any deeper meaning came from other elements that gave the red scar and The Tramway Walker context, and were open to interpretation. One participant found the 'gash of red carpet to be like an open wound flowing with blood'; to another, who had experienced a number of lost pregnancies, the carpet was resonant of 'open wounds [and] the mountain and the body bleeding'.[6]

From wide to focused participant demographics

One participant in *The Gathering* who was facing biological childlessness remarked how the performance 'showed me my own pain head-on but disguised as the ewes' fate!!!'[7] The resonance of the ewes' situation for this participant was significant and fed into my decision to make *Warnscale*. This walking-performance dealt directly and unequivocally – head-on – with the subject and impact of childlessness-by-circumstance and the 'missing' life-event of biological motherhood. The participant quoted above went on to contribute to that project, which placed subject-specific participants at the heart of the creative process. Making *Warnscale* came about, too, because I felt it was time to nail my colours to the mast and test my belief in the tangible and transformative effects of socially engaged and applied scenography.

---

[6] *The Gathering* participant feedback, 2014.
[7] *The Gathering* participant feedback, 2014.

5

Mapping-walks – centring the subject: *Warnscale*

> *Warnscale made the cold, abstract hard-fact of not having biological children into something lived, real, a ritual almost that did have some spiritual significance for me.*
>
> (*WARNSCALE* MAPPING- AND LAUNCH-WALK PARTICIPANT RGI)

In this chapter I explore the extent to which applied scenography can be designed as a transformative experience by enabling participants involved in the creative process and/or the performance to find alternative perspectives on the 'missing' life-event of biological parenthood caused by childlessness-by-circumstance. By 'missing' life-event, I mean the absence of a hoped or planned-for event, and the missing social status or identity that would otherwise have occurred with parenthood. To do this, I analyse *Warnscale: A Landmark Walk Reflecting on In/fertility and Childlessness* (*Warnscale*), a self-guided walking-performance aimed at women who are biologically childless by circumstance. I created *Warnscale* to address directly the missing life-event of biological parenthood by placing it, and people experiencing it, at the centre of the walking-performance. As discussed by the sociologist Celia Roberts in the Foreword to the book, *Warnscale* was designed to 'address a cultural vacuum, or embedded silence around the failure of reproductive technologies to address infertility by creating valuable new opportunities for collective exploration of these difficult issues' (Roberts in Wilson 2015b: Foreword). The book was a scenographic form my practice had not used previously.

In the references for *Warnscale* (Wilson 2015a) refers to the walking-performance (the making of which involved a series of mapping-walks, and a weekend of events to launch the publication of the book used to mediate the walking-performance) and, (Wilson 2015b) refers to that book. Because

Warnscale is ongoing, I refer to the performance in the present tense. Due to their significant contribution to *Warnscale*, I feel it is important to name the mapping-walk and launch-walk participants; however, due to the sensitive nature of the work, they are identified by their initials.

Production credits (for the walking-performance and walking guide/art book) are in Appendix D.

Background – a road map

There are few rites of passage to mark life-event that are hoped or planned for but do not happen, and the missing life-event of involuntary childlessness is no exception. This is an absence that remains broadly underacknowledged by society. It can be isolating and marginalizing, leading to an ongoing state of liminality or in-betweenness akin to Elspeth Probyn's 'outside of belonging' – a state of 'being' that she describes as *beyond* belonging and identity, where individuals might never 'really and truly belong' and in which 'stability' and 'sanctity' of belonging are 'forever past' (Probyn 1996: 8).

There are, however, 'growing numbers of women experiencing childlessness-by-circumstance':

> 1 in 5 women in the UK [have] turned forty-five without having children … it is estimated that … 80% are childless-by-circumstance and [find] themselves living a life never planned for, and for which no one has a roadmap!
>
> (Day 2014)

After a period of silence around my own experiences of IVF and involuntary childlessness, I began to talk to others – and quickly found that the impact of this missing life-event was felt acutely by many. *Warnscale* offers 'a road map' and a means of navigating and transforming the experience into one that is no longer seen and felt as being 'outside belonging', but is rich in significance.

Warnscale is intimate in scale and is mediated through a multilayered walking guide/art book. It involves no formal guide or staged performance or interventions in the landscape. The only 'designed' objects are the book and a geology eyeglass for close-up looking. *Warnscale* can be undertaken by participants walking alone, with a partner or friend, or in a group. The book offers multiple layers of contextualized non-prescriptive materials that enable participants to reflect upon and transform their experience of this missing life-event. The aim is for them to move through the 'inbetween-ness' this

FIGURE 5.1 Warnscale. *Participant with the walking guide/art book on site in the Warnscale Fells, Cumbria. Photographer: Lizzie Coombes*

circumstance can generate and enter a new life stage – in a process akin to a rite of passage – that places them not 'outside', but inside, belonging (Probyn 1996: 8).

My use of no interventions reflects the way that 'In contemporary performance, scenographies are often performative environments that are designed not in the sense of being built but of being edited – selected, determined and curated' (Lotker and Gough 2013: 4). It might be referred to as '"invisible scenography" – a scenography in the scenographer's mind and seen (experienced/felt) by the individual audience member's whole body' (2013: 5). In *Warnscale*, context is everything. Participants experience the landscape and the performance through the lens of involuntary childlessness – this is what makes the 'scene' visible, this is the scenography. Each participant is an expert, witnessing the landscape and themselves in it through the lens of their own story.

Being located and efficacy

The walking guide/art book that was used to mediate *Warnscale* incorporates a distillation of materials gathered from three strands of transdisciplinary research. Each of these strands – site, subject and people affected by the subject matter – is specific and pursued in the context of 'real-life' or 'lived' human experiences relating to an underlying life-event subject. Working in this way brought 'situated knowledges' and raw material from each strand to work with (Haraway 1988: 590). This approach can be understood through the terms 'being located' or 'a view from somewhere', deployed by Haraway to describe how situated knowledge and embodied knowledge provide an account from a specific viewpoint (1988: 581, 590).

The theory challenges essentialism, and argues for a feminist epistemology that makes a social, cultural and political difference not by universalizing, but by finding voices and viewpoints that are different from the established ones. Haraway, however, is not asking for a single, universal perspective, but for a nuanced one made up of distinct points of view, arguing, 'the only way to find a larger vision is to be somewhere in particular', to be located and materially specific (1988: 590). She argues that the dominance of the visual in Western culture has led to a sense of disembodiment and that 'we need to learn in our bodies' rather than 'transcending' them. This is about:

> limited location and situated knowledge, not about transcendence and splitting of subject and object. Images are not the product of escape and transcendence of limits [achieved through the view from above or afar] but the joining of partial views and halting voices into a collective subject position ... of views from somewhere.
>
> (Haraway 1988: 590)

She suggests that we 'Learn how to see from a different or another's point of view ... seeing from the standpoints of the subjugated' and argues 'for seeing from *below* rather than *above*', which she feels is a male-dominated, Western way of seeing (1988: 583–5).

So while all three strands of research worked together and each brought 'situated knowledge' to the making of *Warnscale*, it is the third strand – how to connect to the lived perspective and stories from within/below – that is the main focus of this chapter. This focus led me to working – and walking/'learning in our bodies' – directly with people experiencing biological childlessness-by-circumstance. This chapter reveals how this strand, which took the form of a series of group and one-to-one mapping walks, enabled me to engage directly and explicitly with the underlying subject. This was the first of my projects that involved people affected by the underlying subject matter contributing to the creative process and the content, form, route and structure of the final performance (and the book). My reasons for engaging people in this way were twofold. Firstly, I wanted to make a work that was resonant with others, across a range of experiences. Secondly, I wanted that work to engage participants directly affected by the subject matter. This meant *Warnscale* was made not only for the women who were the target audience, but also with them.

The efficacy of *Warnscale* in creating a *site of transformation* for this group of participants is shown in my use of feedback gathered through questionnaires and email exchanges. This way of collecting feedback reflected another big change, because previously feedback was gathered by the producers, but with this work it was more embedded in the development of the project and extended the performance beyond the walk.

There were three distinct (yet interconnected) groups who provided feedback: mapping-walk participants (identified by their initials); project advisers (fertility, land or social-related); and members of the public who have bought the book. Following each mapping-walk and launch-walk, I gathered qualitative feedback from all the thirteen participants. I did this through a series of questions designed to help assess the outcomes of the project, asking respondents to reflect on their experience of the project and consider what, if any, effect it has had, or continues to have, on them.

This chapter also uses feedback to show how transformation occurred not only for participants but also for groups, and how for some this was significant and immediate, while for others *Warnscale* led to incremental shifts that occurred during and after the performance.

From autobiography to art and walking-performance

Following a miscarriage, the writer Naomi Cumming asked:

> How do you come to terms with the acutely felt loss of something that has never been? ... the loss of hope of a child ... an unconceived child where instead of a person an empty space presents itself.
>
> (Cumming 1997: 1)

Cumming was an earlier documenter of unsuccessful fertility treatment and narrator of the grief of involuntary childlessness. 'Even though it failed', she wrote, she made the 'experience valuable by writing of it afterwards', adding, 'if others have to go through this and suffer, then I will too ... and write of it' (1997: 12). The outcome was the essay 'Grief Unconceived', the writing of which Cumming described as a 'symbolic act' that enabled her to see herself 'in a new way' and make 'peace with a nature beyond control' (1997: 15–16). Like

Cumming, I wanted to make my experience of childlessness-by-circumstance and a failed IVF cycle matter, and be of value to others. So, creating *Warnscale* was, for me, a type of 'symbolic act' through which I not only confronted my own situation but offered others a creative/performative means by which to see their own experiences 'in a new way' (1997:15).

This sentiment is echoed by photographer Elina Brotherus, who writes: 'People these days aren't afraid of talking about sex, psychological problems, alcohol and drugs, but for some reason involuntary childlessness is very much a taboo topic' (Brotherus 2013: 90). As described in Chapter 4, Brotherus documented a five-year-long effort to conceive by IVF treatment in the *Annunciation* series (2009–13). Her reason for recording this process was to 'give visibility to those whose treatments lead nowhere' (2013: 90). Unable to speak of this experience because of the 'deep sadness' she felt, Brotherus' way of 'discussing the matter' was through a series of images, many of which are self-portraits (2013: 90). *Annunciation 24* (2012) shows IVF drugs, syringes and needles in volume, and negative pregnancy tests. In *Annunciation #31 Helsinki 04.03.2013* (2013), created after treatment had failed, Brotherus, face strained, looks unflinchingly out of the frame and directly at the viewer:

> When treatment is unsuccessful, it's not exaggerated to say that it feels like mourning someone who dies. The loss is very concrete. Not only does one lose a possible child, one also loses a whole future life as a family.
>
> (Brotherus 2013: 90)

Like Brotherus, the visual artist Tabitha Moses made a body of work out of her experience of infertility and two unsuccessful attempts at IVF treatment. Comparable to how Cumming described the process of writing about her experience as a 'symbolic act' of renewal and control, for Moses the creative process was a way to 'extract beauty and meaning from an horrific and disorientating experience'.[1] During each round of fertility treatment, Moses described how she thought, 'if I don't get pregnant at least I can make work out of the experience' (Moses 2014a: 32). *Island of Blood and Longing* (2010), a two-dimensional artwork created 'in the weeks following the loss of a much-wanted pregnancy' using menstrual-miscarriage blood on paper, took the form a chart – a map – the making of which helped her 'find her way' through the uncharted grief of this loss.[2] The work *Investment* (2014) comprises three hand-embroidered hospital gowns stitched with symbols and motifs that express Moses' and two other women's experience of IVF.

---

[1] Moses, conversation with the author, 20 September 2021.

[2] Moses, conversation with the author, 20 September 2021.

For example, *Tabitha's Gown* (2014b) includes stitched images of motifs and symbols – a mature egg, sperm, pregnancy test results, vials of drugs, a syringe, a thermometer, four embryos from unsuccessful IVF cycles, blood from miscarriages and menstruation, fertility figurines, the figure of a baby, and tears – that represent both the surgical processes and the rituals of 'hope and disappointment' (2014a: 32). Though deeply personal, Moses' work is exhibited publicly and aims to 'open up a dialogue about fertility treatment, [and] create a space for reflection on a subject that can so often have an isolating and disorientating effect' (Porter in Moses 2014a: 3).

The graphic illustrator Paula J. Knight deals with the subject of childlessness caused by miscarriage in the comic novel 'Heredity' from the collection *X Utero: A Cluster of Comics* as 'a way to process the knowledge that, not having had children and not having siblings, family traits will die out with me' (Knight 2013: 20). Her 'hope in sharing these works was that they might help a little to lift the shroud of silence that surrounds miscarriage' (2013: 20).

A small, but increasing, number of other contemporary artists including Sophie Ingleby (*Seed and Egg Collection*, 2019), Xanthe Gresham-Knight (*Buddha Babies*, 2018), Tina Reid-Peršin (*Photos I'll never take*, 2013 and *Death of Hope*, 2014), and Denise Felkins (*Mum's Not the Word*, 2019) have created autobiographical artworks – photographs, paintings, installations, performances, poetry and prose – as a means to reflect on, share and transform, personal, and often traumatic, experiences of in/fertility and the grief of childlessness. Many, like Cumming, Brotherus and Moses, articulate a desire to reach out to others by revealing publicly hugely personal and intensely private experiences. The need for these writers and artists to share their experiences reflected my own. Where my practice differs is that I reach out through the medium of applied scenography, inviting physical, active and collaborative social engagement with participants. Working with this type of practice enables participants to enter the scene rather than view it from the outside, leading to a physically embodied connection. One person who participated in both the mapping-walks and the launch-walks described how the performance gives a material location:

> a place where we 'belong' … a place that is ours to return to and celebrate/grieve/be … there are plenty of blogs, forums, articles, etc. out there – this was an embodied experience rather than an online conversation (I'm not knocking those, they can be really helpful), but somehow this was different.
>
> *Warnscale* participant (RGi) feedback, 2015[3]

---

[3] From now on, participant feedback will be initials only.

Empty room on a mountain

The clinical emptiness of the egg collection room in the Manchester fertility clinic mirrored the physical and emotional emptiness I felt following my failed IVF. In my imagination it coalesced with the empty ewes at Hafod y Llan Farm being given a black mark and turned away on the mountain. Wanting to address the isolation of involuntary childless and the disturbing and alienating process of IVF, these images of emptiness developed into the idea of creating a walking-performance in an 'empty room' on a mountain – a type of landscape traditionally associated with 'revelation, transformation or inspiration' (Usher 2012: 70). I sought this 'empty room' in the hope of creating a walking-performance that might 'fill the empty' and become *a site of transformation* for others in this situation; a site where material processes and elements might become revelatory or inspirational, in which new ways of looking might lead to new ways of thinking and feeling about the situation, and where the possibility of alternative identities and future life paths, different from those hoped or planned for and outside of biological motherhood, might be contemplated.

The search for an 'empty room' on a mountain took me to Warnscale Head bothy, a slate-built quarryman's shelter nestled into the fellside above Buttermere Lake in Cumbria. The bothy was an intimate single-roomed space with a window that framed the glacial valley and expansive view across it to the lake and the fells beyond. It was there I chose to site the work, and replaced the working title *Empty* with *Warnscale*. This word not only located the performance, but, when broken into component parts, each word created a metaphor for the physical site as well as the context of the work – the word *warn* is meant in the sense of 'to warn off: to keep away (from danger) by timely notice' and the word *scale* relates to the 'act of climbing; a place where one must climb; an ascent' and also means 'A hut or shed ... put up as a temporary protection' ('warn' and 'scale' defined in the *Oxford English Dictionary*). Combined, these words encapsulate the mountainous landscape in which the work is sited, the situation of the bothy and its use in the performance as a shelter, the act of walking embedded within it, and how the project speaks about and raises awareness of circumstances that can lead to involuntary childless, some of which might be avoided if society were to organize itself differently around women's fertility.

My original plan was to create a performance or installation work in and around the bothy. However, because the shelter needs to be accessed at any time of day or night, I was unable to control the space in way a 'staged' performance requires. Instead, I widened my focus to the landscape beyond the bothy, and decided to create a circuitous route into and out of the mountain (fell). Furthermore, I decided not to use performance or design interventions, but create a walking-performance that participants could engage with at a time of their choice and revisit as often as they wished over many years.

Three strands of transdisciplinary research

Strand 1: Site/landscape-specific research

This strand involved an eighteen-month period of on-site research into the landscape around Warnscale Head bothy. During monthly site visits in which I sketched, photographed and recorded the landscape, I logged seasonal changes and searched out routes and distinctive landmarks.

I looked for places (and researched them further off site) that had metaphorical or physical resonance relating to fertility and reproduction – hawthorns in bud, blossom and berry, the sori on the underside of bracken, single-celled flora and microfauna surviving on scarce nutrients in the tarns, trees dying out in waterlogged ground, but other species regenerating in the same conditions and the metamorphic processes that create slate. I worked with people who have expert 'situated knowledge' of that place – a farmer spoke to me about the reproductive cycles of his Herdwick sheep that graze the Warnscale Fells, the geophysicist Mike Kelly showed me the rocks close up through his geology lens, a botanist and a conservationist listed flowers, explaining how native species are returning to the fells, and the local historical society and the Mountain Bothy Association shared research into the slate-mining industry.

FIGURE 5.2 Warnscale. *Strand 1: Site/landscape-specific research, Warnscale Fells, Cumbria – dying and falling trees; this location became 'Landmark/Station 13 – Dying Wood (regeneration)'. Photographer: Louise Ann Wilson*

Strand 2: Life-event/subject-specific research

This strand of research involved the use of photographs and drawings to document my own IVF treatment: scans and examinations, self-injection of hormones, an egg collection operation under general anaesthetic, embryo insertion and a period of waiting for the result. This gave me personal insights into the IVF process from a patient's point of view.

To look at the process from the clinician's point of view, I undertook observational work in fertility clinics. I drew and photographed the embryologists performing egg collection and fertilization using high-powered microscopes, and witnessed embryos cleaving, the cryo-preservation of embryos and implantation surgery. I used a voice recorder to collect biomedical and procedural words. Further reading and collaborative exchanges with social scientists working in the field of reproductive science and technology studies revealed the social effects of involuntary childlessness.

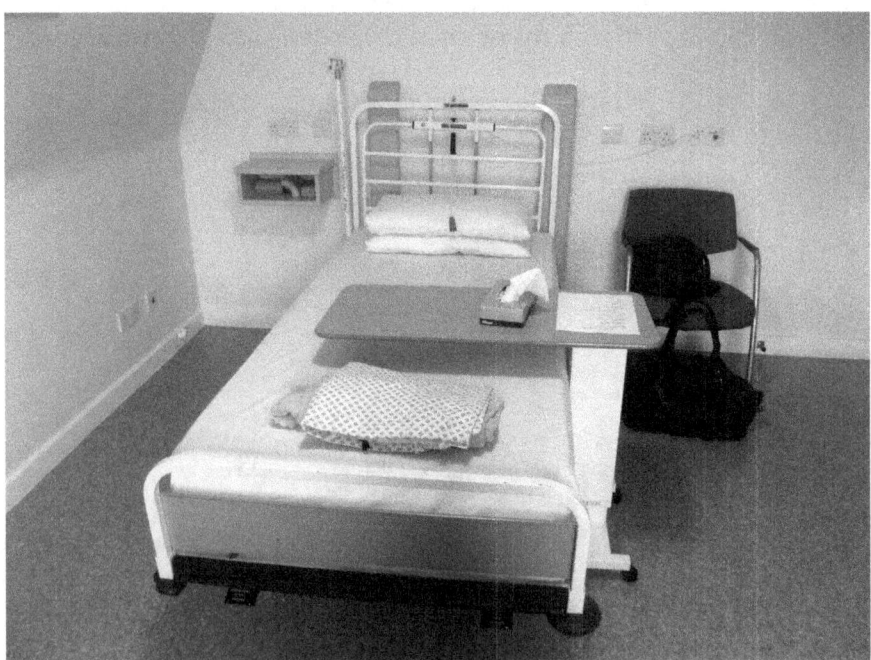

FIGURE 5.3 Warnscale. *Strand 2: Life-event/subject-specific research in fertility clinics – egg collection waiting and recovery room, CARE Fertility, Manchester. Photographer: Louise Ann Wilson*

Strand 3: People/participant-specific research

This strand involved direct research with women experiencing involuntary childlessness – its effects, and the science (fertility, medical, social) underpinning their (and my own) situation. This strand was designed to produce a deeper, more explicit and integrated relationship between the performance and the missing life-event.

To achieve this, I engaged the women in a series of on-site mapping-walks that fed directly into the creation and composition – the scenography – of the walking-performance. Immediately following each mapping-walk, participants recorded their experience on a hand-drawn map, which we then studied and discussed.

Warnscale used the mapping-walks as a tool for participants to address their own autobiographies by acknowledging and expressing their experience of biological childlessness. Through these maps, they were able to show sites in the landscape that were resonant of or acted as a metaphor for the physical and emotional realities and effects of this experience: grief, isolation, missing identity, lack of control.

FIGURE 5.4 Warnscale. *Strand 3: People/participant-specific research, Warnscale Fells, Cumbria – mapping-walk participant stepping into Black Beck Tarn; this location became 'Landmark/Station 5 – Tarn (*waiting*)'. Photographer: Louise Ann Wilson*

140 SITES OF TRANSFORMATION

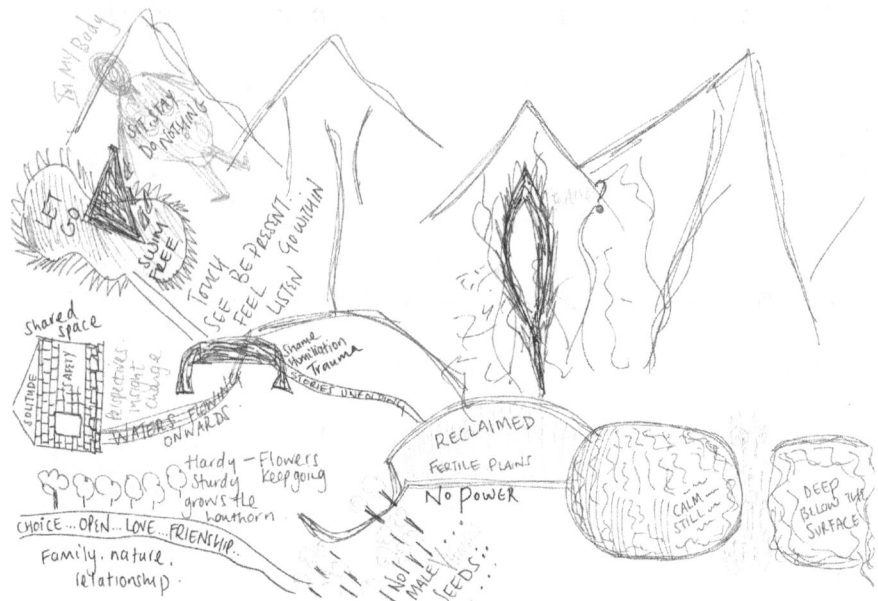

FIGURE 5.5 Warnscale. *Mapping-walk map drawn by participant JF*

Mapping-walks

Call-out and participants

The women who volunteered to join the mapping-walk 'focus group' responded to a call for participants through national fertility networks, clinics and patient support groups.[4] Wanda Georgiades of CARE Fertility Group recognized the social importance of the project:

> Louise has highlighted this very sensitive and overlooked area of life. If her project draws attention and empathy, then it may also give comfort and hope to those couples who look for a way to mark their journey and come to terms with the future. It is important to give a voice to people facing a life without a child – particularly as our society ages, and the age of motherhood is raised, then we should address and help to discuss the issue of failed fertility treatment as well as celebrating the success.
>
> (in Wilson 2015b: Foreword)

---

[4] These included Gateway Women, the Institute for Women's Health at University College London, Lancaster University Women's Studies Network and CARE Fertility Group.

The call-out stated: 'Artist seeks participants for the creation of an interactive mountain walk, created through a mapping exercise which explores the under-represented life-event of involuntary childlessness.' It specifically asked for participants:

> looking at a future that might not involve – involuntarily – having a biological child. This might be due to life or social circumstances, biologically-determined or age-related infertility. You might have attempted, or decided against, fertility treatment.

Approximately twenty women responded to this, revealing not only a desire but also a need to take part in a creative project that acknowledged women who live outside the role of biological motherhood, while not denying a deeply felt desire to parent. Not all respondents felt ready or able to join at the time, however. One participant said it took her 'nine months to get in contact to participate physically but [she] felt [her] participation started when [she] first read about the project' (MZ). For another, the invitation to participate in a mapping-walk 'felt like a permission to articulate the difficulty of [her] circumstantial childlessness' (RG). Later, one participant told me she had wanted to take part in a mapping-walk, but at that time she was not ready; when she felt more 'accepting of her situation', she was ready to undertake the completed walk (ZA).

Thirteen respondents went on to participate in a series of mapping-walks that took place over the following year. The first involved a group of five walkers, but all subsequent mapping-walks were one-to-one with a single participant and me.

The women who took part in the mapping-walks were biologically childless by circumstance for a range of reasons, including biomedical and social/circumstantial factors. A number had had, or were having, IVF through assisted reproductive technologies, some had stopped treatment after multiple attempts, and one participant was considering using donor eggs. Others had adopted children or were in the process of considering this. All talked of an overwhelming sense of isolation caused by childlessness and ongoing fertility treatment. Many were uncertain about their identity – sense of self – outside of biological motherhood. All were making challenging decisions about the next steps, but any choices or future paths lacked the positive outcomes they hoped and longed for. For many, just participating in a mapping-walk was a brave step towards accepting their circumstances. Some wanted to use the mapping-walk process to create a 'ritual' space removed from their everyday lives where they could leave their worries and to which they could return.

Into the mountain – scenography as a border crossing

> We lack – we need – a term for those places where one experiences a 'transition' from a known landscape ... [to] somewhere we feel and think significantly differently ... I have for some time been imagining such transitions as 'border crossings'.
>
> (MacFarlane 2012: 78)

To create a shared space and sense of understanding and trust, I began each mapping-walk by sharing my own story of childlessness-by-circumstance. Then I stressed to each participant that the mapping-walk was a time for them to bring their uniquely personal experience and situation of this circumstance to bear. They were the focus of the walk; my role was to hold the space and guide them carefully into, and out of, the physical (known) landscape, and also to 'transition' them across a symbolic threshold in a landscape of the imagination where (through the collision of both) they might 'feel and think significantly differently' about their situation. This was scenographic technique used to make a 'border crossing' (2012: 78) – a way of working that built on my previous work, but took it much further.

The mapping-walks began in the valley bottom and ascended 'into the mountain' and finally to the summit. My route choice was guided by a number of factors – the circuitous route was devised to take in a range of potential sites and features such as cairns, bothies, streams and tarns that participants could respond to and the scenography could incorporate. It passed through three geological timeframes and rock types before descending back into the valley bottom. The route at this stage was not fixed; instead, I kept it open, trying different approaches to see which path mapped best for the underlying subject matter. I gauged participants' reactions to different routes and approaches. Steep and hard first? To the bothy early? Down the gentler way? The route and distance varied depending on how much we sat to talk and on the weather, which at times meant the walk had to be rerouted due to raging rivers, flooded paths or high winds. All these factors spoke to the subject matter, as each walk was unique to the day and the person.

While walking, I noticed the threshold or transition places in the landscape, some of which were common to, or typical of, each walk: places where we entered into deeper, knottier conversations, typically after a strenuous climb, on a bridge or by running water, sheltering from the wind or cold, or somewhere we could sit with an expansive view. In some places there were emotional shifts and a fuller immersion into the landscape and the underlying subject matter, typically when something unexpected, unanticipated or bodily happened – for example, needing a pee leading to conversations about nuns and fertility drugs, finding frogspawn heaving in a puddle or drying out in the sun, and seeing a tree or a flower managing to grow, or water being contained through man-made intervention. Other places were conducive to quiet and reflection, typically at a tarn, inside the bothy, around a boulder, under a hawthorn bush or in the shelter of a wood.

Dorothy Wordsworth as a tool for engagement – framing the mapping-walks

One tool I used to guide and frame the mapping-walks was reading selected extracts from Dorothy Wordsworth's *Grasmere Journals* (discussed in Chapter 1) that I divided into scenographic categories – visual, material, sonic, spatial, action, feeling and metaphor. These readings were designed to encourage 'moments of being' (Woolf [1972] 1978: 81). They served to frame the walk and encourage observational, embodied and multisensory engagement with the landscape, and also drew attention to the material of the environment, fleeting phenomena and our 'impotence in the face of forces of "nature"' ([1972] 1978: 84). My aim in using them was to make the whole landscape a work of art experienced in the context of the underlying subject.

At the start of each walk I read an extract written on the same date over 200 years ago, and as we walked I read excerpts selected in response to landscape features, the weather or the season. In response to unfolding conversations, I chose excerpts that became significant to a particular person. Later, mapping-walk participants said the readings helped them focus on the landscape and the process of walking:

> Louise bringing ... readings from Dorothy's journal of a walk on the same date years ago [was] very enriching on the walk and established my engagement at a different level than a standard walk ... Dorothy's words, mixed with other text, also creates an atmosphere and is thought provoking.
>
> (PG)

For some, the independent and unbidden character of Dorothy Wordsworth herself became a powerful and inspiring link across generations of women. Combined, these positive responses and the effectiveness of her writing informed my decision to use extracts to frame each section of the walking guide, and the geology lens for magnifying rocks, plants and lichens.

The mapping-walk and my use of Dorothy's words invited participants to become immersed in the landscape and environmental phenomena – to listen, observe, touch – and through that reflect on their circumstance and feelings.

During one mapping-walk, a stream running off the fell, under a bridge and out into the lake became a metaphor for a limited fertility window, that time was running (or had run) out and having a child biologically was now too late. A dying wood that could not rejuvenate, its roots waterlogged, spoke to the distress one participant felt because her lack of childbearing was disappointing for her parents and grandparents. The weight of this was increased by the awareness that her family line, name and genetics would end with her.

For one mapping-walk participant, the 'remote and stark' landscape:

seemed like an appropriate place to do the walk – quite intimidating at times to be out in nature, but amazing to know that you are part of creation. That had the effect of putting things into perspective a bit. Seeing some frogspawn in a puddle was quite incredible but poignant as it reminded me that I won't reproduce.

(RGi)

For another, the frogspawn acted as a painful reminder of human oocytes that could not/would not become embryos or children, and pointed to the possibility/inevitability of using donor eggs.

I used Dorothy Wordsworth's acute awareness of the life and death forces of nature and how *she* noticed nature's struggle to survive as a metaphor to encourage walk participants to think metaphorically and symbolically so that they could feel, express *and* share personal stories that were highly complex and often too painful to put into words. For example, during one mapping-walk, a wind so strong it blew us off our feet and floored us became a metaphor for years of failed IVF treatment, and the physical effort of ascending the fell and balancing over sharp rocks became a metaphor for the arduousness of IVF treatment and the physical, emotional and psychologically draining effects of childlessness. On another walk, drenching rain hid tears of sorrow and frustration. Rivers so torrential they diverted our route, shortened our walk and cut off our path into the mountain became metaphors for options for motherhood, including adoption, being closed off.

There were also signs of renewal, metamorphosis and transformation seen in rocks, flowers, animals, seasons and weather; using Dorothy's words, I invited participants to notice these – anticipating they might become reflective and transformative for them. For one participant, a solitary viola, growing in the shade of a rock, became a means to reflect on feelings of isolation, but as more violas appeared – becoming a family – she recognized that she was not alone in her experience. A tree somehow managing to grow on a steep scree slope reflected not only isolation but also a determination to survive:

> *rain ... blown across ... stripy curtains*
> *barren ... scree ... slopes*
> *ghost trees ... isolation ... loneliness ... bent over ... dwarfed ... finding a way to live*
>
> (Wilson 2015b: View Point iii)

For this participant, the geology of the landscape spoke to the pain of her situation:

> There's a line in a John Grant song about a landscape being carved by the glacier moving through it – carving deep valleys and enriching the soil with minerals. The pain of childlessness felt something like that – it had a depth I have never experienced before.
>
> (RG)

To encourage participants to view the landscape from different physical perspectives, for example by lying down or becoming immersed in the sensations of the place by stepping barefoot into the water of a tarn, I invited mapping walkers (and launch-walk participants) to use a geology lens for close-up study of the material of the landscape.

FIGURE 5.6 Warnscale. *Participant using geology magnifying glass for close-up looking, Warnscale Fells, Cumbria. Photographer: Lizzie Coombes*

In the *Warnscale* book, images of magnified human oocytes, single-cell diatoms and microfauna living in Black Beck Tarn sit next to images of the lining of the uterus (endometrium) thickening in preparation for the implantation of an oocyte, then emptying when implantation has failed. For one participant, this close-up looking was contextualized, enabling her to 'notice the creativity and growth in the smallest details and most "barren" areas' (RG). Another said how she 'loved engaging with the environment both microscopically and through the lens. It connected me to the here and now. Created a different perspective to the typical one' (MZ). Another remarked how she 'really engaged with the microscopic exploring of the plants and flora', and found it:

> fascinating to see beauty in such small places. Observing pattern, growth, emergence and the force of nature, uninterrupted by over thinking or fears!
>
> (AD)

Along with other research materials, the mapping-walks and maps, the words and the feelings, images, symbols and conversations they evoked informed my choice of locations for the landmarks/stations and viewing points, and within those locations where was a good place for conversation, reflection or action. Selected words from the maps were distilled into the pages of the book.

Phases and landmarks/stations

Warnscale is divided into four phases – named after phases of the moon – *empty*, *waxing*, *full* and *waning*. These phases provided a dramaturgical structure and divided the walk into stages that can be undertaken at different times. Moving from one phase to the next marks a threshold that transitions participants into another phase of the performance, and their own story – physically and metaphorically. Within each phase are a number of Landmarks/Stations – thirteen altogether – each focusing on a theme or issue raised by biological childlessness and located in a place chosen for its physical, visual or metaphorical/symbolic resonance. These Landmarks/Stations work scenographically with ice, tarns, lichen, violas, hawthorn in bud, bloom or berry, frogspawn and cairns, and with forces that form the landscape, such as volcanic activity, metamorphosis and glaciation. They also work with the effects of everyday phenomena: the power of the wind to blow people over, and of rain to soak and block paths. How each participant chooses to use these landmarks/stations is personal and unique to them, but the book (and the scenography) places them in context.

Thirteen landmarks/stations

At 'Landmark/Station 1 – Bracken Yew (*mire*)', participants' attention is drawn to the fertility of the landscape, flora and fauna as seen in the bracken and the ewes.[5] In the book there is a line drawing of the skyline detailing the crags, gills, gullies, becks, ridges and tracks.

'Landmark/Station 2 – Wooden Bridge (*transition*)' uses the metaphor of the water flowing off the fell, under a bridge and out into the lake to prompt reflections on time, fertility and hope of becoming a biological parent running out. In the book, images of water running off the fell are layered with reflections on 'time and fertility running out'.

At 'Landmark/Station 3 – Warnscale Head Bothy (*riven*)', a series of juxtapositions explore the precarious fragility of fertility, the reality of fertility treatments *and* how alienating, physically intrusive and distressing undergoing treatment can be. The bothy window frames the view down the valley and becomes a means by which participants are invited to review their 'walk – physical and emotional – to this place'.

FIGURE 5.7 Warnscale. *View/review from the window of Warnscale Head bothy over the valley bottom to Buttermere Lake, Warnscale Fells, Cumbria. Photographer: Lizzie Coombes*

---

[5] Unless another author's work is referenced (other than Dorothy Wordsworth), all the quotes in this subsection are from the *Warnscale* book (Wilson 2015b) and are not cited individually.

At 'Landmark/Station 4 – Great Round Howe (*hope*)', Dorothy Wordsworth's words 'feasting with silence ... sate down upon a rock Seat ... lingering long looking into the vales' are designed to encourage stillness. This station is located in a wide, open boggy area, with standing pools of rainwater and outcrops of boulders, chosen to reflect the unbounded feelings of hoping against hope for an embryo to be sucessfully implanted following fertility treatment. Here, participants are invited to 'sit on one of the rocks ... look into the vales ... at the collecting pools of water and the expansive sky ... with the hand-held lens study the lichens growing on the rock you are sitting on'. A drawing of an embryologist looking at embryos through a magnifying glass sits next to a series of printed images that show the magnified endometrium (the womb lining which makes implantation possible), as it 'changes from a non-receptive to a receptive state, ready for an embryo to implant'. These images – the form and texture of which look uncannily like the magnified lichen – are layered into the words of the anthropologist Sarah Franklin, 'All reproductive technologies are hope technologies' (2006: 213) and Naomi Cumming, who wrote: 'I could not believe in, nor withhold some hope for, a positive outcome – a child' (1997: 1).

'Landmark/Station 5 – Black Beck Tarn (*waiting*)' emplaced the protracted ten-day wait for the results of treatment (a pregnancy test), the uncertainty of which is reflected in the black depths of the tarn and the hidden oligotrophic and single-cell life forms it supports. It aligns these with the desire of those undergoing treatment to reclaim their bodies from 'medical' intervention and regain a sense of self. Dorothy Wordsworth's words encourage participants to become absorbed in the landscape by listening to it and watching the play of light and wind on the tarn: 'We amused ourselves for a long time in watching the breezes ... brushing the surface ... growing more delicate ... thinner ... paler ... until they died away'. Participants are invited to 'step into the water and feel the sensation of it, listen to the rhythm of its movement, climb the rocky outcrop, lie on top of it and change their perspective' both on the landscape and through it on their situation.

'Landmark/Station 6 – Innominate Tarn (*heaf*)' reflects on the 'liminal', 'outside belonging' and 'void' effects of a negative pregnancy test and the questions they raise about what to do, or not do, next – 'further treatment, donor eggs, nothing, adopt?'. The possibility of belonging is suggested through the use of the word *heaf*, reflecting the process by which 'The Gatesgarth flock graze here throughout the year' and hold an embodied knowledge of the land they inhabit and the way the fell is a site of mothering:

1 April – last year's lambs put to *heaf*
Late May – ewes with single lambs put to fell to *heaf*
July – ewes with twins put to fell to *heaf*
20 December – all ewes on fell

However, an image drawn in the book showing the oval-shaped window of a pregnancy test with the red line of a negative result is laid over and intersects with the cut-out shape of a waning moon; this sits next to a photograph of a ewe whose fleece is marked with a line of red to show she has been tupped and is pregnant. Participants are invited to 're-imagine mothering in a way that includes everyone who gives love and comfort to others'.

'Landmark/Station 7 – Haystacks Summit (*geld*)' uses the spiny, sharp, rocky hardness of the summit ridge as a metaphor for the hard questions about breaking out of IVF treatment cycles. Participants are invited to consider 'the arduous physical and emotional effort it has taken to reach this place (literally and metaphorically)' and the 'cycles we might be trapped in', 'the uncertainty of biological childlessness' and how 'There are well-trodden routes into IVF yet the routes out of treatment are more obscure'.

'Landmark/Station 8 – Summit Tarn (*vitrify*)' uses images of the frozen tarn and frozen embryos and eggs to raise awareness of the need for a 'cultural ... social ... rethink' around women's fertility.

'Landmark/Station 9 – Dubs Hut (*metamorphosis*)' works with the metamorphic processes by which slate is formed as a metaphor for human metamorphosis and transformation.

'Landmark/Station 10 – Warnscale Beck and Cairns (*landmark*)' uses actual pathways as metaphors to suggest the 'future life-paths you might follow and the alternative stories you might live' outside of biological motherhood. It works with the downward gravity and flow of the landscape, water and stone. Guided by a series of cairns that mark the way off the mountain, participants are invited to 'acknowledge their powerlessness to control the forces of nature within and around'. A defintion of the word *landmark*, 'a turning point, a watershed ... an event marking a unique change', sits juxtaposed with words from the mapping-walks:

> *uncertainty ... which direction?*
> *choosing life path ... luck ... belief*
> *fertility is cruel*

'Landmark/Station 11 – Hawthorn Bower (*heart*)' reflects on the need for courage and invites participants to think about renewed, but different, hope.

'Landmark/Station 12 – Solitary Viola (*solitary*)' reflects feelings of isolation and lack of community, asks questions about identity and challenging social norms, and sees the possibility for different sorts of families and communities. In the book, a photo of a solitary viola is montaged into a repeat pattern. Participants are invited to notice the violas 'struggling but surviving in cradles in rocks'. However, one solitary viola, and then another, 'begins to make a family'. This is designed in response to the way women felt less alone in their experiences after participating in *Warnscale*.

'Landmark/Station 13 – Dying Wood (*regeneration*)' works with processes of destruction and repair. The station reflects on family lines ending/dying out, but is attentive to the 'renewal, resurrection, rebirth' taking place in the landscape by inviting participants to 'look for signs of renewal and live the life unimagined ... on the other side of nothing ... of resurrection'.

The book as a scenographic tool
Multilayered storyboard-style montage

Despite being mediated through the walking guide/artbook, the actual process of designing *Warnscale* compared closely to that of designing a staged/live performance. In both instances, I used drawing, mapping and storyboarding as research tools as well as a means to develop my ideas, and share them with others. However, whereas with works prior to *Warnscale* these scenographic techniques remained part of the design process, in *Warnscale* they became incorporated into the final work – the book.

To gather materials for the book I spent time photographing, making digital voice recordings and drawing, in the landscape but also in fertility clinics where, with consent, I drew people at work or performing an action or activity. In sensitive environments, or when working closely with people affected by a life-event, I tend to draw because it is less intrusive than photography. Drawing is a quick way of catching fast-moving scenes and activities, and the intensity of looking that is required often captures the essence of things and people.

The materials gathered in each strand of research were juxtaposed and interlayered in the pages of the book using an assemblage method comparable to the storyboard-style montages I made for *The Gathering*. Choices about the book's design and composition were guided by multiple factors, both practical and creative.

Practically, the book was designed (shape and size) to fit into a map-carrying case and contained route maps, walking instructions and grid references for all viewpoints, tracks, routes and landmarks/stations as well as facts and figures on terrain, altitude and distances. Original photographs and drawings from my fieldwork and the mapping-walks were combined with topographical, geological, historical, botanical and farming texts, maps and illustrations specific to each landmark/station. These sit with original photographs and drawings from my fieldwork in clinics, in turn layered with biomedical, social science and reflective texts, charts and illustrations about in/fertility processes, cycles, fertility treatment and involuntary childlessness.

The solitary figure – drawn into the page

Within each storyboard montage is a simple line drawing of a solitary figure or groups of figures, drawn from the photographs I took during the mapping-walks. Using drawing does not limit the human presence to a specific person, but acts as a stand-in for the participant-performer. These figures walk through the landscape and across the page or stand in stillness and look, their gaze drawing the viewer into 'the scene', see Figure 5.8 on page 152.

In other 'scenes', a drawn figure is seen crouching beneath the wind, lying on a rock, stepping barefoot into a tarn, lighting a candle in a bothy, following a line of cairns, and using a geology magnifying glass to look closely at plants, flowers and lichen and the volcanic rock on which it grows. The actions of the drawn figures reflect the actions participants are invited to perform. They are designed to encourage participant-performers to slow down, to bring them closer to the landscape and experience it through all their senses – to look, to listen, to feel their emotions and reflect on the elemental forces around and within, and in doing so to contemplate and shift their perspective on the environment *and* their circumstance.

The drawings are laid over other images and in relation to texts/words on the page – everything is balanced and composed. The texts range from words from the mapping-walks distilled into abstract reflective texts/poems to invitations to become immersed or perform a series of sited actions – to sit or lie down to find an alternative perspective or look through a geology eyeglass. These invitations are drawn from the mapping-walks and Dorothy Wordsworth's way of walking, looking at and dwelling in the landscape.

Self-guiding, revisiting, conversation and sharing

The book form means *Warnscale* is able to achieve a number of outcomes and effects that a 'traditional' performance could not. For example, it is repeatable and can be revisited either physically *or* in the memory, or in the imagination as new markers are found – a need which recognizes that:

> Acceptance of childlessness may be achieved at a particular time, and yet needs to be re-enacted when new markers of loss are found.
>
> (Wilson 2015b: Landmark/Station 10)[6]

---

[6] *Warnscale* quotes Cumming (1997: 5).

vitrify
to convert/be converted to glass

alter, change, modify – cause to change
cause a transformation
become different in essence
losing one's original nature

the action of natural forces (rather than by the intent of human beings) such as volcanic activity

single raven, single rock, cloud

take time, pace yourself, be where you are

apple, mammoth, paying female employees eggs, embryos, frozen, delay fertility IVF success rates poor gambling, child-bearing future
the answer...?

cultural, social, retime, change

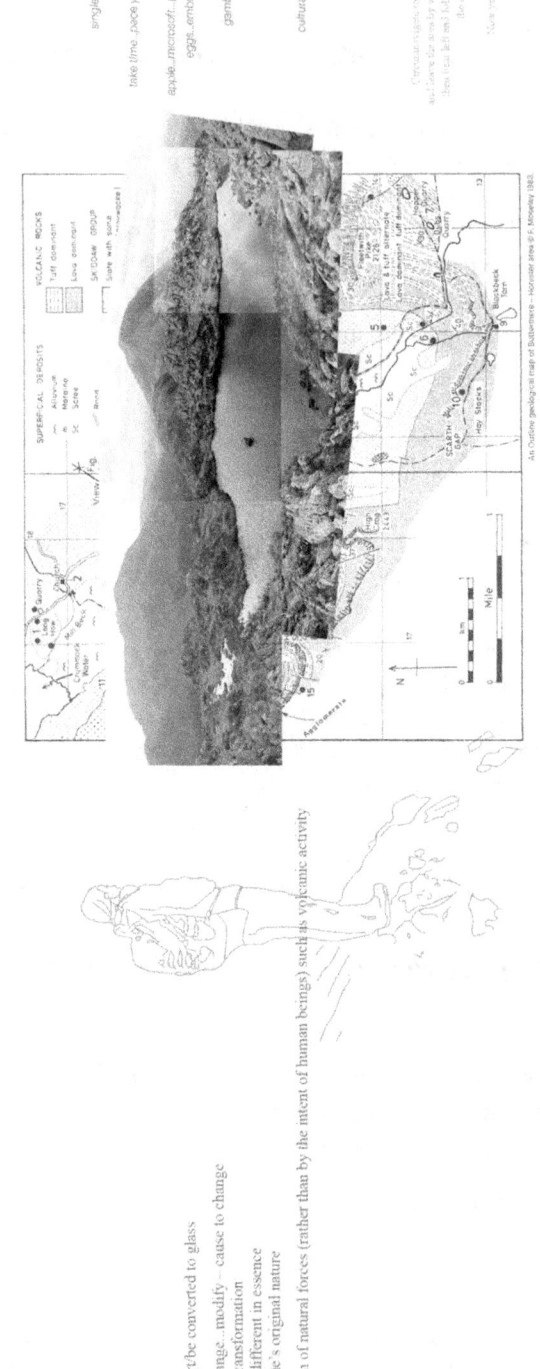

FIGURE 5.8 Warnscale. *Book page from 'Landmark/Station 8: Summit Tarn (vitrify)'. Designed by Louise Ann Wilson*

For one participant, the fact that *Warnscale* can be 'done again and again' not only gave it a 'lasting legacy', but was also a factor in it working as a repeatable 'ritual' that can be undertaken as a 'physical act of doing' to 'mark an important life-event' (RGi). Another described how she would 'go back to, and to dip in and out of sections ... the book is a very beautiful reminder of the walk, but also feels like a deeper resource for thinking about land, children, belonging'. These reactions show how *Warnscale* can be used by participants over time, and as perspectives and life circumstances change, different meanings will be found.

Another commented that the 'layout and imagery of the book is immediately intriguing and engaging', adding that 'it also asks to be revisited and browsed repeatedly and new things can be found on each revisiting' (JK). These comments suggest that the book acts as memory trigger – akin to a pilgrimage artefact – that can be used away from the site as an aid to help participants revisit the landscape in their minds. The book form also enables participants unable to travel to the site in person to engage off site and in their imagination – they read the book but do not do the walk.

Initiating conversation, understanding and change

> The more women and men talk about their own realities – in a more open atmosphere – the more others will be inspired to do the same.
>
> (MZ)

When asked if they could imagine undertaking *Warnscale* (with the book) in the future, a number said they had already revisited and rewalked the performance:

> Absolutely. I would particularly like to do the walk on my own and with my partner, to share the time, the journey and reflect on the unique beauty of this particular place and experience.
>
> (AD)

One said she could 'imagine taking others on the walk and using the book to introduce both the ideas and concepts behind [it]' (JK). Another remarked on the way *Warnscale* 'has helped her feel able to speak about the walk and its importance to me with greater confidence', adding that she has 'gifted a book to my ex-husband and plan to walk with him next week. I want to share the walk with him and give us a chance to reflect on our shared loss' (ZA). She 'plans to revisit the walk annually' and sometimes with her Gateway Women 'mentorship group'. Another wrote how she would:

> love to do the walk again – either alone, or with close friends who are also childless, or with another group of childless women. Although it might

feel difficult, I think I would also like to do it with my sister, who has two children, in order to share some of this with her and think about our places in the family.

(RGi)

A participant who later conceived a child through donor eggs wrote 'I would like to repeat the walk by myself at first, then again with my partner and child', and then a further time when the child was older and the participant could 'talk about my experiences when she would have some deeper understanding of the choices we made to have her and how we went about this process' (JH).

As well as working as an artefact to help participants to reconstruct the performance, feedback suggests the book works as a tool for them to 'walk' someone else through it. This enables them to share both the performance *and* most crucially their experiences of biological childlessness. In this respect, *Warnscale* has opened up conversations – back at home – that might otherwise not have happened, and with friends in similar circumstances:

> I return to the book, to remind myself of an issue that still feels unresolved to me, and hope very much to return to the walk soon. It is definitely something I will share with others in the same position as and when it arises.
>
> (RGi)

For this participant, *Warnscale* 'allowed her to look at her own experience afresh', added to which her '*need*' to take part 'opened up a space between myself and my husband – I was able to talk about the experience with him' (RGi). A week after participating, she emailed me to say:

> It's been interesting the effect that doing [the mapping-walk] has had on my close family: it has somehow given childlessness a frame and a focus and a way of talking about it. It has opened up some quite deep conversations with my husband this week too, and I think we're getting closer to a final decision on which path to take.
>
> (RGi)

These reflections suggest that the effects of *Warnscale* echo how 'pilgrims' return to their everyday lives, families and friends with the 'stories' from afar that trigger sharing and conversation in the real world (van Gennep 1960: 20). In doing so, participants become 'an agent of change by spreading new ideas gleaned on the journey' either domestically, within their immediate circle of family and friends, or in wider society (Coleman and Elsner 1995: 206).

Beyond the direct effect *Warnscale* has had on individual participants and the significant ripple effects that have occurred as a consequence of their participation, *Warnscale* has affected wider society by contributing to current debates and dialogues on the subject of in/fertility, fertility treatment, the social constructs and inequalities around fertility, and the implications and impact of involuntary and biological childlessness-by-circumstance. For example, Kate Brian, editor of the *Journal of Fertility Counselling* in which *Warnscale* was featured, described the project as being of 'huge interest to counsellors working in the field of in/fertility and biological childlessness' (Brian 2015: 24). As a resource used by individuals and groups but also by clinicians, sociologists, counsellors and therapists, *Warnscale* has contributed to the raising of awareness and dialogues about the subject of in/fertility. In the summer of 2016, I presented *Warnscale* and *The Gathering* at the Fertility Fest 2016, 'the first ever festival of work in the UK' exploring topics including 'facing the diagnosis of infertility, IVF, donation, surrogacy, the male experience, egg freezing, involuntary childlessness and alternative routes to parenthood' (Fertility Fest 2016).[7] The festival posed the questions: 'What happens when IVF is and isn't successful? What are going to be the effects of this science on future generations? How far as a society are we prepared to go in our pursuit of parenthood? It also placed centre stage the visual artists, performance makers, playwrights and poets who were asking these questions in their work.

Complex layers of information

The clean design aesthetic and multiple – transdisciplinary – layers of material within the book were important parts of its appeal. For example, in response to the way *Warnscale* layered the site, medical, subject and participant research, Wanda Georgiades (CARE Fertility) wrote:

> We focus so much on achieving 'success' having that much wanted child, beating the odds to become parents through IVF. We probably don't acknowledge adequately the number of patients who will not have a baby this way – ever. This project shows in a graphic form how different people cope with the loss of the baby they may never have, the grief for something that will never be. It is a beautifully executed book pulling together strands of treatment into strands of landscape.[8]

---

[7] I presented my work and ran a mapping/drawing workshop with men experiencing infertility and involuntary childlessness at Fertility Fest 2018. The workshop used *Warnscale* as a model and invited participants to consider the types of landscapes and environments into which they would emplace their experiences – with a view to creating a version of *Warnscale* for men.
[8] Wanda Georgiades (CARE Fertilty) email to author, 18 July 2015.

The coalition of performance (action), landscape, science, images and words brought together in multiple layers in the book's pages was a factor in how *Warnscale* engaged participants physically, intellectually and emotionally. However, *Warnscale* leaves space for the walkers to interpret the materials and make their own meaning. One participant found the way she could 'add [her] own thoughts and experiences, was particularly helpful' (RGi). For another, the book worked on several levels and had a 'resonance beyond the walk' that she found 'tremendously engaging':

> [It] strikes a powerful balance between presenting information and ideas and allowing space for the reader to make their own connections. The way it is organised means there is both a freedom and a guiding structure. This means that navigating the book and understanding the way in which the elements fit together leads you to draw personal conclusions and make links between the elements in an entirely individual manner.
>
> (JK)

Walking and standing together – finding solidarity and community

As well as giving a physical place to 'belong', *Warnscale* created a social space that brought people together in communitas and solidarity – in person, but also through knowing other people were out there. As one participant remarked, childlessness-by-circumstance 'can be isolating, so to feel you are not alone can be very positive' (HW). Involvement in *Warnscale* showed one participant she was 'not alone' and that 'it was good to be able to both literally and metaphorically walk the same path alongside others':

> [The] public nature of the performance starts to combat some of the shame around childlessness. It's important to give childless women a voice – they are shamed into hiding themselves and staying silent. The more we make art, publish and speak out about our circumstances the better it will be for all of society.
>
> (RGi)

Others echoed this feeling. One contributor said *Warnscale* helped her 'feel a bit less alone in my sense of loss at not having a child' and placed her 'experience in the context of a wider community of contributors' (LE). For her, 'speaking with women who have had similar childless stories' validated her 'feelings and emotions', but also provided a way of connecting to 'other women who have come to terms with their circumstances' (LE).

Warnscale's incorporation of a range of experiences created a space for participants to connect. One found the solidarity of walking in the company of other women 'from different ages' with experiences of biological childlessness-by-circumstance inspiring and helpful. She appreciated 'the chance to meet people who had obviously created beautiful and interesting lives without their own wishes to have a child fulfilled' (JH). For many, the performance became a means of 'individual acceptance and acknowledgement' and the book 'makes the images and reflections on this issue more public, and hopefully stimulates debate or a reframing of the issue' (JH). For this participant, *Warnscale* provided a space to 'acknowledge herself more positively *and* be more positively acknowledged by others and society ... Projects like this one acknowledge and support what "we" went and are going through as people living with this loss' (JH).

The way *Warnscale* brings people together can be understood as an application of what the philosopher Gayatri Chakravorty Spivak refers to a 'strategic essentialism', where it becomes 'advantageous for a group to temporarily "essentialize" themselves [in order to] achieve certain goals' (Ashcroft 1998: 159–60). This concept recognizes how a 'minority group acting on the basis of a shared identity' comes together – strategically and in solidarity – for the purpose of social action (Buchanan 2016).

Change and alternative life paths

Warnscale invites participants to consider the 'future life-paths you might follow and the alternative stories you might live' (Wilson 2015b: Landmark/Station 10). It brought one participant 'one step towards becoming more open about my situation' (RGi). Since taking part, she has 'done a course with Gateway Women', written a 'feature about childlessness for the church for *Church Times*' and 'set up a peer-to-peer support group for local childless Christians, male and female' (RGi). For her, the mapping and launch-walk became:

> part of a process over about 2 years of small steps to face up to this frankly quite devastating loss and to do something positive with it. I enrolled for an MA in art history last September ... this has been about doing something with the money that was put aside to spend on IVF/egg donation.
>
> (RGi)

Following the mapping-walk, another participant decided to pursue an alternative life path: 'since the walk I contacted our local adoption service in the local authority and started the process' (LE). Another said the mapping-walk 'led her to reconsider the future life-paths she *might* choose', and she chose to 'try IVF with donor eggs':

At the point of the walk, I was almost moving on to trying IVF with donor eggs – I couldn't have not tried this option and I'm sat here holding my baby and writing this and I don't know what I would have done or how many times I would have tried IVF if it hadn't worked. ... Vivienne's middle name is Rowan – the name conjures up craggy northern landscapes and wet boggy turf – the kind of landscape where *Warnscale* exists.

(JH)

Site of transformation – physical (literal) and metaphorical

For some, the Warnscale Fells have become a *site of transformation* into which they have emplaced difficult thoughts and feelings, knowing they can be left there to be revisited physically or in memory, using the book to aid this. For one participant, this landscape 'has helped her process of recovery', and she described feeling 'strengthened by having a place that enables my feelings of loss to be expressed and worked through':

> The barrenness of the landscape and beauty and timelessness helped me recognise that my grieving and pain would pass in time ... I have already begun to flourish.

(ZA)

Another participant who had undergone repeated fertility treatment described how 'the landscape she walked through':

> evokes personal memories of hard walks and sore feet, tiredness and distance travelled. This connects with my journey to have a child – although the emotional hardship and patience required were so much harder. I had to let go of my own wish for my own biological daughter, and ask myself what did I really want?

(JH)

The sense of recognition and validation, the conversation with family and friends back at home, the life-changing decisions and the impact on wider social and counselling networks all point to *Warnscale* being an ongoing *site of transformation* created through purposeful and intentional scenography.

6

Giving a voice – centring people and place: *Mulliontide*

Mulliontide really gave me a voice and was a great chance to talk about something I feel really passionate about. I feel my involvement confirmed my feelings and made them urgent.

(*MULLIONTIDE* COLLABORATOR AND PERFORMER WENDY WILLIAMSON)

In this chapter I explore how a community-led walking-performance created with and performed by the residents of a coastal village in Cornwall placed 'real' people at the heart of a project. It shows how the performance-making process enabled those involved to voice and express their views, concerns and feelings in a way that brought unique and specific insights to the underlying subject matter. It also explores the concepts of autotopographical scenography which uses locations and objects specific to each contributor and deploys existing interests and skills, such as photography, drawing, storytelling and stitching, as tools with which each contributor can share their lives and views.

Originating in the visual art world, the 'concept of "autotopography" refers to autobiography while also distinguishing itself from the latter. It refers to a spatial, local, and situational "writing" of the self's life in visual art' (Gonzalez 1995: 133). Recognizing the significant role that place and objects associated with place play in a person's sense of self and identity, Gonzalez remodelled the term auto*bio*graphy by replacing the word *bio* (self) with *topo* (place). Within the field of performance studies, Deirdre Heddon applies the term 'autotopographic' to 'performances that fold or unfold autobiography and place, particularly outside places … as being', reminding us that:

'Topos' comes from the Greek word for place, whilst 'graphein' means to scratch, to draw, to write; topography, then, signifies the writing of place.

(Heddon 2008: 90)

Further, the term recognizes how objects associated with a place, such as 'trophies, photographs, travel souvenirs, heirlooms, religious icons, gifts', not only hold meaning but also come to signify an 'individual's identity' (Gonzalez 1995: 133–4). *Mulliontide* (2016a) used a combination of autotopographical life stories, objects and locations as a means to voice deeply felt experiences of life, loss and recovery – human and landscape. Specific to each contributor (some through making and some through performing), these materials became vibrant and powerful scenographic tools. When placed within an overarching and symbolic structure (also informed by the landscape and the people), autotopographical scenography can produce visceral and impactful responses among contributors and participants alike.

Mulliontide was a three-hour processional walking-performance that led twenty-five participants on foot for a two-mile walk along the coastal path from Poldhu Cove to Mullion Cove and harbour on the Lizard Peninsula in Cornwall, UK. En route, the procession stopped at fifteen stations, where it was met by a local person who spoke to participants about the significance of that location to them and their personal experiences of adapting to change. *Mulliontide* was created with and performed solely by local people who were residents of Mullion. The performance was commissioned by Golden Tree Productions (GTP), a Cornish arts organization, as part of a project entitled *Miss You Already*, and was performed twice over a weekend in October 2016.

Mulliontide revealed how, in different ways, the life of each person involved is deeply rooted in the landscape through time and memory, but also how that landscape is threatened by rising tides, devastating storms and coastal erosion. The performance created a scenographic space within which performers and other contributors could express these feelings through image, word, song, action, object and site. Working closely with me, each person involved as a performer and contributor chose what they wanted to say or make. They included care home residents, fishermen, a cliff walker, a palliative care nurse, a National Trust warden, a trio of singers and a choir, a local historian, a botanical artist and tea-room owners. Behind the scenes, a sculptor of flotsam and jetsam created a miniature of the harbour, a florist made wreaths, needleworkers stitched a flag, a baker cooked biscuits, a chocolatier crafted chocolate fish and a café served high tea.

Many involved had themselves adapted to change or helped others to adapt, and each contribution was very personal and considered how, in our own lives, we might prepare for change, loss, death and dying. These contributions in turn became a metaphorical means by which to reflect on the loss of a much-loved coastal landscape, the possibility of that loss increasing in the future and the uncertainty this causes locally.

The title *Mulliontide* was designed to be resonant in several ways. It was suggestive of the ebbing and flowing rhythms of the tides, of local concerns over rising sea levels and destructive tides in the cove and along the coast. Furthermore, because *Mulliontide* was designed to be a repeatable performance the title was also suggestive of daily, monthly and seasonal rhythms such as eventide and noontide, April-tide and New-Year's tide, summertide and wintertide, agrarian rhythms such as 'harvest-tide, and the rhythms of annual and religious festivals such as Eastertide, Whitsuntide and Passiontide.

The process of repeatability was aided through tools that were created for and used in *Mulliontide*. These include a pack of items given to participants during the performance and a printed guidebook, *Mulliontide: A Guide for Walkers* (2017), produced following the live event. This guide incorporates maps, walking instructions, texts, photographs, drawings and a series of actions that distil the original work. Both the pack of items and the guidebook can be used by those unable to join the live walk, or who want to re-create the performance and incorporate their own stories and concerns.

Feedback referenced in this chapter was gathered through email correspondence with the author and feedback forms and follow-on interviews with collaborator-contributors, collaborator-performers and participants undertaken by the producers (GTP and Louise Ann Wilson Company) and Bryony Onciul, Associate Professor of History at the University of Exeter. Unless otherwise stated, this feedback was received in 2016. Where I do not have access to a participant's name, I use the reference (anon.). Extracts from the performance 'script' included in this chapter were performed live in *Mulliontide* (Wilson 2016a), and many can be found in the guidebook; when that is the case, they are as indentifed as (Wilson 2017). Further details about the production can be found in Appendix E.

Socially engaged performance: 'real' places and people

The ability of site-specific performance to not only immerse participants in the work but also engage and embed people and communities in the creative and performative process has seen national theatre companies in the UK move out of theatre buildings to make *and* perform work not just in 'real' places, but with 'real' people and communities. Taking inspiration from the 'theatre without walls' policy of the National Theatre of Scotland (2013), National Theatre Wales (NTW) left the building-based model of London's National Theatre to produce an 'itinerant national theatre, concerned with moving identities, moving practices and moving sites' (National Theatre Wales 2013). This saw NTW mobilize communities to create works specific to and/or staged in specific places, a socially engaged approach to making and performing work that reflects how in 'socially engaged, contemporary performance the "spectator" participates in the making/creation of the piece' (Mosley 2017: 51).

In 2011, NTW and Wildworks staged *The Passion of Port Talbot*, an 'epic re-telling of the Passion of Christ that took place across the streets of the town of Port Talbot in South Wales, UK, with the support of over 1,000 community volunteers' (National Theatre Wales 2011). It was performed by choirs, schools, social clubs and gymnasts together with professional actors. Because the community were involved in both the processes of making *and* performing *The Passion of Port Talbot*, and large numbers of the town's residents came on to the street to witness it, the lines separating performance, performer and audience became blurred. This blurring had echoes of how in *The Gathering*, also produced by NTW and discussed in Chapter 4, the local people (shepherds, schoolchildren and a brass band) performed with and alongside a company of professional actors to 'tell' a 'story' created in response to the site, animals and people of Hafod y Llan Farm. One audience member, who described herself as a 'farm girl', wrote that the performance was 'very special indeed' in the way it showed 'Our ordinary lives … as a piece of art' (*The Gathering* participant, 2014). Both of these works reflect NTW's policy of producing community performance works that sought to 'make a real change to the lives of people in Wales and beyond and instigate action through art' (National Theatre Wales 2013). Furthering their pursuit of a purposeful and democratic type of 'people's performances', NTW set up a series of 'Assemblies' that involved communities across Wales. These Assemblies led to the 'Big Democracy Project', which considered 'how art and creativity can play a part in helping communities across Wales to re-engage with the democratic process' (National Theatre Wales 2014–16). For example, *The People's Platform: Merthyr* took place in a social club and celebrated the people of Merthyr Tydfil by inviting them to 'join NTW for an evening of performance to celebrate our community, hear our stories, questions and hopes for the future' (National Theatre Wales 2016).

Work of this nature has historic roots that can be traced back to Welfare State International, an experimental theatre group based in Ulverston in Cumbria between 1968 and 2006, which created celebratory art and large-scale participatory 'theatre in landscape, lantern processions, spectacular fire shows, community carnivals and participatory festivals' that 'allowed collaboration rather than spectatorship' as local people became involved in the making of the work (Welfare State International 2006). The company's 'interest in rites of passage moved between the intimate, private celebrations associated with birth, marriage and death ... to the production of large-scale public events and rituals responsive to the community contexts in which they were created' (Shaughnessy 2012: 23).

More recently, in the year-long project *Field of Wheat* (2015–16) the artists Anne-Marie Culhane and Ruth Levene, with farmer Peter Lundgren, brought together a collective of people who became 'active stakeholders in a field of wheat in Lincolnshire, England' (Culhane and Levene 2016). This collective included members of the public, people working in the food industry and from the farming community, as well as artists and researchers. Together, they engaged in a process of 'Collective Enquiry' that 'explored nature and culture, land ownership and stewardship and the future of farming' (Levene 2016). Using art, ritual and performative interventions as dialogical tools, the collective made shared decisions about how to farm and harvest the 22-acre field of wheat. Another project that brought together a disparate group of individuals to create a temporary community is the company Curious' *UpRoot* (2019). Taking the form of 'gardening related workshops with recent immigrants, including refugees, to the UK', Curious employed 'rooting and uprooting' as a metaphorical means with which to talk about 'leaving and finding home' (Artsadmin 2019). Underpinning the work was a 'commitment to community engagement [that] prioritises speaking "to" and "with" rather than "for" and "about" immigrants' (2019).

Working 'from the premise that people have a deep knowledge of their own locality', performance-makers Katie Etheridge and Simon Persighetti (Small Acts) create live participatory projects such as *Public House* (2018–ongoing) and *Future Feast* (2019–20) that reveal the 'interrelationships between people and places' and recognize 'that the people who live and work in a place are the experts' (Small Acts 2021). Common to the site- and people-specific work of these companies and artists is the centring, highlighting and noticing of the local, in such a way that quietly and skillfully magnifies wider environmental, ecological and socio-political issues.

Multiple viewpoints and intergenerational performance

Building on my use of dialogical processes (with site, subject and participant experts) and social engagement, *Mulliontide* took these aspects of my practice in a direction that leaned the work towards a type of socially engaged art practice aiming to 'help [a] community work towards a common goal, raise awareness and encourage conversation around issues, or perhaps to improve their physical or psychological conditions' (Tate Gallery 2020a). In *Mulliontide* my use of the term 'giving a voice' was literal. The performance made no division between performance, place and people – all were interwoven and centre stage. Whereas previous works such as *Fissure* and *The Gathering* involved professional actors performing alongside people of the site and/or subject-specific experts, *Mulliontide* was performed solely by residents of Mullion. Each performer chose the site, clothes, objects and words or song that best portrayed them and the stories, memories or concerns they wanted to voice of real-life experiences and situations on the ground. Although each performance was framed and curated by the scenography, which provided the overarching themes of life, loss and recovery and the structural form, the dramaturgical shape of the whole and the cohesive design of the framework and content were people-led. This methodology – in which the scenographer, the processes of scenography and the people meet – exemplifies how:

> Proactive scenographic performance is increasingly being used as an active intervention to register and empower the collective and individual memories of local communities. Through space, objects, memorabilia, playful procession, dance and clothes – all essentially scenographic qualities, intangible, ephemeral and transient – memories may be generated and archived. In abandoning theatre buildings, scenography is taking to the community its skills of modelling, graphic representation, costume and public celebration, alongside sophisticated new technologies and digital archiving skills. [...] Scenography is offering a paradigm of performance whereby communities may collaborate with artists and work to develop skills to record and celebrate thoughts, memories and emotions collectively experienced.
>
> (Baugh 2013: 235)

By involving as many people as wanted to engage in the process, *Mulliontide* deliberately gave a space for multiple viewpoints and perspectives on the landscape (and loss), as experienced by a wide range of local residents. Wendy Williamson, a resident who performed in the project said:

> *Mulliontide* really gave me a voice and was a great chance to talk about something I feel really passionate about. I feel my involvement confirmed my feelings and made them urgent.[1]

Jonny Pascoe, a third-generation fisherman who also performed in *Mulliontide*, said he was motivated to get involved in the project because it:

---

[1] Wendy Williamson, collaborator/performer feedback (interview), *Mulliontide*, 2016.

gave him a chance to speak out about his life growing up in Mullion Cove and its fishing industry ... it's always nice to tell a story to those who are interested in hearing it.[2]

Contributor/performer feedback showed that *Mulliontide* created a space for speaking and listening that led to greater levels of awareness, appreciation and understanding among those involved in the project as makers, performers and participants. This demonstrates how, 'As well as a means of giving voice, autobiographical performance is a form through which we can understand and embody the perspectives of others' (Shaughnessy 2012: 76). For example, Justin Whitehouse, the National Trust's Countryside Manager for the Lizard and Penrose area and a performer in *Mulliontide*, remarked how through the performance he 'understood the local community more'.[3]

Mulliontide also brought together people from across the generations whose voices and stories might otherwise not have been heard in the same space. They ranged from eighty-year-old retirees living in a care home to a twenty-year-old fisherman working out of Mullion Cove. In this regard, the project provides an example of how intergenerational performance 'is used increasingly to bring together different age groups ... in creative collaboration' (2012: 76). In creating an intergenerational space, the performance brought about an awareness of how important and fundamental the landscape of Mullion's coast and coves was to each performer's or contributor's sense of personal, or autotopographical, identity.

One participant, Dominica Williamson, later remarked how during the performance 'lots of conversations were struck [up] amongst the participants, many of whom shared stories between the stations'. By the end of the performance, which culminated in the tea-room in Mullion Cove, Porthmellin, where all involved came together, a palpable feeling of community had developed among the local people who voiced and shared their lives during the performance, and extended to the participants who came to listen.

The depth of connection, understanding and empathy generated during the performance is perhaps best demonstrated in the number of long-term friendships that were formed between people, including one participant who reported how they continued to visit 'new friends' at the care home long after the event.

Another legacy highlighting the deep connection people made with the work is the repeat performances of *Mulliontide* led by local residents that have

---

[2] Jonny Pascoe, collaborator/performer feedback (interview), *Mulliontide*, 2016.
[3] Justin Whitehouse, collaborator/performer feedback (interview), *Mulliontide*, 2016.

continued to take place each year since the original event. Gail Lyons, a resident who performed in the original work and now co-leads these performance walks, remarked that *Mulliontide* has had a 'lasting impact on the village'.[4]

Background: from Yorkshire to Cornwall

In early 2016, I was approached by GTP to create a walking-performance in Mullion Cove as part of *Miss You Already*, a weekend of artistic events at three different coastal sites in Cornwall that would:

> creatively imagine how we can cope with rising sea levels and coastal erosion, which has accelerated over the past decade [due to] extreme weather events which are occurring more frequently.
>
> (Golden Tree Productions 2016)

Miss You Already was a partnership with the National Trust, which as an organization was concerned about the social impact of its proposed policy of managed retreat, which means that 'as part of caring for a place they are gradually letting go of it' (2016). During a research trip, and later in the performance, Justin Whitehouse explained that, in the case of Mullion Cove harbour:

> With anticipated rising sea levels, and increasing severity of winter storms, repairs are going to become increasingly unsustainable until a tipping point is reached when it would be necessary to call a halt to further repairs. Whilst everyone hopes the harbour will survive for as long as possible, we do need to be realistic and understand that, at some point in the future, the harbour will no longer be here.
>
> (in Wilson 2016a: Station 11 and 2017: 46)

GTP and the National Trust recognized that, despite the local community and other stakeholders being consulted over the 'managed retreat':

> what has been missing from the decision-making process has often been the 'contemporary histories': the personal and emotional meanings that residents and visitors attribute to these places.
>
> (Golden Tree Productions 2016)

---

[4] Gail Lyons, email to the author, 25 September, 2019.

My symbolic use of landscape and walking as a metaphorical means to reflect upon human loss in *Fissure* was resonant with the concepts of 'palliative curation' for GTP's associate director, Natalia Eernstman. She wanted me to apply a similar thinking process to the creation of a new performance work that looked at landscape loss. My response was to work with both human loss *and* landscape loss as interlinked and interchangeable themes. Beyond that, I felt it was important to work site-specifically and without preconceived ideas. This is typical of my practice, but here I felt the need to be particularly sensitive and respectful, not least because, as a stranger who lived hundreds of miles away, I was reluctant to enter what was for some people an understandably fraught and emotional situation.

The concept of palliative curation was developed by the cultural geographer Caitlin DeSilvey, believing that intervention/art 'creates opportunities to say "goodbye" to loved landmarks and landscapes, and allow them [the place] to die with dignity' (DeSilvey, Naylor and Sackett 2011: 56–7). For me, while the idea of palliative curation helped me understand the producers' formation of the *Miss You Already* project, my creative process could not be concept-led, but needed to be entirely responsive. This was because I did not feel it was my role or place (nor was it my creative purpose or strength) to advocate on the National Trust's behalf for managed retreat or explicitly prepare the people of Mullion to accept a possible future without the harbour and the coastline by saying 'goodbye' and letting their harbour and coast 'die with dignity'.

Going into the project, my sense was that before the potential loss of a place or person can be accepted, their intrinsic value and significance must first to be recognized and celebrated. This might take time, and not be straightforward. Rather than setting out to prepare the community for loss, my approach was to find out what Mullion Cove, the harbour and coastline meant personally, practically and emotionally to local residents. This approach was designed to understand better, and publicly acknowledge through the making of a performance work, the impact of any future loss on individuals, livelihoods and the community. It was an approach designed to recognize the interconnectedness that exists between people and the place they inhabit.

Close-up looking, listening and noticing

Having undertaken some preliminary background research into Mullion and the Lizard Peninsula, I deliberately arrived in Mullion without a preconceived idea of what I would make. I did not at this stage know that the work would be called *Mulliontide*, that it would take the form of a coastal walk, that it would be performed by local people telling their own story in the location of their own choice, that it would engage local groups, individuals, businesses and makers in the creation of bespoke objects, or that it would be staged using only the landscape, the people and objects specific each person to a create a series of scenes. Rather, my approach was to put residents and the landscape centre stage and adapt my creative thinking in response to what they wanted, or needed, to say about the place, and how that place was woven into the fabric of their lives and identities. This adaptive approach, though typical of my scenographic practice, was in *Mulliontide* central to the creative process. I worked co-creatively and democratically, without favouring one voice over another, by creating an inclusive space within which multiple voices with unique viewpoints, perspectives and concerns would be heard, and as many people as wanted could make a contribution.

Since time was short, being limited to a total of three weeks on the ground, I had to move quickly and follow the leads as they presented themselves. I met people through a mixture of quick planning and happenstance, and largely found that one person led me to another person or group. My creative methodology centred around the scenographic technique of close-up looking, listening and noticing that is designed to encourage alternative ways of seeing, thinking and feeling about a situation. This involved looking at the sites people took me to, listening to the heart of what they were saying and noticing the detail of the objects they showed me, or made, that for them embodied their story and landscape.

To begin conversations (which often led to walks) I used two questions as prompts:

1   Is there a place in the landscape that is special to you?
2   If the tides or times were to take that place away, what, for you, would be lost?

The first question established a significant site and the second question brought the idea of loss into the frame, but avoided making direct references to the harbour or assumptions about which places might be significant. In all cases, people then led me to their site where they told me more about its significance. Working this way (and not focusing on the harbour) meant all residents became involved, not just those whose lives were connected to or located in the harbour. The discussion triggered by the questions widened out to activities relating to that place and objects associated with it. Everything in the final walking-performance (locations, actions, objects, costumes/clothes, content, routes and stations) came from these meetings and site visits.

Despite my concerns, perhaps coming from outside the community and therefore being unaware of established hierarchies and opinions meant that

I did not have preconceived ideas and residents were willing to share things with me, knowing I had no agenda and they had autonomy over what they said and in what location. Plus, I think people sensed my interest was genuine; for example, Johnny Pascoe later said:

> what was really poignant was that Louise engaged so much with us ... the local community and the local people. It really promoted enthusiasm for a project. It got to the point when I was like: Wow, you're so interested and so enthusiastic about this that I just want to help you in any way I can.[5]

Another contributor and performer, Gail Lyons, who sang in the trio and the choir, valued what she later described as 'my gracious sensitivity towards people and place ... and attention to detail when planning the project and bringing it all together'.[6]

It immediately became clear that each person wanted to share their love and passion for a specific place and the activity they did there. It also became clear that the loss of those interconnected and inextricably linked things – person, place and activity – would be immense. For many, these intense and deeply embedded feelings reflected a complex weave between their lives and the place they inhabit going back generations. This can perhaps be best understood by the term *topophilia*, which literally means love of place, and is described in cultural geography as 'the affective bond between people and place or setting' (Tuan 1977: 4).

What emerged was that expressing topophilia was more important to residents than discussing the future of the harbour and ideas of managed retreat, which many felt had become a dominant narrative. That is not to say they were without concerns and uncertainties for the future, but first and foremost what each person wanted to share was their love for that place, in the here and now, informed by history and the past but more as part of their everyday life.

In parallel to thinking about each individual story, location and intervention, I looked for where one person's story linked to another's, and to make a dramaturgically coherent and structured whole, I sought forms (and structures) that I could use to bring and hold all the voices and contributions together.

Dramaturgical form and structure

The sites and issues identified by close-up looking, listening and noticing suggested structuring the performance in a linear route along the coastal path,

---

[5] Jonny Pascoe, collaborator/performer feedback (interview), *Mulliontide*, 2016.
[6] Gail Lyons, collaborator/performer feedback (interview), *Mulliontide*, 2016.

using places of particular importance as stopping points. This evolved into a processional walk from station to station. Among the songs loved by the local choir, one – The White Rose – was particularly powerful and resonant with the subject matter of love and loss, so I saw an opportunity to use it at certain stations as a second way of giving the performance structure. The third structural element of *Mulliontide* was based on a palliative care model (not connected to the concept of palliative curation discussed previously) that I had become aware of while working on *Fissure*. I will now look at each of these in turn.

Processional walk, stations, objects and Mulliontide *flag*

Developing *Mulliontide* as a processional walk along the coastal path was a response to the local tradition of coastal processions that take place in the harbour and on the cliffs to mark liturgical festivals such as Eastertide and during the summer.

In another echo of a liturgical or processional walk, before we set off I gave each participant a waterproof zip bag containing a booklet in the style of a funeral service leaflet, inside which was a map of the route, the location of each station, the name of the performer they would meet there and the theme of that place. This booklet was the first of a number of autotopographic objects handed out to participants during the performance at different stations – a song-sheet booklet, a series of photographs and botanical drawings printed on cards, chocolate fish, home-made biscuits and a scallop shell. Along with other interventions experienced en route (choral singing, wreath laying, storytelling, palliative care interventions and physical actions), each site, person, object and action served to deepen the story being communicated at each station and prompt connections across the whole performance – making a dramaturgically meaningful and coherent whole.

By the end of the performance, participants – like pilgrims collecting souvenirs of their journey – had accumulated a collection of objects and a series of embodied experiences, which were designed to act not only as mementos of the day, but also as prompts to aid remembering and reconstruction of the walk away from the site or on repeat visits. One group of participants remarked on this: 'It's so great to have the pack, we will now walk with this material and share it with our walking group'.[7] In this respect the work created its own autotopographical objects.

Another autotopographical object was the *Mulliontide* flag. The idea of using a flag to lead the walk was inspired by seeing the banners in St Mellanus Church in Mullion village that are used in local and regional ceremonial processions and festival parades. I invited members of the Mullion Women's Institute

---

[7] Anon., *Mulliontide* participant feedback (form), 2016.

Arts and Crafts Group to create a flag for the *Mulliontide* walk. Designed collectively and hand-stitched by the women, the two-sided *Mulliontide* flag had a vivid folk-art aesthetic and featured images of landmarks, objects, animals and plants that were significant to each individual as well as motifs which they said everyone from the area knew. It showed images of: Mullion Cove harbour and stone-built piers; the view from the bench placed in memory of one stitcher's husband, with Mullion Cove's distinctive rock formations and clifftop flora; a sunset over the sea created in an array of coloured silks ranging from orange, pink and yellow to purple, blue and turquoise; a chough with dense black feathers, red bill and claws and a bright gleaming eye; silvery herring fish; gulls (Mullion's symbol); a fishing boat; the Cornish flag; and heather, gorse and tamarisk. The collective endeavour of designing and stitching the *Mulliontide* flag led 'to the sharing of thoughts and discussions amongst the group'.[8] Later, during the performance, for one participant (Dominica Williamson) the flag bearing was particularly poignant because it 'brought back memories of her father', who had formerly been the priest at St Mellanus Church, 'carrying out services on the cliffs and at the harbour'.[9]

Mulliontide's progression along the coastal path, stopping at a series of locations, or stations, where performers shared their stories, had echoes of a pilgrimage or processional walk. My use of this linear form and the 'stations' was a direct reference to the Eastertide tradition of Stations of the Cross, during which worshippers progress along a path and at a series of stations are told the next phase of the story of Christ's crucifixion. For example, at 'Station 2: Poldhu Care Home', participants met in the conservatory, lounge and dining room and talked to residents who spoke of places in the landscape they loved and longed for: the coastal paths they walked, the beauty of the heather-covered cliffs, the Cornish hedges they built, the coves where they swam and body-boarded. No longer able to do these things, Sidney Francis Jenkins said: 'Never mind, I have the memory of it' (in Wilson 2016a). They also talked of the lives they once led, and showed photographs of a younger self wearing a nursing uniform, as a dancer, collecting a service award from the Queen, showing a pedigree cow. One resident talked of becoming a widower aged fifty-three, and another, Marie Withers, about being widowed after sixteen years of marriage. 'This is life!', she said, and explained when she 'moved in five months ago', she:

> didn't want it at first. It was the hardest, most traumatic decision I've ever had to make. You come in at a low ebb. After two weeks I felt better. I had to accept it.
>
> (Wilson 2016a: Station 2 and 2017: 10)

---

[8] Beryl Cullen, *Mulliontide* collaborator feedback (form), 2016.
[9] Dominica Williamson, *Mulliontide* participant feedback (form), 2016.

FIGURE 6.1 Mulliontide. *Wendy Williamson greeting participants at 'Station 4: Kissing Gate – Meres Cliff', Mullion, Cornwall. Photographer: Andy Hughes*

At 'Station 4: Kissing Gate – Meres Cliff', participants were met by Wendy Williamson, who handed out chocolate fish to each person as they passed through the gate and asked, 'Chocolate fish are safe to eat [...] but what about the fish swimming in the sea? Are they safe to eat?' (in Wilson 2016a and 2017: 20–1). The chocolates were pulled out of what Wendy called her 'Nelly bag', knitted by Nelly, a neighbour, from cut-up Tesco carrier bags in protest against single-use plastics and the dominance of the supermarket over local shops. Dressed in an ankle-length purple coat with staff in hand, looking distinctly like a pilgrim, Wendy led everyone along the cliff path she walked every day, pointing out sea-lions in the water below and sharing her concerns about plastic pollution and the fate of birds, fish and other sea creatures, before stopping above Polurrian Cove. At this location, where the cliff is covered in a snowy-white blanket of sea campion, she guided everyone's gaze to the opposite cliff where two houses once stood. She then told the story of a friend who, when eight years old, watched as 'the cliff seemed to rear up … Black mud squelched out, the cliff shrank, the houses twisted and groaned then crashed onto the rocks below' (in Wilson 2016a and 2017: 20).

At 'Station 7: Love Rock – Carrag-Luz', where local botanical artist Diana Davis spends hours observing the flora, participants were given a picture of a sea campion in bud, bloom and seed, drawn by her for *Mulliontide*. The choice of flower was deliberate, and a caption on the card, 'Sea Campion (also known as Dead Man's Bells) should never be picked, for fear of tempting death', is a reference to the flowers' habit of growing on the precarious edges of sea cliffs (in Wilson 2016a and 2017: 33–4).

At 'Station 8: View of Mullion Cove – Henscath Head', participants met local historian Bob Felce, who explained how the harbour below them was built in 1868 due to stormy conditions causing loss of ships and lives, adding: 'When it goes it will be a sad day' (in Wilson 2016a and 2017: 35). Each participant was given a card with a triptych of photographs taken by Bob between 2013 and 2014, showing the harbour deluged by storm waves, the devastation and damage they caused, and workmen repairing the break-walls.

At 'Station 12: Barry Mundy's Scallop Shells – Northern Quay' in Mullion Cove harbour, participants listened to an audio recording of Barry Mundy, a fifth-generation fisherman, who expressed the need for the harbour, built by his ancestors, to be preserved as a 'testament to the men that built it':

> I'm fully aware that in life, in general the 'Lord giveth and the Lord taketh away'. It is a possibility that we get what they call the one in 200-years storm where the harbour would be completely obliterated. Well then, you wouldn't expect anyone, the National Trust or any other organisation to re-build it because it just wouldn't be viable. So, at that point the Lord would taketh again. But, in saying that, I think we could hang on to it for generations to come.
>
> (in Wilson 2016a: Station 12 and 2017: 47–8)

Participants were given a black-and-white photograph of men building the west pier in around 1891 and, as a memento of the harbour and Barry's story, a scallop shell (symbol of a pilgrim), fished for by Barry and sold by him from a weathered box on the harbour wall.

At 'Station 13: The Fishing Boat "Laurie Jean" – Slipway', in Mullion Cove harbour, participants surrounded Jonny Pascoe as he sat in his boat and discussed the fragile future of fishing out of the cove. Wanting to get away from conversation around 'how much money [the harbour] costs … from the aesthetics of the harbour wall … if it falls down or if they have to use concrete', he talked about and wanted participants to think about its history and 'what or who we are potentially keeping it there for' (in Wilson 2016a). He described how he 'started going out fishing with his Dad when he was seven years old':

> It's a generational thing, fishing is in my blood. This is my home port. I feel this tug towards the cove and fishing. I almost feel it a duty to continue

FIGURE 6.2 Mulliontide. *Fisherman Johnny Pascoe speaking to participants at 'Station 13: The Fishing Boat "Laurie Jean" – Slipway' in Mullion Cove harbour, Cornwall. Photographer: Andy Hughes*

what has been such an important part of the Cove's history. Whatever happens, I will always be deeply connected to this place and my family's history within it – my homeport, Mullion Cove.

(in Wilson 2016a: Station 13 and 2017: 51–2)

One resident, Gail Lyons, who performed in *Mulliontide* was herself related to the fishermen in Mullion Cove harbour and, with her siblings, had learned to swim there:

[My] father, a builder, repaired the piers when I was a child ... and [my] stepfather and his father and brother have had fishing boats there for years.[10]

Perhaps because of the way the harbour had 'featured largely in [her] family's life', Gail found Johnny Pascoe's description of the importance of the harbour to him, representing another, younger, generation for whom the loss of the harbour would be hard, to be deeply moving and 'resonant in meaning'.[11]

---

[10] Gail Lyons, collaborator/performer feedback (form), *Mulliontide*, 2016.
[11] Gail Lyons, collaborator/performer feedback (form), *Mulliontide*, 2016.

At 'Station 14: Heavy Cake and Tea' in Porthmellin tea-room, participants were served tea and Cornish *Hevva*, or heavy cake, containing no eggs and traditionally made by fishermen's wives to welcome their men home from the sea. The cake, made from a family recipe, was served by the Pearson family who had opened the café in 1947 and whose ancestors had lived there since the nineteenth century. Each participant was given a black-and-white photo showing Kitty, the grandmother, as a girl watching her father making traditional lobster pots from tamarisk and willow. Many of the contributors and performers joined the gathering, designed with reference to a traditional funeral tea at a wake. To bring everyone together, songsheet booklets were placed on the table and the choir led participants in singing 'Calm Is the Sea' and 'Cornwall My Home'. The singing was deeply felt and full of meaning for performers and participants alike. As one participant said: 'Quite a few people had tears in their eyes.'[12]

'The White Rose' song, wreaths and lost landscape

The second structural element was my use of 'The White Rose', a well-known Cornish folksong often sung at funerals. The song uses the life cycle of a

FIGURE 6.3 Mulliontide. *Gail Lyons, Russ Stanland and Charlotte Douglas of the St Mellanus Singers singing and laying a wreath of white roses at 'Station 10: Closed Path – Mullion Cove', Cornwall. Photographer: Andy Hughes*

---

[12] Anon., participant feedback (form), *Mulliontide*, 2016.

rose as a metaphor for youthfulness, ageing, death, sorrow and the promise of return in the spring. In the performance, one verse was sung by a trio of Cornish singers from Mullion's St Mellanus Singers at three stations where the signs of landscape loss were clearly visible: a path lost to a fast-crumbling cliff, a wall which is all that remains of the two houses that fell off the cliff, and a landslide into the sea with a view of the storm-damaged harbour.

After the singing, a circular wreath of white roses was laid at the site of loss. These interventions were a reference to the laying of wreaths to mark a memorial site or a person's place of rest, and were designed to reflect on time passing, impermanence and change, bringing human loss and landscape loss into the same frame. One of the sites of landscape loss was adjacent to a series of memorial benches, making the connection to remembrance and passing clear. For Gail Lyons, one of the trio of singers, the song took on a deeply personal significance: 'In singing the "White Rose" I was able to express my love of the place.'[13] She had inherited Cornish singing from her mother and involvement brought another layer of personal meaning, because at the time of the event she was helping to care for her mother with dementia:

> It's now heartbreaking that memories of those wonderful years [of singing and spending time in the cove] have gone from her.[14]

The sequence of verses at different stations was rounded off by the whole choir singing the final verse at Mullion Harbour.

The three-phase palliative care model

When a person is terminally ill, a three-phase palliative care model is used in end-of-life care to support patients and their families as they go through the three phases of diagnosis, illness, and finally death and bereavement. I first had conversations regarding the importance of talking about dying and death with palliative and end-of-life care researchers at Lancaster University when making *Fissure*. When developing *Mulliontide*, I met Saul Ridley, a palliative care nurse who worked with the model. He interpreted the three phases as diagnosis and change, preparation and uncertainty, and the importance of truth about dying and death. I discovered that he had a comparable way of working with the landscape symbolically, as I did in *Fissure*. He was also a surfer on the Mullion coast, and joined the project 'motivated by relating

---

[13] Gail Lyons, collaborator/performer feedback (interview), *Mulliontide*, 2016.
[14] Gail Lyons, collaborator/performer feedback (interview), *Mulliontide*, 2016.

change of landscape to the existential changes that can happen to people facing the end of their life'.[15]

We indentified three locations (all coves with sandy beaches) where Saul would meet participants and use the landscape to explain the palliative process in a material and metaphorical way.

At 'Station 1: Beach and Surf – Poldhu Cove', Saul – who, having just emerged from the sea, wore a wetsuit and carried a surfboard – used the wide expanse of sandy beach and dunes that are constantly being weathered and moved by wind and water to explore the first phase of the palliaitve process – that of adaptation. He invited participants to consider how change can be challenging and explained how his work recognized the need for, and importance of, preparing for loss and death:

> Everything changes all the time – there is no standing still. Think of your own life, and all the changes you've experienced, and have witnessed in other people's experiences. Some planned, others like bolts from the blue which strike you unexpectedly. Some changes are easy, others seem nigh on impossible to survive, so we adapt, we have to, we have no choice in that ... when people are told they are incurably ill, they adapt to the progression of their disease. It goes: wellness – deterioration – death. My job is to help them to adapt and accept.
>
> (in Wilson 2016a: Station 1 and 2017: 5–6)

He then asks the participants 'that you see, hear, smell and think a little more – and talk less' (in Wilson 2016a and 2017: 6).

Their next meeting with Saul – now dressed as he does for work in smart but casual clothes – was at 'Station 5: Sand and Sea – Polurrian Cove' to explore the second phase of the palliative process – that of 'uncertainty and truth' (in Wilson 2016a and 2017: 23). This is a place where one of his terminally ill patients, a mother aged thirty, confronted the end of her life and filmed a 'goodbye' video for the small children she would leave behind, telling them all about her and her relationship with their father. Saul's telling of the event was a revelation, which immediately shifted the participants' view of the cove and its significance in the palliative process. Pointing to the beauty of the place, he then invited them to:

> Just take it in. Breathe it, smell it, feel it. Really 'feel' this place, be entirely 'in the moment'. But feeling that alive means you can be heightened to a sense of death – just how close it always is. In my job you never know when someone is going to ask you whether they will still be alive at Christmas ... The only

---

[15] Saul Ridley, collaborator/performer feedback (interview), *Mulliontide*, 2016.

right answer is the truth, even though the books teach you to deflect that by asking the questioner why they asked, or what they think! Uncertainty is often the hardest aspect of living with incurable progressive illness. It causes more distress than the truth ... What holds families together is honesty, the truth.

(in Wilson 2016a: Station 5 and 2017: 24)

Saul then invited participants to take off their shoes and socks and led them across the sand into the cold, clear seawater. This action brought them an acute awareness of the feel and sensations of the sand and water. Emerging from the sea, their view of the cove, now seen from a different perspective, had been altered and their own sense of aliveness heightened.

At 'Station 14: Rock and Tide – Cave' in Mullion Cove, Saul stepped out from the darkness of a tunnel-like cave and reflected on the third phase of the palliative process – that of helping the dying person and their loved ones through the death:

Some changes are gradual; very slow, without you barely noticing. Others come out of nowhere. Others still are seen, anticipated, engaged with, and leave people feeling empowered and strong. In specialist palliative care we

FIGURE 6.4 Mulliontide. *'Station 14: Rock and Tide – Cave'*, *participant emerging from the tunnel out of Mullion Cove, Cornwall. Photographer: Andy Hughes*

try to do the latter – we help people 'through a tunnel', the tunnel being the dying journey. But people can easily become preoccupied with the tunnel – therein lies danger, and can get stuck. Usually, the reason for that is simply fear. Fear of what the landscape of their life is going to look like on the other side. There is no 'right or wrong' life on the other side, it's just different ... All has changed.

... I really want you all to feel the experience of going from one place to another in a condensed form. To do that, let's go into this cave – and realise it's a tunnel – and cross to the other side, with no idea of what is there, feel how uncomfortable that can be. The journey itself, in the dark, over rocks and through puddles is the process ... The landscape on the other side will be different.

(in Wilson 2016a: Station 14 and 2017: 55–6)

Saul then led the participants into the cave; in this journey they had to move slowly and use all their senses to feel their way through the darkness. To make this physical journey, some had to overcome feelings of fear and anxiety about the unknown terrain of tunnel, and all were encouraged to offer each other a helping hand and give their bodies and eyes time to adapt. The gleam of sunlight emanating from the sandy cove at the far end of the tunnel – only accessible for a short time during low tide – drew participants on. As they emerged from the cold, dark tunnel into the warm, bright cove, many expressed a sense of wonderment at the glow of the golden sand, the sunshine glinting in the lapping sea, the blue sky, and gulls wheeling overhead.

With a sense of communitas achieved by hours of walking together and the collective and personal effort of making it through the tunnel, participants became quiet and reflective. They soaked up the atmosphere and the alternative and unfamiliar point of view this rarely-visted cove gave them on the sea, the harbour walls and the cliff. This place, and the materials and phenomena that formed it, became a *site of transformation* in which participants could contemplate their relationship to the living and dying processes. This contemplation and the feelings participants shared with each other were given time and space to develop, but soon the incoming tide made it necessary to leave the cove before it became cut off again.

The palliative care model was used as a tool to reflect on human loss at specific stations; it was also important to the work as a whole, because it provided a meta-structure. By this I mean that it enabled me to place all the individual stories into a larger metaphoric and symbolic framework and provided a lens through which all the components of the whole could be viewed.

Reassemblage and lasting legacy

The extent to which the contributors became invested in the work can be seen in the way two performers (Gail Lyons and Wendy Williamson) regularly lead *Mulliontide* 'walks and talks with singing' for local groups, including the Mullion Mothers Union and Mullion Methodist Monday Club. Using the *Mulliontide: A Guide for Walkers* book as a score, they 'led folks through the whole performance'.[16] During these performances, they gather the necessary objects, visit the care home, meet some of the original performers en route and end in the tea-room with singing. Each performer draws out aspects that are particularly important to them (belonging, impermanence, environmental pollution) as well as themes of interest to the specific group they are leading. This repeated reassembling and performing of *Mulliontide* demonstrates their sense of ownership of the work and how performance like this can be applied in a range of places and situations.

---

[16] Gail Lyons, email to the author, 24 March 2020.

7

Applied scenography – multiple applications: *Dorothy's Room* and *Women's Walks to Remember*

No need of motion or of strength
Or even the breathing air
I thought of nature's loveliest <u>scenes</u> – <u>haunts</u>   ?
And with memory I was there.

(DOROTHY WORDSWORTH, TRANSCRIBED FROM THE *RYDAL JOURNALS*)

Most things disappear out of my memory these days, however, the feeling of them [the fells] is still there and revisiting them in my mind, I more or less experience the occasion of walking.

(HAROLD POTTER, POLDHU CARE HOME, MULLION, CORNWALL, 2016)

This chapter explores how scenographic-led walking-performance can be transformative even when a participant cannot access the physical site. Much of my practice is predicated on scenographic walking both as a way of engaging participants and as a component of the transformative experience, where walking is used symbolically and dramaturgically. This chapter looks at how scenography can bring a landscape indoors through the act of surrogate walking or the design of a multimedia immersive installation. It points to a type of therapeutic one-to-one scenography.

I consider two interconnected 'surrogate walking' projects that recognized and celebrated Dorothy Wordsworth's walking legacy and the walking lives of present-day Lake District women who due to ageing, incapacity, illness or circumstance are no longer able to walk as they once did. The first is *Dorothy's Room* (2018), an immersive multimedia installation centred on and around Dorothy's sickbed that I originally created for Dorothy Wordsworth's bedroom at Rydal Mount, Ambleside, Cumbria, where she lived from 1813 to 1850. The installation made material her deeply felt longing to be outside and, when, due to illness, she was bedroom-bound for long periods, she used her memory and imagination to 'walk'. The second project is *Women's Walks to Remember: 'With memory I was there'* (2018–19), a one-to-one applied scenography project I created with present-day women in the Lake District who had been keen walkers in the past, but have lost mobility. I worked with them to materialize a significant walk they vividly remembered and deeply longed for but could no longer manage. In *Women's Walks to Remember* I invited these women to draw an at-home memory-map of a longed-for walk, then used these maps to rewalk the landscape on their behalf – as a surrogate walk. Walking like this, in the footsteps of these women, enabled me to get as close a view as possible of the landscape they remembered. Following each walk, I distilled my findings into a bespoke storyboard-style card (one for each memory-walker) that together made a collection of 'walks to remember'. This collection valued the individual walkers and their walks, and can be used by others to walk in their footsteps.

The project title, *Walks to Remember*, had a double meaning. It refers to both the way remembered walks are to be valued and not forgotten, and how they can be used to help participants to remember, recollect and re-enter longed-for landscapes – and in so doing leave the mental or physical confines of a space or circumstance.

Women's Walks to Remember built on how, as discussed in Chapter 5, some *Warnscale* participants who were not able to access the site physically used the book to experience and/or share the walking-performance, and still found the work immersive and transformative. For example, for one participant in Tasmania:

> the layers and layers of this book insinuate themselves so deeply into the self – words, images, maps, medical processes and emotional turmoil – all with the exquisite writings of Dorothy Wordsworth and the metaphorical and physical appreciation of the landscape – I love the way all these layers interplay (I can almost *hear* it).[1]

---

[1] MM, email to the author, 3 November 2015.

Women's Walks to Remember saw me develop and apply the drawing and storyboard techniques used as creative and methodological tools in *The Gathering* and the multilayered montaged images that created the pages in the *Warnscale* book. The project also adapted the on-site mapping-walk technique first used in *Warnscale* into an 'at-home' memory-mapping activity. The memory-mapping process for *Women's Walks to Remember* valued the voices and landscapes of the women involved who were no longer able to walk as they once had. It recognized the importance of their particular walk, the part it played in their daily, family or community life and their identity, health and sense of well-being. The storyboard/memory cards made the remembered walks and the landscapes in which they are located visible to others, and brought a further level of significance.

The chapter looks at my use of scenographic techniques and co-creative methodologies for making one-to-one applied scenography. Beyond map-making, these techniques included the use of photographs, objects and stories as prompts to remember a landscape physically, visually, sonically, emotionally and kinaesthetically. I look at how the storyboard form can be used as a way of collating these materials – stories, images and words – to make bespoke and co-created scenography. The chapter also considers how scenography can be used to:

- reveal the effects and impact on health and well-being caused by the loss or lack of ability to access a landscape (or a longed-for place); and

- return that landscape/place to a participant to counter these effects and bring positive and transformative outcomes (short, medium and long term) for the individual and others – family, friends, carers and the community.

Feedback referenced in this chapter was received through letters and email correspondence with participants, who are identified by first names, full names or initials. The chapter includes short transcriptions of conversations that I recorded in notebooks or on a digital voice recorder during the creative process – these are identified but not given an in-text reference. The chapter also includes extracts from the bespoke storyboard/memory cards I created for each of the *Women's Walks to Remember* 'memory-walkers' – these are unpublished, bespoke materials. Also included are extracts from Dorothy Wordsworth's *Rydal Journals*. These extracts come from two sources: the scholar Carl H. Ketcham's partial (unpublished) transcription of the journals written in 1978, and the original journals that are housed in the archive at the Wordsworth Trust (Wordsworth Grasmere), Cumbria, UK.

Production credits for *Dorothy's Room* and *Women's Walks to Remember* are in Appendix F and Appendix G.

Harold Potter: a walk to remember

While creating *Mulliontide*, a number of residents in the Poldhu Care Home in Cornwall shared memories of walks along the coast, pools they had learnt to swim in and coves where they used to body-board. The two activity workers at the home (Julie and Gemma) later told me that, during my research visits to the care home, they heard 'residents share stories they hadn't heard before'.[2]

One resident, Harold Potter (1923–2019), told me, 'When I kick the bucket, I'll have my ashes scattered near Haweswater in the Mardale Head area of the Lake District', which he described as 'my favourite place'. I was surprised at this Cumbrian location, hundreds of miles from Cornwall yet not too far from where I live in North West England, but Harold told me he was born there and it was his 'favourite place'. I asked Harold if, when I returned home, he would be happy for me to walk in his footsteps to his find his beloved landscape then send him photos of my journey and findings – an idea he loved!

FIGURE 7.1 Walks to Remember. *Louise Ann Wilson surrogate walking 'Harold Potter's Mardale Head Walk: "When I kick the bucket, I'll have my ashes scattered at Mardale Head"', Cumbria. Photographer: Nigel Stewart*

---

[2] Julie Bird and Gemma Conroy, interview, *Mulliontide*, 2016.

A few months later, on an icy January day, with Harold's precise and vivid instructions in hand, I set out in search of a series of waterfalls above Haweswater – the place where he wished for his ashes to be scattered. As I walked, I marked the route on an Ordnance Survey map and took photographs to capture the landscape, key features and close-up detail – icicles, berries, frost patterns and lichen – in the hope of bringing Harold as close to the landscape as possible, from afar. Following my walk, I sent him all my findings. A few days later, the care home reported that the items I had sent were 'bringing back many happy memories' for Harold and had prompted conversations with him about his early life and the landscape he loved and longed for that they would otherwise not have had. It seemed that this exchange gave them a deeper, more nuanced understanding of Harold, for whom the Cumbrian landscape formed a large part of his identity.

Since that first walk, I followed in Harold's footsteps in Kentmere and Greenholme, and until his death in 2019 we Skyped regularly to talk about them and the Cumbria landscape. I posted him maps that he marked up and I followed. After each surrogate walk I sent him photos and drawings of the houses he had lived in, the school he had attended and the land his family had farmed. I also used film to capture the sounds of the landscapes – streams bubbling, shepherds calling and lambs chorusing – and to gain a more intimate, deeper and slower perspective of the place. My aim was to return the landscape, and the feeling of it, to him not just visually but also haptically and sonically.

FIGURE 7.2 Walks to Remember. *Harold Potter and Louise Ann Wilson talking via Skype. Photographer: Louise Ann Wilson*

The care home staff noticed that Harold came alive during our Skype conversations and was always keen to 'talk again', and every Skype meeting ended with him singing to me in a faltering but expressive voice a song that he retrieved from deep within. Following our conversations, the staff described how 'Harold is buzzing':

> [He has] really made a connection with you and clearly enjoys the interaction, revisiting old walks and reliving his life up North. He was happy throughout the talk! It's simply wonderful to see Harold this way. It's amazing he spoke with you for 45 minutes![3]

Central to our connection was a common knowledge of the landscape and of sheep farming, and we imagined walking the Cumbrian fells together. Through memory-walking, Harold described how he could 'see the place' as if he were physically there, and was able to 'remember the fells off by heart':

> Most things disappear out of my memory these days, however, the feeling of them is still there and revisiting them in my mind, I more or less experience the occasion of walking. My memory is not very good these days. I make the excuse of being 96 years old. I still have visions of the wonderful Mardale Head and all the fells around there.[4]

This act of memory-walking – prompted by me walking as a surrogate for Harold and returning with materials – reflects the way that the:

> action and effort of walking brings the walker into the present yet also allows them to make an internal journey into memory, imagination, feeling, being and knowing.
>
> (MacFarlane 2012: 26)

Harold's walking was internal and took him into inner landscapes of 'memory, imagination, feeling, being and knowing' that were embedded and embodied within him. Through memory-walking, he visited, and shared, personal stories and childhood memories – of Haweswater being flooded, tickling trout in the stream, the school bell ringing and hurrying to school late, of days spent running wild in the fells 'on and off the beaten track ... led on by my elder

---

[3] David Sanders, activity coordinator, Poldhu care home, email to the author, 15 February 2018.
[4] Harold Potter, Skype conversation with the author, 15 February 2018.

sister Elsie'.[5] He also shared stories of sheep farming, poverty, harsh winters and a snowfall that suffocated his father's flock of sheep.

Harold's vivid and immediate recollections revealed the landscape that had shaped him and framed his life – he carried the fells within him, and was able to retrieve and return to them and the events and people who ghost them. This process of remembering vivid site-specifc 'moments of being' (Woolf [1972] 1978: 84) aligns with William Wordsworth's concept of 'spots of time'. 'In his autobiographical poem *The Prelude*, Wordsworth emphasises the positive power and shaping influence of key moments in his life, which he calls "spots of time"' (Bainbridge 2013: Part 1). Many of these 'spots' occurred in the landscape of the Lake District and, for Wordsworth, reflection on them 'was a vital and positive process and had what he describes as a restorative, nourishing and repairing effect (2013: Part 1). Eventually, I distilled all the photos and maps, along with other findings – songs, drawings, Harold's family tree and a poem written using his words – into a storyboard/memory card and sent it to him. This physical object – which, reported the care staff, 'put a big smile on his face and we had a good chat about it all' – meant that Harold could share his walk with others.

'Walking to remember' was for Harold a 'vital and positive' process and one that he was proud of – he enjoyed being the focus of a creative project, and loved the idea that his places and stories would be written about and shared with others. This placed value on the landscapes and on Harold himself, and was a process that led to 'Harold of the Cumbrian lakes and fells' becoming more visible.

Dorothy Wordsworth: it was perfect healing

While walking Harold's 'walk to remember', I read Dorothy Wordsworth's *Rydal Journals*. Written between 1824 and 1835 while she was living at Rydal Mount with her brother William, his wife Mary and their daughter Dora, the journals were a daily record of her life. Her *Grasmere Journals*, explored in Chapter 5 of this book, were written over twenty years earlier while she was living at Town End (now Dove Cottage) in Grasmere, and show how this radical and adventurous walker *needed* to be outside, to move her body, to become immersed in her surroundings, to observe closely, to listen intently, to think deeply and to find equilibrium with herself and communion with others.

---

[5] Harold Potter, Skype conversation with the author, 15 February 2018.

Written two decades later when she was in her mid-fifties, Dorothy's *Rydal Journals* reveal that initially she remained an active walker, pursuing solitary rambles, sociable walks with family, friends or visitors, or calls on neighbours, often routing her walk via waterfalls, quarries, tarns, bridges and lakes, and repeatedly returning to 'personal landmarks in the landscape' (Bainbridge 2015: 4.1). Many of these landmarks were associated with the past and with specific people – John's Grove, named after her beloved brother John Wordsworth, killed at sea; the Wishing Gate or Sara's Gate, named by and after Sarah Hutchinson; and Dora's Field (The Rash), a memorial 'garden' named for her niece Dora who died of tuberculosis aged forty-three at Rydal Mount.

When Dorothy was aged only fifty-eight years old, however, 'illness began twenty-six years of physical and mental decline' (Woof 2015: 157). During her first period of illness in 1831–2, she was 'for five weeks confined to her room', but this period lengthened until, as reported by her brother William in a letter to his friend and travel companion Robert Jones, she 'had been for nearly 8 months confined to her room with sickness and debility' (2015: 157). Over the months and years that followed, her walking became limited to the garden and terrace at Rydal Mount and 'in the house' (Wordsworth 1978: 83).

Dorothy's bedroom window framed the view on to the fells she knew intimately and, with observational powers reminiscent of the *Grasmere Journals*, she noted how a 'hail shower falls from dazzling silver & dark clouds' and the visual effects of 'glittering showers travel over the house (1978: 79). These visceral observations not only 'cheered' her but were also therapeutic, serving as a type of healing to deliver her from the solitary hours she spent imprisoned in her lonely room. One evening, she wrote how she:

> prudently contented myself with sitting before the window and was never more cheered – with sun-set and moon-rising – and clouds gathering and melting away … It was perfect healing.
>
> (Wordsworth 1978: 16)

Sound also imaginatively transported Dorothy out of the bedroom. On Christmas Day 1834, she wrote, the sound of 'thickly falling rain' and the sight of a rain-soaked William Wordsworth brought the 'remembrance of many a moist tramp' (1978: 92). A few weeks later, on New Year's Day 1835, the 'brilliant' light brought recollections of 'Xmas days' past: 'One especially when we sate on the side of Nab Fell to sun & rest ourselves' (1978: 93).

Family and visitors found other ways of bringing the outside in to her: 'pictures lined the walls and pots of flowers lined her window ledge and plants grew around her window' (Woof 2015: 158). On Tuesday 23 April 1833, Dorothy wrote:

Two glowing anemones and a snow-white companion are in a pot on my window ledge, and two knots of blue primroses of the Alpine purple ... Rooks busy – all the Birds of sky and earth are singing – & all is wrapped up in happy brightness.

(Wordsworth 1978: 78)

Dorothy's indoor 'garden of *all the* seasons is visited by the Bees who solace me with their gentle humming while the birds warble sweetly' (1978: 79). In the winter months she was moved to tears by visits from her 'companion Robin' who, she wrote, 'treated me with his best song' and 'cheered my bedroom with its slender sublime piping' (1978: 117, 119). However, in a letter to her friend Jane Marshall 'written in April 1834', she lamented that 'the sun shines so bright and the birds sing so sweetly that I have almost a painful longing to go out of doors and am half tempted to break my bonds and sally forth into the garden' (Woof 2015: 162). This longing to be outside appeared in a number of journal entries at this time, revealing her 'desire to be free of the open air!' and how she feels the pull of 'Sunshine to make me long to go to & feel it' (Wordsworth 1978: 92).

Unable to escape the physical bounds of her bedroom, writing on Saturday 29 July 1832, Dorothy's journal shows how she freed herself from being 'a prisoner in this lonely room' and entered her longed-for landscapes by using the 'power' of her imagination through which she 'trod the Hills again':

No need of motion or of strength
Or even the breathing air
I thought of nature's loveliest <u>scenes</u> – <u>haunts</u>   ?
And with memory I was there

(Wordsworth 1824–35: (DCMS 118.3–0029))

Her use of memory to transport herself into the landscape was reminiscent of Harold leaving the physical confines of the care home by remembering. Together, these two Cumbrian fell walkers inspired two new interconnected projects.

Dorothy's Room: empathy and immersion

To create *Dorothy's Room*, I rewalked the walks Dorothy Wordsworth mentioned in the *Rydal Journal*s and used digital film and a recording device to bring the sights, sounds and atmosphere of the landscapes back into her bedroom, as she had done through memory.

Working in this way, *Dorothy's Room* picked up Dorothy's aliveness-to the human and other-than-human material of the everyday seen in her *Grasmere Journals*. Her aliveness continued to be seen in her early *Rydal Journals*, where she described 'bright gleams & startling flashes of sunshine', Snow drops in warm places hanging their bead like heads', a 'hail shower falls from dazzling silver & dark clouds', the sound of 'warbling birds' and how 'grass grows so fast & so green you do indeed "almost *see* it growing"' (Wordsworth 1978: 82–94). On Thursday 22 May 1834, she expressed her delight at the sight of Grasmere Lake:

> never more beautiful – the oaks changing their first yellow to the purest of bright green hues – all things partook of life & happiness ... – there was a calm brilliancy surpassing any thing I ever saw at that hour (between 2 & 3).
>
> (Wordsworth 1978: 96)

From the digital film footage I shot while walking in Dorothy's footsteps, I created a semi-abstract film in which layers of imagery and sound morphed, like memories and dreams, from bedroom to window and garden, then outwards beyond the grounds of Rydal Mount to the lakes, fells, tarns and sea. Within the film, pools reflect upside-down trees, rivers flow and sea ripple, light reveals the colour and texture of rock, flowers glow with vivid hues. Figures of women I met whilst walking in Dorothy's footsteps – leaping across stepping-stones, singing in a cave, striding out alone, laughing and trooping along with friends and paddling in the sea – were also layered into the film. Like the figures who walk across the pages of the *Warnscale* walking guide/art book, these women brought a human presence to the landscapes captured in the film that was designed to ghost Dorothy walking through it, place present-day walking-women into the frame and draw the viewer into the scene. Throughout the film, the image of the bedroom window returned repeatedly. This was designed to remind the viewer that the places they were moving through were experienced from within an interior space, and that what they were seeing was imagined and constructed through memory. When installed in the semi-darkness of Dorothy's bedroom at Rydal Mount, the film was projected over pillows stitched with words of escape, release and longing extracted from her journal pages. Objects mentioned in the journals or that I found when walking in her footsteps were placed around the bed and tucked into the sheets, which were twisted to suggest visually what she described as a constant aching or a 'dragging' and 'twisting' pain, which at times became a 'piping agony' (1978: 27, 92).

Each object was full of stories and associations drawn from the journal: a sheep jawbone and teeth suggestive of false teeth, birds' feathers suggestive of writing quills but also Dorothy's loss of freedom, needles and threads suggestive of the mending she did in bed and the way she stitched her journals together, but also of her stitching herself into the bed with her words. Together the sheets, pillows, blankets and objects were placed in a way to suggest a body lay within the bed. Two red books, suggestive of a mouth, were placed in a crack between two pillows that were dented to look as if a head had laid there for hours, and a pair of reading spectacles placed close by could be constructed (brought together) into a head and face. Coal tongs suggested an arm, teaspoon fingers a hand, and a stone water-bottle was placed to suggest legs. The twisted sheets wound across the centre of the bed like a contorted body, and placed within nests made by these windings in a way that suggested the abdomen and internal organs of the body were hand-dyed Easter eggs, a gaggle of medicine bottles, a cup containing tea, screwed-up threads and sharp-stabbing needles.

Underscoring the installation was a soundtrack of a cave echoing with footsteps and dripping water, bees buzzing, rivers flowing, waves washing, birds singing and a cuckoo clock ticking and sounding; the noises emerged and fell away. This visual and sonic morphing captured how the present recedes into the background when we move outside of ourselves into memory and imagination, and then emerges again.

The layering of the film, sound and objects in and over the physical bed was a collision that from some angles caused the bed to appear like a scaled-down version of the landscape with mountains, lakes and coasts in which Dorothy walked. At other times this collision gave the illusion that a ghostly thin figure was lying in the bed.

Making the bed involved a number of skilled craftspeople from the community, some of whom used traditional Cumbrian techniques such as that of making decorative Pace Eggs at Easter by wrapping eggs in spring flowers and onion skins and then boiling them to create patterns and colours as natural dyes. Other local people (along with a small team of needleworkers from my home town) were involved in stitching the extracts from the *Rydal Journals* into the bed linen, and described how the slow, precise stitching gave them a closer understanding of Dorothy. For one needleworker, who 'over a period of three weeks spent a couple of hours most days reproducing one page of her journal', the stitching immersed her in Dorothy's remembered walks, while another described how the stitching drew her closer in:

> the character and life of Dorothy began to emerge as a real person with both friendships and concern about her health very much at the front of her mind.[6]

---

[6] Jean Simpson and Liz Bagley, Sanctuary Guild member, Lancaster Priory Church, emails to the author, 2018.

The needlework team were proud of their work and their responses suggest how this sort of creative social engagement (also seen in *Mulliontide*, for example, with the making of the flag) generates an empathetic immersion that brings participants closer to the subject matter and points to scenographic processes having a value and transformative significance of their own.

Effects of Dorothy's Room

Dorothy's Room was exhibited at Rydal Mount for the summer season of 2018. The installation became a means by which people could empathize with Dorothy's circumstance and how she became limited to a single room. For one visitor guide at Rydal Mount (Hazel Seddon), the installation:

> showed a great understanding of the effects of dementia – or an inability through ill health to no longer be able to continue with things they enjoyed in the past – but how, with prompts, through words and objects – could remember and reminisce.[7]

Hazel went on to say how 'the visual imagery of Rydal [the room, house and garden] overlaid with images of memories' was resonant and moving because her father-in-law was 'very unwell with dementia'.[8]

One visitor to *Dorothy's Room*, Wallace Heim, wrote how, for her, the 'film and the spilling and embroidered bed' became an 'embodiment of Dorothy's imagination … she, and the need for and recompense of poetry and memory, felt very close'.[9] Wallace's empathy for Dorothy and her situation was poignant because Wallace was herself no longer able to walk the fells as she once had.[10] Later she described the installation and its themes to her neighbour, Joanna McLaren, who, once an avid walker, responded by saying: 'That's exactly what I'm going through!'[11] This moment of exchange between two frustrated walkers, along with Joanna's recognition of Dorothy's plight, led to her, like Wallace, participating in *Women's Walks to Remember*.

Siting *Dorothy's Room* in an interior space within a visitor attraction meant I was able to create an immersive environment that a large number of viewers could access, including people who were themselves unable to walk extended distances or in rural terrain. Furthermore, though site-specific in its original

---

[7] Hazel Seddon, Rydal Mount visitor guide, email to the author, 30 August 2018.
[8] Hazel Seddon, Rydal Mount visitor guide, email to the author, 30 August 2018.
[9] Wallace Heim, email to the author, 16 December 2018.
[10] Wallace Heim was a *Women's Walks to Remember* participant.
[11] Wallace Heim, email to the author, 10 October 2018.

form, because the installation does not involve a live performance element and is made of easily transportable component parts, it can be relocated to other comparable spaces, including in galleries and visitor sites, but also in care homes, hospices and other healthcare settings. The ability to relocate this work adds to its accessibility and therapeutic reach.

Women's Walks to Remember – surrogate walking

To find participants for *Women's Walks to Remember*, I put a call out asking recipients to contact me if they had a significant walk that they are no longer able to manage but remember vividly. The women who volunteered were no longer able to walk due to the effects of ageing, illness or being a full-time carer. All felt the loss and impact of no longer being able to walk, and genuinely longed for the fells. Some women who made contact were close to the end of their life, and some were recently bereaved and remained overwhelmed by the feelings and memories their walk would bring. Some participants became involved through serendipity and chance meetings. For example, whilst walking in the footsteps of Dorothy Wordsworth, I had an unplanned meeting with the Tuesday Walkers. This group, explained their leader Sue Faulkner, was 'started about 34 years ago by an amazing walker called Jill Peel but now, aged 89 this week, Jill couldn't do the walks with us anymore'.[12] The group continues though, and walks 'every week whatever the weather':

> We just love walking. We're all over 60. I'm over 70. It's just women that walk. You chat to everybody about things that have gone wrong, by the time you've got to the end it's all sorted out.[13]

I explained to Sue and the group why I was out walking – in the footsteps of Dorothy Wordsworth – and that I was looking for present-day women walkers who were no longer able to walk as they once had, and who might therefore be interested in participating in a memory-walking project. Jill, who had dedicated much of her life to long-distance fell walking in the Lake District and Scotland, and had changed many women's lives through the Tuesday Walkers, would be ideal and enthusasitic about the idea of the project. A few days later, I was sent Jill's contact details and permission to telephone her. A few weeks

---

[12] Extracts from an audio recording I made of my conversation with Sue Faulkner and the Tuesday Walkers.
[13] Extracts from an audio recording I made of my conversation with Sue Faulkner and the Tuesday Walkers.

after that, I drove to Jill's house in West Cumbria where she undertook the memory-walk mapping process.

Co-creation – memory-walk mapping

Before meeting each memory-walk participant, I sent a series of questions designed to gather walk-specific and person-specific information, and to help the participant begin the process of remembering details about their walk and gathering associated materials such as photos and objects:

1. Where did the walk begin and end, and what route did it follow?
2. How often did the walk happen, what were its reasons and purpose, and did the participant walk alone or with others?
3. Were there any specific features, sights, sounds, stopping points or activities associated with the walk?
4. Why was the walk no longer possible?

When meeting each participant, we worked through their answers and talked. I made voice recordings of these conversations, not to share publicly, but for my own record and to avoid the distraction of taking notes during the dialogue. Following a detailed conversation about the remembered walk, enhanced by photos and objects, each participant drew a memory-map that could be pictorial, graphic or abstract and used line, colour or symbols. After each meeting I transcribed the conversations and used them to write a poem, which later became a layer in the storyboard/memory card that externalized the remembered landscapes and made them visible, firstly to the participant involved and then to others who saw the cards when I showed them in a number of exhibitions – sharing the walks in this way gave them a further level of significance and exposed them to a wider audience.[14]

Together, the memory-mapping and distillation formed a process of co-creation that valued the voices and landscapes of the women involved. This process recognized the importance of each particular walk, the part it had played in the participant's daily, family, work or community life, and how it formed part of their identity, health and sense of well-being. The reasons and purposes for walking and the impact of not walking were varied, and the loss of walking was one that many were still adjusting to.

---

[14] Exhibtions include: *This Girl Did: Dorothy Wordsworth and Women's Mountaineering* (1 September–23 December 2018), Wordsworth Grasmere; *Landlines* (4–14 September 2019), Royal Geographical Society, London; *'Moments of Being': Mountain, Cave, Coast* (7–27 November 2019), Archive Gallery, Heaton Cooper Studio, Grasmere.

'Margaret Crayston's Upper Eskside Walk: "As a child I walked this valley every day"'

Margaret Crayston explained how walking was part of her life going back to her childhood, when she walked 'to run errands, to take sheep to the fell, to feed the hens, to play-out with my six siblings, to pick bilberries for a pie,

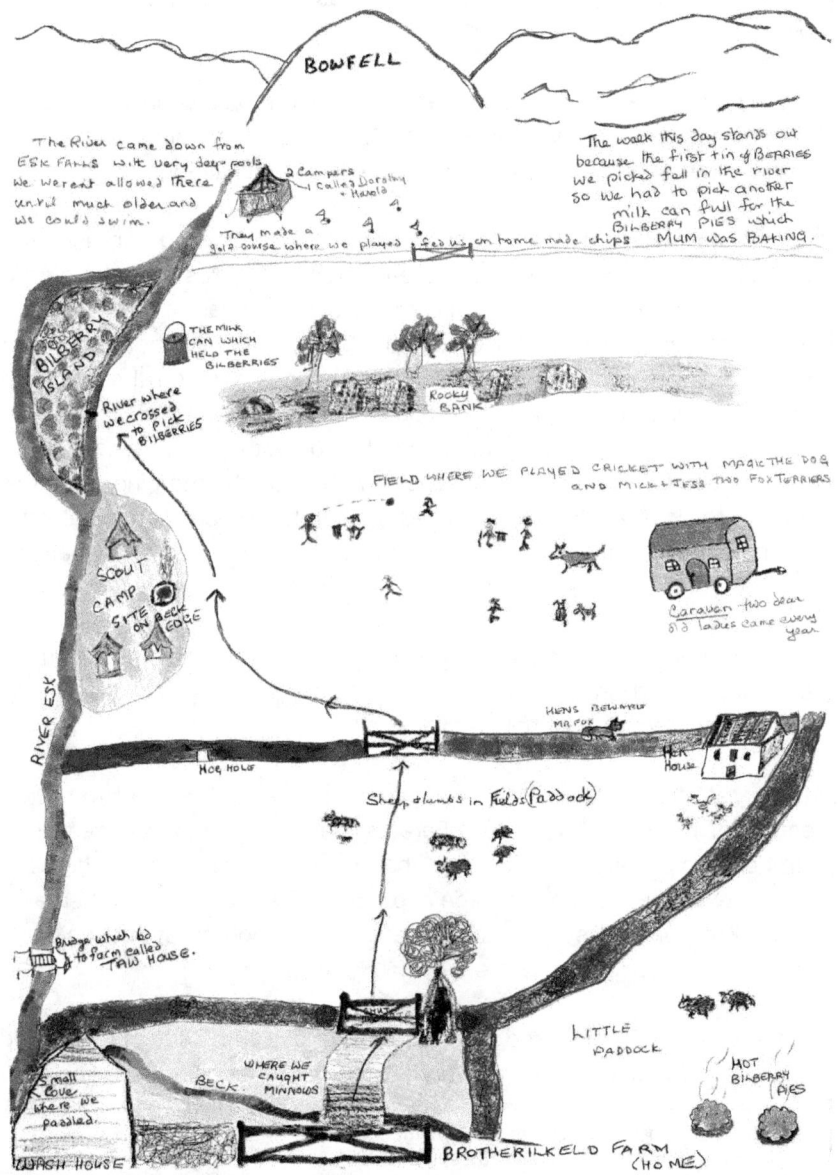

FIGURE 7.3 Women's Walks to Remember. *'Margaret Crayston's Upper Eskside Walk: "As a child I walked this valley every day"'. Drawn by Margaret Crayston*

to reach deep pools in the river where we went swimming'. Now, however, being less mobile and the sole carer for her husband, she 'didn't get out much' and, as her daughter Linda Broughton explained, she 'had lost some sense of her as her own person'.[15] Being involved in the project took her:

> back to happy times and memories and seemed to give her a confidence boost and an adventure of her own, that was about her, as a person in her own right, not about her roles.[16]

During my first meeting with Margaret, she took me on a short walk into the valley she visited every summer, a 'place full of so many happy memories'.[17] Her map, drawn following our trip to Eskdale, was pictorial with written annotations – it showed trees and rocks, the river and the bilberry island, tracks and gates, tents in the Scout camp, children playing games, foxes, sheep, hens outside a henhouse and steaming bilberry pies. At the top of the page was Bowfell and the skyline of other fells at the head of the valley.

The photographs Margaret shared were from her family photo album and were taken in the early 1950s. These sepia images showed the landscape features and objects, activities and people she had included in her map, and one of her as a child with her two sisters. Her object was a milk-can used to take milk to campers, collect berries and carry tea. On the morning of my walk with Margaret, her family 'noticed the change in her mood', and speaking on the phone she 'sounded so much more positive and upbeat, in anticipation of the outing'.[18] This positive impact:

> lasted for several weeks and created a space where seated at the kitchen table she talked and laughed with her family recalling, as if yesterday, stories and memories of her Eskside Walk.[19]

For Margaret and her family, the project gave space for Margaret to have an adventure of her own, but also a shared experience – a joint endeavour of remembering a place of significance – that had a positive effect on the whole family. For example, her object made another link between her and her family that prompted shared stories, conversation and laughter, about which her daughter, Linda Broughton, wrote:

> a battered milk can was used for so much through Mum's and my childhoods as well. Talking about it me and my brother were laughing recalling some

---

[15] Linda Broughton, email to the author, 18 September 2018.
[16] Linda Broughton, email to the author, 18 September 2018.
[17] Linda Broughton, email to the author, 18 September 2018.
[18] Linda Broughton, email to the author, 10 July 2018.
[19] Linda Broughton, email to the author, 10 July 2018.

memories of taking tea to Dad in the fields when it was haytime and using the same can to pick blackberries.[20]

'Wallace Heim's Low Wood Walk: "My heart goes out with you"'

For Wallace Heim, walking was a 'time to reflect, look around and ease [her] thoughts' following a morning spent writing. But arthritic knees had made walking painful – she was trying, but having 'a lot of trouble' accepting that she did not 'walk anymore'. For her, the impact of this loss was 'huge' and was reflected in her choice of the pair of walking boots that now sit unused on the shelf as an object.

As I set off on her walk, following her map, Wallace said she felt a 'bit of melancholy' but also that: 'It's great to have somebody do the walk … At least the places that know my feet … will know somebody else's feet.'

'Joanna McLaren's Catbells Walk: "My last Wainwright"'

Joanna McLaren started walking when she moved back to the Lakes following a divorce. Walking, she said, gave her 'something for herself', and she soon found she loved traversing the fells she had lived in as a child and still called home. But osteoarthritis had made walking impossible. 'My joints are too bad. It's painful, and I'm slow', she said. 'Now, I walk in my memory.'

Joanna's map used a looped line to show the circuitous route of her significant walk, which she marked with stopping places for lunch, coffee and playing games with her grandchildren. She also used crosses to mark the places where her father's, mother's and brother's ashes are scattered. She shared sepia-coloured photographs from her family album that showed her as a toddler in the valley and with her father and mother, as well as photos she had taken on her last Catbells walk with her grandchildren. Her named object was the 'memories of a very happy day' she held inside.

'Harriet Fraser's Brigsteer Woods Walk: "Once daily, and the holders of years"'

Facing the possibility that she 'might have had [her] last walk' due to the immobilizing effects of what at the time was diagnosed as ME (now referred to as Chronic Fatigue Syndrome (CFS)), Harriet Fraser mapped (and took me on) a walk that led to many trees. One tree, the Brigsteer beech, dominated her map. On days when she could walk a few steps, she would visit this tree and lean into it, letting it support her body for a time and nourish her spirit. Her

---

[20] Linda Brougthon, email to the author, 10 July 2018.

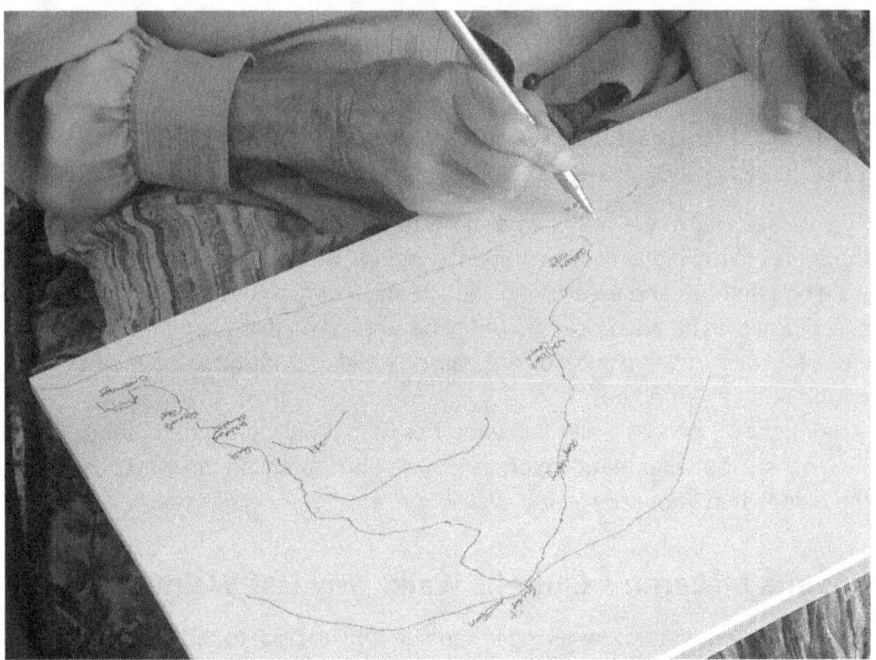

FIGURE 7.4 Women's Walks to Remember. *Jill Peel drawing her memory-map: 'Black Combe Circuit Walk: "I envy you going for a walk"'*. Photographer: Louise Ann Wilson

object was a fossil and her photo, taken from a lying-down position, captured a summer meadow teaming with wild flowers. For Harriet, the walk, the tree, the fossil and the meadow now hold memories of illness and recovery.

'Jill Peel's Black Combe Circuit Walk: "I envy you going for a walk"'

Jill Peel walked Black Coombe, her chosen fell, 'every day as practice before walking across Scotland'. Walking was a central feature of her life and identity. She had 'walked all the fells in Cumbria', giving up gradually as she entered her late eighties. Her walking also played a significant and beneficial role in the lives of others. Her group, the Tuesday Walkers, brought health, companionship and a 'different way' of looking and thinking to many other women, and she felt pride when the local doctor told her 'you've done more for the women of Millom than all the pills I've given them'. As I set off to follow in her footsteps, she said: 'I envy you going for a walk.'

Jill's map used a series of simple lines and three colours – blue, yellow and black – to suggest precisely and graphically the contours and shape of the physical landscape. She used place names to locate each line. As she drew, it became clear she was remembering every footstep, turn, rise and feature – this was a long walk – and her spatial mapping captured the distances and the step ascents and descents. She shared photo albums and a logbook in which she had 'recorded all the people who've ever been up Black Combe and other Lakeland Fells with her, and there were many'.

Storyboard/memory card – returning the walk to the rememberer

Once the walks were mapped and rewalked, my next step was to turn all the materials gathered into the bespoke storyboard/memory cards. My intention was to make a tangible and visual artwork, to validate each person's experiences of walking and not walking, and to collect a permanent record of walks linking people to places that can be shared with others. The project and the cards also brought a sense of companionship to the women who took part, even though they didn't meet each other. One participant, Wallace Heim, described how 'it felt good to be accompanied by the other women whose walks you walked'.[21]

These memory cards were folded to form a many-sided concertina-style card that incorporated multiple layers of montaged material that together created a visual palimpsest that captured both the physical landscape of the remembered walk and also the walker's internal (remembered) terrain.

On one side of the card was the walker's name and the title of their walk. Set next to this was a photograph sent to me by the walker that encapsulated a significant memory: a smiling girl and her mother by a drystone wall, a blue doorway surrounded by sweet peas, a flower meadow lit by golden sunshine, a montage of photos showing the 'Tuesday Walkers' out in the fells, a sepia photo of three children (sisters) huddled in front of a farmhouse. Overlaying these photos – on semi-transparent paper – was a line drawing of the object, significant to each walk: a heart-shaped rock found by a cairn, a pair of walking boots, a fossil found in the flower meadow, a milk-can used to collect blackberries, a logbook detailing decades of walking trips.

On another page, a geographical map showed the route and describes key features and stopping places, activities that can be undertaken on the way (paddling, brambling, hide and seek, lying down, picnicking, collecting stones) and sights and sounds to look and listen for. This information was overlaid with another line drawing: Margaret on a narrow path by the river, Wallace gathering vegetables in her allotment, Harriet leaning into her beech tree, Joanna's hands searching her Wainwright route guide, Jill's hands drawing her memory-map. On the other side of the card, there was a present-day photograph of each woman and a copy of her hand-drawn memory-map, then another photograph: a close-up of harebells, heather and blackberries, the curved line

---

[21] Wallace Heim, email to the author, 16 December 2019.

and texture of a fossil, a view from a summit showing the patterns of fields below and the vast sea in the distance, a collection of sepia photos taken in the 1950s showing a family on holiday in a caravan, children playing in the stream and a closed gate onto Bowfell (a Lake District mountain). Further along the page, a poem that distilled the walker's words and memories and captured their remembered walk was overlaid with a line drawing of Brotherilkeld (Margaret's family farm) and Bowfell, Harriet's hand feeling the bark on a tree, Wallace cutting flowers in her allotment and the front of her cottage, the house Joanna was born in that nestled under Catbells, a mountain in the Lake District, which she called:

A place of sanctuary where my father's ashes were scattered.
A place of beauty where my mother's ashes were scattered.
A place of happiness where my brother's ashes were scattered.
A place of happiness that now, I walk in my memory.

(Wilson 2018–19)

The words above, spoken by Joanna and written as a poem by me, are an extract of a longer poem layered into her storyboard/memory card. After receving the card, Joanna wrote me a postcard to say: 'I was so very pleased to have your card & the work you have done on my Catbells Walk. So lovely to relive that afternoon'.[22] In a further letter sent later in the year – when due to the COVID-19 pandemic lockdowns she was house- and garden-bound – Joanna wrote to say her apprecation of the project continued and the storyboard/memory card had prompted her to walk the fell in her imagination 'many times and from all approaches'.[23]

Memory-mapping – multiple applications

The potential applications of the *Walks to Remember* methodology are significant and multiple. To date, as well using memory-mapping with walking, creative and writing groups, I have applied the technique in clinical, care and community/social settings such as care homes, hospices and hospitals, where maps can be drawn on behalf of a person unable to make one themselves. The project offers an accessible methodology that can be applied when working one to one or in groups, in person or via digital platforms (Zoom, Skype, Teams, etc.), and across a range of situations and circumstances – medical,

---

[22] Joanne McLaren, postcard to the author, postmarked 30 April 2020.
[23] Joanne McLaren, letter to the author, 23 August 2020.

therapeutic and social – where mobility is limited and/or physical distancing is required. Furthermore, as the population ages and mobility is challenged, loneliness increases and periods of isolation arise or are required – such as lockdowns imposed during the global COVID-19 pandemic.

For example, during the first UK lockdown in March 2020, I applied the memory-mapping methodology to a project entitled *Walks to Remember During a Pandemic* that invited participants to map or draw a memorable walk or place using abstraction, words, lines, symbols or pictures and with materials close to hand: pencil, crayon, felt-tip or a combination. Some worked alone, liaising at a distance with family, friends, students and colleagues they were unable to visit due to lockdown restrictions. Some used the mapping process to return to places of significance from times past, while others drew places such as Cornwall, Italy or China that ordinarily they would have visited in person. For one memory-mapper, not only did the drawing 'engage her with place memories', but it also led her to 'go through many of the photographs I took from the neighbourhood, which made my own memory walk even richer'.[24] Another remarked how 'Just imagining the route and my thoughts around it has been very absorbing',[25] later adding 'what a labour of joy and love it [the memory-mapping] has been … there are so many memories of people woven into the walk'.[26]

During the national *Creative Adventures in Dementia: A Life More Ordinary* festival (2018), I led a series of memory-mapping workshops with people living with dementia, family and carers, healthcare professionals, researchers and artists working in the field of dementia and healthcare. One workshop participant, Jenn Mattinson, who, in her role as an intergenerational creative practitioner at Theatre by the Lake in Keswick, Cumbria, works with people living with dementia, found that the memory-mapping methodology offered her 'great insight into the very flexible and freeing way [of working]', adding that it offered 'an approach which has the potential to open up a world of discovery' that she would take forward into her own practice.[27]

The flexibility and liberating nature of the memory-mapping process, as expressed by Mattinson, means the technique can be applied in other social settings and situations where verbal communication may not be possible – for example, with marginalized individuals or groups such as displaced people, refugees and migrants, adoptive families, and ill or traumatized children for whom words and language are not always available or adequate.

---

[24] Madlen Kobi, email to the author, 2020.
[25] Awena Carter, email to the author, 20 May 2020.
[26] Awena Carter, email to the author, 30 September 2020.
[27] Jenn Mattinson, email to the Dukes Theatre, Lancaster, 25 May 2018.

Drawing it out – collaborative scenographic drawing and mapping

The various scenographic mapping/drawing methodologies I have developed from *Warnscale* to the present have been taken up and applied practically by social scientists. One such researcher is the social anthropologist Stine Willum Adrian (Aalborg University, Denmark) who now uses my drawing/mapping techniques as part of her research process with interviewees taking part in the research project entitled 'Technologies of Death and Dying at the Beginning of Life (Technodeath)' (2019–current). These techniques, she reports, have allowed her to 'extend her interview-based approach with parents who have lost a child due to hypoplastic left heart syndrome' and in so doing 'explore more deeply the technological decisions they have taken in relation to the death of a child'.[28] The mapping/drawing approach she has now adopted has been:

> exceptionally good as it enables exploring new layers of thought and emotions, including conceptual and personal thinking together, that speaking does not do.[29]

Willum Adrian's adoption of drawing/mapping techniques began when she joined a practical memory-mapping workshop I led as part of an exhibition of my practice curated to coincide with a European Association for the Study of Science and Technology (EASST (STS)) Conference in 2018 at Lancaster University, and found the process 'eye opening'.[30] Using the Warnscale mapping-walks as examples, the workshop invited participants to draw a mind-map of a life event that had particular significance to them. In response, Willum Adrian drew a map in which she emplaced, through drawing, her experience of the death of her baby son due to hypoplastic left heart syndrome (a birth defect that affects normal blood flow through the heart). The map she drew, and named 'What If, What Then, What Now?: Landscapes of Grief', showed a hybridized landscape that morphed the real and the imagined, and used images, shapes, symbols and words: a heart with long spider-like tendrils that became paths and led to a multi peaked

---

[28] Stine Willum Adrian, email to the author, 15 August 2019.
[29] Stine Willum Adrian, email to the author, 29 July 2018.
[30] This exhibition (at the Peter Scott Gallery at Lancaster University) was entitled 'Sites of Transformation: Creating Life-Event Walks – A Meeting of Art, Landscape, People and Science' and explored the theme of 'meetings' from my perspective as a practicing scenographer and researcher.

and pointed mountain range, a box-like hospital building outside which ambulances blare, an intensive-care baby unit, a cloud of uncertainties, stick-figure children playing, and a memorial tree in bloom. Willum Adrian had never drawn-out her experience before, and the map revealed – to herself – unworked-through feelings and questions around a series of 'what ifs'. What if she had known more/had different information about her son's condition during her pregnancy? What, if anything, might she have done differently? Following the conference, Willum Adrian made contact, saying:

> There was so much in your work that resonated with my thinking on so many levels. Not least, I am trying to think of how I can further develop a methodology that catches the 'what ifs'.[31]

Working via Skype, over the next six months, we undertook regular, one-to-one creative and research exchanges during which we used scenographic drawing methods to pursue shared themes of loss in relation to motherhood. Both of us created multiple drawings that took us deeper into the inner – and at times painful – terrain of our experiences. Working together but at a distance, we were able to hold the space for each other and both dared to draw these inner landscapes, and internalized feelings, out onto the page, without censorship. Willum Adrian described how each of these 'mappings made me think a lot, not least that I need to get deeper into the emotions at stake', adding:

> Although I am not used to drawing or maybe because of that – drawing has enabled thoughts and ideas that I would not have learned otherwise [and] gives time to 'explore the places' that otherwise would be forgotten – it is those places where the important issues are at stake.[32]

In time, the drawing process served both as a preparation for the interviews, and an auto-ethnographic work Willum Adrian undertook with 'her interviewees' – parents who like her had lost children to heart disease. The process became a technique in those interviews for 'accessing and making visible experiences that were hard to grasp and voice, partly forgotten, or buried deep within'.[33]

---

[31] Stine Willum Adrian, email to the author, 15 August 2019.
[32] Stine Willum Adrian, email to the author, 15 August 2019.
[33] Stine Willum Adrian, email to the author, 15 August 2019.

Final reflection

The methodologies explored in this book show how the scenography and social science elements of the process have become inextricably linked, co-existent and co-creative. Used at all stages of a project, from the making to the delivery of a final performance work, these multimodal methods are designed to transcend language by incorporating two- and three-dimensional image making in mapping and drawing exchanges, montage and storytelling, objects and performance – a process that connects directly with participants and enables them to share or express their own life-event story.

My approach builds on the growth of arts-based research in social science contexts that understands art as 'a way of knowing, problem solving, healing and transformation' (McNiff 2013: xiii) and as sharing close affinities with social science research methods, 'including keen observational skills, analytic skill, story-telling proficiency, and the ability to think conceptually, symbolically and metaphorically' (Leavy 2015: 18). The collaborative methodologies I discuss match calls for 'forms of attentiveness that can admit the fleeting, distributed, multiple, sensory, emotional and kinaesthetic aspects of sociality' (Back and Puwar 2012: 28).

The scenographic creative methods I use in my practice – mapping-walks, memory-mappings and drawing exchanges – engage and connect directly with people, and enable individuals and groups to voice their own stories. These methods can be applied to a range of life-event subjects, situations and circumstances, beyond the subject matters that my practice has pursued. Though my practice largely focuses on performance works made in rural landscapes, the techniques and methods explored in this book are applicable to scenography made across any number and type of places and environments – rural, urban, domestic, private and public.

Furthermore, because scenography is a visual, spatial and multisensory art form that transcends language, work made in this way can engage transient groupings or create temporary communities that come together to give a voice to a specific concern. The book has sought to demonstrate that the possibilities for socially engaged and applied scenography are multiple. It points towards a field of practice that is not only rich in significance but also diverse in its purpose and application.

Appendices

Appendix A – production credits: *Fissure* (2011), Ingleborough Fells, Yorkshire Dales, Yorkshire, UK

Creator, director, designer and scenographer: Louise Ann Wilson
Writer: Elizabeth Burns
Choreographer: Nigel Stewart
Composer: Jocelyn Pook

Neurological consultant/collaborators/performers:
Michael Brada (neuro-oncologist), formerly Professor of Clinical Oncology, Royal Marsden Hospital, London (currently Professor of Radiation Oncology, University of Liverpool), Andrew McEvoy (neurosurgeon), The National Hospital for Neurology and Neurosurgery, Chris Clark (neurophysicist and imager), Professor of Imaging and Biophysics, University College London

Landscape consultants/performers: Dr Mike Kelly (geophysicist) Colin Newlands (conservationist, Natural England), Duncan Morrison (caver, Above and Below), a team of Mountain Leaders

Liturgical structure and Norber Erratics consultant: Professor John Rodwell
Palliative Care consultant: Professor Shelia Payne, Lancaster University

Dancers: Fania Grigoriou, Jennifer Essex, Julia Griffin, Luisa Lazzaro, Noora Kela, Sonja Perreten
Musicians and singers: Alice Grant, Martina Schwarz, Mikhail Karikis, Olivia Chaney, Sally Davies, Vivien Ellis
Choral singers: Alisun Pawley, Jeff Wallcook, Cara Curran, Sarah Wallcock
Bell ringers: St James Church, Clapham and Kirby Lonsdale Handbell Ringers

Commissioners and producers: Artevents as part of 'The Re-Enchantment' (2010–11) (http://www.artevents.info/projects/current/the-re-enchantment) with Louise Ann Wilson Company Ltd (LAW Co.)
Supporters: Yorkshire Dales National Park, Ingleborough Nature Reserve, Natural England, Ingleborough Estates, Ingleborough Cave and Settle to Carlisle Railway
Funders: Arts Council England, the Performing Rights Society and the Paul Hamlyn Foundation

Appendix B – production credits: *Ghost Bird* (2012), Langden Valley, Trough of Bowland, Lancashire, UK

Creator, director, designer and scenographer: Louise Ann Wilson
Choreographer: Nigel Stewart
Sound designer: Lisa Whistlecroft
Film editor: Janan Yakula
Dancer: Julia Griffin
Pointing People: Jim Hendley, Lowri Jones, Alastair Walker
Life models/performers: Carol Ackroyd, Gill Ainsworth, Lucy Archbould, Charlotte Bizsewski, Linda Bradshaw, Michael Bradshaw, Sarah Durham, Robert Ferguson, Karen Forshaw, Susan Hill, Janet House, Rob Hudson, Lisa Hunn, Anne Lees, Dandy Lion, Les Mac, Howard Mansfield, Julie Moosburg, Frances Panchoo, Steve Ritter, Martin Rowe, Yvonne Rowe, Mo Schofield, Neil Schofield, Caf Smith, John Tunney, Nick Verrall, Sheila Winstanley, Richard Worral, Neil Younghusband
Landscape Consultants: Jude Laine (RSPB) and Dr Mike Kelly (geophysicist)

Production manager: Peter Reed
Project assistant: Lowri Jones
Stage managers: Lesley Chernery, Craig Davidson, Shona Wright
Installation assistants: David Honeybone, Carla Monvid, Dorrie Scott
Front of house coordinator: Ele Kinchin-Smith
Front of house assistants: Dominic Halladay, Derek Tarr

Supporters: landowners (United Utilities) and their tenants, Forest of Bowland Area of Outstanding Natural Beauty, RSPB hen harrier experts
Commissioners and funders: Green Close Studios and Lancaster Arts as part of Lancashire Witches 400 Programme (https://greenclose.org/lancashire-witches-400/)
Producers: LAW Co.

Appendix C – production credits: *The Gathering* (2014), Hafod y Llan Farm, Snowdonia, Wales, UK

Creator, director, designer, scenographer: Louise Ann Wilson
Writer: Gillian Clarke
Additional writing: Louise Ann Wilson
Choreography: Nigel Stewart
Music consultation: John Hardy Music
Sound and film recorder, director, designer: Louise Ann Wilson
Additional sound recording and editing: Tic Ashfield
Film technical editing: Janan Yakula
Assistant designer: Dorrie Scott

Actors: Ffion Dafis, Emyr Gibson, Gwyn Vaughan Jones, Gwion Aled Williams, Meilir Rhys Williams
Aerial artist: Kate Lawrence
Shepherds: Bryn Griffiths, Roger Hughes, Elgan Jones, Trefor Jones, Arwyn Owen, Tudur Parry, Andrew Roberts, Arthurs Williams and their dogs
Musicians: Deiniolen Band
Archive photographs presented by the children of Beddgelert School

Production manager: Jacob Gough
Project manager: Fiona Curtis
Costume supervisor: Angharad Matthews
Design assistants: Ruby Spencer-Pugh, Phoebe Tonkin, David Honeybone, Stefan Gwyn
Tramway inclines aerial rigger: Simon Edwards

Hafod y Llan Farm office manager: Wynn Owen
Ecologist: Sabine Nouvet
Additional members: Stage managers, guides and mountain leaders
Family history adviser: Bleddyn Williams
Local history adviser: Gwenant Roberts
Producer and funders: National Theatre Wales with Migrations and LAW Co.
Supporters: the Hafod y Llan Farm team and the National Trust, with additional support from Snowdonia National Park

The Gathering formed part of my Practice as Research PhD in Theatre at Lancaster Institute for the Contemporary Arts, Lancaster University, UK

Appendix D – production credits (launch-walk and published walking guide/art book): *Warnscale* (2015), Warnscale Fells, Buttermere, Cumbria, UK

Creator, writer, designer and scenographer: Louise Ann Wilson
Publisher: LAW Co. Ltd, Leeds
Printer: Bowmans, Leeds
Digital book layout: Gareth Dennison, Morph Films, Lancaster
Producers: Peter Reed and Louise Ann Wilson

Mapping-walk participants: SB, AD, LE, PG, RG, RGi, JH, JK, NK, KS, MZ
Fertility and social science consultants: Joyce Harper, Institute for Women's Health, UCL; Celia Roberts, College of Arts and Social Sciences, Australia National University (formerly Lancaster University); Jody Day, Gateway Women; Wanda Georgiades and CARE Fertility Group; embryology team, Centre for Reproductive & Genetic Health, London; Archivists, Wellcome Trust

Landscape, literary and local consultants and support: Mr Richardson, Gatesgarth Farm; Honister Slate Quarry; Old School House, Buttermere; Museum of Lakeland Life and Industry; Mike Kelly (geophysicist); Mark Astley, National Trust; Jean Johnston (botanist), Natural England; Denis Mollison, Mountain Bothies Association; Helen Turton (mountain leader); Armitt Museum; Jeff Cowton (curator), Wordsworth Grasmere; Simon Bainbridge, Lancaster University

Funders: Arts Council England, the Arts & Humanities Research Council and the Seedbed Trust
Supporter: the Lancaster Institute for Contemporary Arts, Lancaster University

Warnscale formed part of my Practice as Research PhD in Theatre at Lancaster Institute for the Contemporary Arts, Lancaster University, UK

Appendix E – production credits: *Mulliontide* performance (2016) and published guide book (2017), Mullion, Lizard Peninsula, Cornwall, UK

Creator, director, designer and scenographer: Louise Ann Wilson
Collaborators and performers: Mullion Women's Institute Arts and Crafts Group: Beryl Cullen, Carolyn Marshall, Kay Woodall, Margaret Evans, Suzanne Stephens; residents and staff at Poldhu Care Home: Evelyn Sly, Muriel Woods, Sidney Francis Jenkins (Francis), Marie Withers, Vera Wilton, Elaine Wicks, Harold Potter, Gemma Conroy, Julie Bird; Saul Ridley (surfer and specialist palliative care nurse); Justin Whitehouse (Countryside Manager, National Trust, Lizard and Penrose); Mary Cooper Brown and St Mellanus Singers: Gail Lyons, Russ Stanland and Charlotte Douglas; Wendy Williamson (walker of Meres cliffs); Diana Davis (botanical artist); Bob Felce (photographer and local historian); Barry Mundy and Jonny Pascoe (fishermen); Hannah Hawkins (flotsam and jetsam artist, Seacoast Studio); Paul and Patricia Pearson and Joanna Cummings (Porthmellin Tearooms); Briony Tonkins (Mullion Flowers)

Project assistant: David Honeybone
Production assistants: Amos Jacob with Soča Kodrič, Mája Ditrtová, Tasha Plant, Giedrė Makauskaitė

Producers: Golden Tree Productions with LAW Co.
Part of *Miss You Already* produced by Natalia Eernstman for Golden Tree Productions
Funders: the National Trust, the Culture Capital Exchange, the University of Exeter, FEAST and the Real Idea Organisations

Appendix F – production credits: *Dorothy's Room* (2018), Rydal Mount, Ambleside, Cumbria, UK

Creator, designer, scenographer: Louise Ann Wilson
Project assistant: David Honeybone
Hand embroiderers: Liz Bagley, Catherine Bartlett, Lois Kirtley, Jean Simpson
Pace Eggs maker: Anne Wills
Film and sound director: Louise Ann Wilson
Film editor: Janan Yakula
Sound editor: Lisa Whistlecroft

Producer: LAW Co.
Funders: Wordsworth Grasmere, the Faculty of Arts and Social Science (Diversifying Wordsworth Project) Arts Strategy Fund and a FASS impact grant from Lancaster University, Lancaster Arts at Lancaster University, wilson+wilson, Women's Studies and Sociology, Lancaster University, EASST

Appendix G – production credits: *Women's Walks to Remember: 'With memory I was there'* (2018–19), Wordsworth Grasmere, Grasmere, Cumbria, UK

Creator, designer, writer: Louise Ann Wilson
Walk rememberers: Linda Broughton, Margaret Crayston, Jill Peel, the Tuesday Walkers (led by Sue Falkner), Wallace Heim, Harriet Fraser, Joanna McLaren, Harold Potter

Funders: Wordsworth Grasmere, the Faculty of Arts and Social Sciences at Lancaster University, Lancaster Arts at Lancaster University, wilson+wilson
Producer: LAW Co.
Supporter: Rydal Mount and the Wordsworth family

References

Andrews, Malcolm (1999), *Landscape and Western Art*, Oxford: Oxford University Press.
Aronson, Arnold ([1981] 2018), *The History of Environmental Scenography*, Ann Arbor, MI: UMI Research Press.
Ashcroft, Bill (1998), *Key Concepts in Post-colonial Studies*, London: Routledge.
Back, Les and Nirmal Puwar (eds.) (2012), 'A Manifesto for Live Methods: Provocations and Capacities', *Sociological Review*, Monograph Series, 6–12.
Bainbridge, Simon (2008), *Romanticism: A Sourcebook*, Basingstoke: Palgrave Macmillan.
Bainbridge, Simon (2013), *Wordsworth Walks in Three Parts Including 'Reflections on My Life's Journey'*, Grasmere: Wordsworth Trust (Wordsworth Grasmere).
Bainbridge, Simon (2015), 'William Wordsworth: Poetry, People and Place: 4.8. The Rock of Names', *Future Learn / Lancaster University*. Available online: https://www.mooc-list.com/course/william-wordsworth-poetry-people-and-place-futurelearn?static=true (accessed 1 September 2021).
Banham, Simon, Michael Brady, Sarah Hunter and Renny O'Shea (eds.) (2019), *Summer. Autumn. Winter. Spring. Staging Life and Death*, Manchester: Manchester University Press.
Barbauld, Anna Laetitia (1773), 'On the Pleasure Derived from Objects of Terror from Pieces in Prose' in 'Anna Letitia Aikin (later Barbauld) and John Aikin', *University of Pennsylvania*. Available online: http://www.english.upenn.edu/~mgamer/Etexts/barbauldessays.html. (accessed 8 June 2014).
Barone, Tom and Elliot Eisner (2012), *Arts Based Research*, London: Sage.
Barrett, Estelle (2007), 'Experiential Learning in Practice as Research: Context, Method, Knowledge', *Journal of Visual Art Practice*, 6(2): 115–214.
Battersby, Christine (2007), *The Sublime, Terror and Human Difference*, Abingdon: Routledge.
Baugh, Christopher L. (2012), 'Scenography with Purpose: Activism and Intervention' in Arnold Aronson (ed.), *The Disappearing Stage: Reflections on the 2011 Prague Quadrennial*, Prague: Institut umění – Divadelní ústav, 36–49.
Baugh, Christopher L. (2013), *Theatre, Performance and Technology: The Development and Transformation of Scenography*, 2nd edn, Basingstoke: Palgrave Macmillan.
Baugh, Christopher L. (2017), 'Devices of Wonder: Globalizing Technologies in the Process of Scenography' in Joslin McKinney and Scott Palmer (eds.), *Scenography Expanded: Contemporary Perspectives on Performance Design*, London: Methuen Drama.
Beer, Tanja (2021), 'About', *Tanja Beer*. Available online: http://www.tanjabeer.com/about (accessed 4 May 2021).

REFERENCES

Bellis, Kate and Sally Matthews (2005), *Gathering: Hill Farming, People, Animals and Landscape*. Powys, Wales: Little Fish Press.

Bennett, Jane (2010), *Vibrant Matter: A Political Ecology of Things*, Durham, NC: Duke University Press.

Bennett, Susan (1990), *Theatre Audiences: A Theory of Production and Reception*, London: Routledge.

Berger, John (1972), *Ways of Seeing*, Harmondsworth: Penguin.

Bernstein, Jay Hillel (2015), 'Transdisciplinarity: A Review of Its Origins, Development, and Current Issues', *Journal of Research Practice*, 11(1): Article R1.

Bowen, Keith (1997), *Snowdon Shepherd: Four Seasons on the Hill Farms of North Wales*, Carmarthen: Gomer Press.

Brian, Kate (2015), 'Introduction to "Warnscale: A Landmark Walk Reflecting on In/Fertility and Childlessness" by Louise Ann Wilson', *Journal of Fertility Counselling*, 22(3): 24–8.

Brotherus, Elina (2013), 'Elina Brotherus' in *Home Truths: Photography and Motherhood*, ed. Susan Bright, London: Art Book Publishing, 84–93.

Brotherus, Elina (2015), *'Annunciation'* (2009–2013) (series of photographs) in *Carpe Fucking Diem*, Berlin: Krehrer Heidelberg.

Buchanan, Ian (2016), *A Dictionary of Critical Theory*, Oxford: Oxford University Press.

Burns, Elizabeth (1999), *The Gift of Light*, Edinburgh: Diehard Poetry.

Burns, Elizabeth (2011), *'Fissure*: cycle of poems' in Louise Ann Wilson (2011), creator and dir. *Fissure* (unpublished performance script), Yorkshire Dales, Yorkshire, England: Artevents with LAW Co.

Butterworth, Philip and Joslin McKinney (2009), *The Cambridge Introduction to Scenography*, Cambridge: Cambridge University Press.

Cade, Rosana (2011), '*Walking: Holding*', *Rosana Cade*. Available online: https://www.rosanacade.co.uk/walking-holding (accessed 2015).

Carlson, Ann (2011a), 'Picture Jasper Ridge Performance Hike', *Jasper Ridge Preserve, Stanford University*. Available online: https://jrbp.stanford.edu/news/picture-jasper-ridge-performance-hike (accessed 16 February 2020).

Carlson, Ann (2011b), 'Picture Jasper Ridge. A performance hike by artist, Ann Carlson.' [Vimeo], *Stanford Arts Institute*. Available online: https://vimeo.com/41388304 (accessed 16 February 2020).

Casey, Sarah and Gerald Davies (2015), 'Lines of Engagement: Drawing Walking Tracking', *Journal of Visual Art Practice*, 14(1): 72–83.

Chadwick, Whitney (2002), *Women, Art, and Society*, New York: Thames Hudson.

Clarke, Gillian (2014), '*The Gathering*: cycle of poems (The Woman's poems)' in Louise Ann Wilson (2014), creator and dir. *The Gathering / Yr Helfa* (unpublished performance script), Hafod y Llan Farm, Snowdonia, Wales: National Theatre Wales with Migrations and LAW Co.

Clarke, Gillian (2017), *Zoology*, Manchester: Carcanet Press.

Coleman, Simon and John Elsner (1995), *Pilgrimage Past and Present: Sacred Travel and Sacred Space in the World Religions*, London: British Museum Press.

Collier, Tony and Kate Green (2018), *Mindwalks* (exhibition catalogue).

Collins, Brigid and Kathleen Jamie (2013), *Frissures*, Edinburgh: Polgon Books.

REFERENCES

Collins, Jane and Andrew Nisbett (2010), *Theatre and Performance Design: A Reader in Scenography*, Abingdon: Routledge.

Culhane, Ann-Marie and Ruth Levene (2016), 'A Field of Wheat. What Was the Project About?', *Field of Wheat*. Available online: http://fieldofwheat.co.uk/about-the-project/ (accessed 10 October 2019).

Curious (2019), 'Artists' Projects: Curious, *Uproot*', *Artsadmin*. Available online: https://www.artsadmin.co.uk/project/uproot/ (accessed 10 July 2019).

Curran, Stuart (1993), *The Poems of Charlotte Smith*, New York: Oxford University Press.

Cumming, Naomi (1997), 'Grief Unconceived', London: Naomi Helen Cumming Foundation.

Day, Jody (2014), *Gateway Women*. Available online: http://gateway-women.com/ (accessed 1 January 2014).

De Sélincourt, Ernest (1933), *Dorothy Wordsworth: A Biography*, Oxford: The Clarendon Press.

DeSilvey, Caitlin, Simon Naylor and Colin Sackett (eds.) (2011), *Anticipatory History*, Cornwall: Uniform Books.

Di Benedetto, Stephen (2012), *An Introduction to Theatre Design*, Abingdon: Routledge.

Donald, Minty (2021a), 'Minty Donald', *Performance Ecology Heritage*. Available online: https://performanceecologyheritage.wordpress.com/portfolio/minty-donald/ (accessed 9 September 2021).

Donald, Minty (2021b), 'Professor Minty Donald. Research Interests', *School of Culture & Creative Arts, University of Glasgow*. Available online: https://www.gla.ac.uk/schools/cca/staff/mintydonald/#additionalinformation,researchinterests (accessed 9 September 2011).

Doughty, Karolina (2013), 'Walking Together: The Embodied and Mobile Production of a Therapeutic Landscape', *Health and Place*, 24: 140–6.

Fertility Fest (2016), *Fertility Fest*. Available online: https://fertilityfest.co.uk (accessed 1 April 2016).

Franklin, Sarah and Celia Roberts (2006), *Born and Made: An Ethnography of Preimplantation Genetic Diagnosis*, Princeton, New Jersey: Princeton University Press.

Fraser, Harriet and Robert Fraser. (2017), 'Yellow at the Wasdale Oak, May 9–15, 2016' in *The Long View: Two Years with Seven Remarkably Ordinary Trees*, Kendal: Somewhere Nowhere Press, 138–9.

French and Mottershead (2016), '*Woodland*', *French and Mottershead*. Available online: http://frenchmottershead.com/works/woodland/ (accessed 21 September 2021).

Fusco, Maria (2015), 'Maria Fusco's *Master Rock* from inside a Scottish mountain, presented with BBC Radio 4. Artangel', *e-flux Announcements*. Available online: https://www.e-flux.com/announcements/28842/maria-fusco-s-master-rock-from-inside-a-scottish-mountain-presented-with-bbc-radio-4/ (accessed 4 October 2021).

Gardner, Lyn (2014), '*The Gathering* review – sheep are the stars in Snowdon theatre show', *Guardian*, 15 September. Available online: https://www.theguardian.com/stage/2014/sep/15/the-gathering-review-national-theatre-wales-hafod-y-llan-snowdonia (accessed 15 September 2014).

Gatrell, Anthony C. (2013), 'Theraputic Mobilities: Walking and "Steps" to Well-Being', *Health and Place*, 22: 98–106.
Gesler, Wilbert M. (1992), 'Therapeutic Landscapes: Medical Issues in Light of the New Cultural Geography', *Social Science & Medicine*, 34(7): 735–46.
Gesler, Wilbert M. (1996), 'Lourdes: Healing in a Place of Pilgrimage' *Health & Place* 2(2): 95–105.
Golden Tree Productions (2016), *Miss You Already*, Cornwall, UK: Golden Tree Productions.
Gonzalez, Jennifer (1995), 'Autotopographies' in Gabriel Braham, Jr. and Mark Driscoll (eds.), *Prosthetic Territories: Politics and Hypertechnologies*, San Francisco, CA: Westview Press, 133–50.
Green, Kate (2017–2018), '*Mind Walks*', *Kate Green*. Available online: http://www.kate-green.co.uk/installation/4594182921 (accessed 1 September 2021).
Grosenick, Uta (ed.) (2001), *Women Artists in the 20th and 21st Century*, Cologne: Taschen.
Grout, Paul (2013), 'The Summerhouse at Rydal Hall', *Paul Grout Associates*. Available online: http://www.paulgroutassociates.co.uk/projects/rydal-summerhouse/ (accessed 7 June 2013).
Haedicke, Susan (2021), *Performing Farmscapes*, London: Palgrave Macmillan.
Hann, Rachel (2018), *Beyond Scenography*, London: Routledge.
Haraway, Donna J. (1988), 'Situated Knowledges: The Science Question in Feminism and the Privilege of Partial Perspective', *Feminist Studies*, 14: 575–99.
Haraway, Donna J. (2016), *Staying with the Trouble: Making Kin in the Chthulucene*, Durham, NC: Duke University Press.
Hawkins, Kirsten (2015) '*Lesions in the Landscape* by Shona Illingworth. A Report from Fact Liverpool', *Digicult*. Available online: http://digicult.it/news/lesions-in-the-landscape-an-interview-with-shona-illingworth/ (accessed 1 May 2019).
Heddon, Deirdre (2008), *Autobiography and Performance: Performing Selves*, Basingstoke: Palgrave Macmillan.
Heddon, Deirdre (2012), 'Turning 40: 40 Turns', *Performance Research*, 17: 67–75.
Heddon, Deirdre and Cathy Turner (2010), 'Walking Women: Interviews with Artists on the Move', *Performance Research*, 15: 14–22.
Heddon, Deirdre and Cathy Turner (2012), 'Walking Women: Shifting the Tales and Scales of Mobility', *Contemporary Theatre Review*, 22: 224–36.
Heddon, Deirdre, Carl Lavery and Phil Smith (2009), *Walking, Writing and Performance: Autobiographical Texts*, Bristol: Intellect Books.
Herbert, Jocelyn (1993), *Jocelyn Herbert: A Theatre Workbook*, London: Art Books International.
Hills, David (2017), 'Metaphor', *Stanford Encyclopedia of Philosophy* (Fall 2017 Edition), ed. Edward N. Zalta. Available online: https://plato.stanford.edu/archives/fall2017/entries/metaphor/ (accessed 1 July 2020).
Howard, Pamela (2002), *What is Scenography?*, London: Routledge.
Iball, Helen and Joslin McKinney (2011), 'Researching Scenography' in Helen Nicholson and Baz Kershaw (eds.), *Research Methods in Theatre and Performance*, Edinburgh: Edinburgh University Press, 111–36.
Jamie, Kathleen ([2008] 2012), 'Pathologies: A Startling Tour of Our Bodies' in *Sightlines*, London: Sort of Books, 21–41.

REFERENCES

Jeder, Daniela (2014), 'Transdisciplinarity – the Advantage of a Holistic Approach to Life', *Procedia – Social and Behavioural Sciences*, 137: 127–31.

Jones, Ffion (2010), 'Woollying the Boundaries: Perceptions of, and Interventions into, Upland Sheep Farming in Wales: Artistic and interdisciplinary methodological approaches to rural research', PhD thesis, Department of Theatre, Film and Television Studies, Aberystwyth University, Aberystwyth, Wales, UK.

Jones, Ffion (2010), *The Only Place We Ever Knew*, Cwmrhaiadr Farm, Powys/Ceredigion, Wales.

Kenyon, Simone (2019), 'About', *Into The Mountain*. Available online: http://www.intothemountain.co.uk/about/ (accessed 1 September 2021).

Knight, Paula J. (2013), 'Heredity' in *X Utero: A Cluster of Comics*. London: Word Press.

Lancaster Castle (2020), 'Lancashire Witch Trials', *Lancaster Castle*. Available online: http://www.lancastercastle.com/history-heritage/a-dark-history/lancashire-witch-trials/ (accessed 1 July 2020).

Leavy, Patricia (2015), *Method Meets Art: Arts-Based Research Practice*, London: Guilford Press.

Lehmann, Hans-Thies (2006), *Postdramatic Theatre*, trans. Karen Jurs-Munby, London: Routledge.

Lemon, Lee T. (1965), *Russian Formalist Criticism: Four Essays*, Lincoln, NE: University of Nebraska Press.

Levene, Ruth (2016), 'A Field of Wheat', *Ruth Levene*. Available online https://ruthlevene.co.uk/works/a-field-of-wheat (accessed 30 September 2021).

Levin, Susan. M. (1987), *Dorothy Wordsworth & Romanticism*, New Brunswick: Rutgers, The State University Press.

Lotker, Sodja and Richard Gough (eds.) (2013), 'On Scenography: Editorial', *Performance Research*, 18(3): 3–6.

MacFarlane, Robert (2012), *The Old Ways: A Journey on Foot*, London: Hamish Hamilton.

Machon, Josephine (2013), *Immersive Theatres: Intimacy and Immediacy in Contemporary Performance*, Basingstoke: Palgrave Macmillan.

Machon, Josephine and Louise Ann Wilson (2013), 'Immersed in the Environment: Off the Beaten Track' in Josephine Machon (ed.), *Immersive Theatres: Intimacy and Immediacy in Contemporary Performance*, London: Palgrave Macmillan, 229–40.

Madni, Azad M. (2007), 'Transdisciplinarity: Reaching beyond Disciplines to Find Connections', *Journal of Integrated Design and Process Science*, 11(1): 1–11.

Marranca, Bonnie (1976), *Theatre of Images*, Baltimore, MD: Johns Hopkins University Press.

McCracken, David (2013), 'WALK ON Highgreen: Farm Walk, David McCracken', *Visual Arts in Rural Communities*. Available online: http://varc.org.uk/projects/walk-on-highgreen-farm-walk (accessed 1 October 2013).

McKinney, Joslin (2013), 'Scenography, Spectacle and the Body of the Spectator', *Performance Research*, 18:(3): 63–74.

McKinney, Joslin (2017), 'Seeing Scenography' in *The Routledge Companion to Scenography*, ed. Arnold Aronson, Abingdon: Routledge, 102–18.

McKinney, Joslin and Scott Palmer (eds.) (2017), *Scenography Expanded: Contemporary Perspectives on Performance Design*, London: Methuen Drama.

McNiff, Shaun (ed.) (2013), 'Preface' in *Art as Research: Opportunities and Challenges*, Bristol: Intellect, xiii–xvi.

Mosley, Terrence I. (2017), 'Social Practice' in Stephen M. Eckert, Philip Gates, Rachel Karp, Sara Lyons, Terrence I. Mosley (authors) and Caden Manson (ed.), *Currents: The Contemporary Performance Think Tank*, New York: Contemporary Performance, 51–60.

Moses, Tabitha (2014a), 'A Note on Investment' in *Tabitha Moses Investment* (exhibition catalogue), Liverpool: Tabitha Moses.

Moses, Tabitha (2014b), *Tabitha's Gown* (embroidered artwork) in *Tabitha Moses Investment* (exhibition catalogue), Liverpool: Tabitha Moses.

Miles, Robert (1995), *Ann Radcliffe: The Great Enchantress*, Manchester: Manchester University Press.

National Theatre of Scotland (2013), 'Theatre Without Walls', *National Theatre of Scotland*. Available online: http://www.nationaltheatrescotland.com/content/ (accessed 1 October 2015).

National Theatre Wales (2011), '*The Passion*: About', *National Theatre Wales*. Available online: https://www.nationaltheatrewales.org/ntw_shows/the-passion/#about_ (accessed 1 September 2013).

National Theatre Wales (2013), 'We Are National Theatre Wales', *National Theatre Wales*. Available online: https://www.nationaltheatrewales.org/about-us/we-are-ntw/ (accessed 1 September 2013).

National Theatre Wales (2014–16), 'National Theatre Wales Community: The Big Democracy Project', *National Theatre Wales*. Available online: https://community.nationaltheatrewales.org/group/the-big-democracy (accessed 1 October 2016).

National Theatre Wales (2016), 'National Theatre Wales Community: The People's Platform: Merthyr', *National Theatre Wales*. Available online: https://community.nationaltheatrewales.org/events/the-peoples-platform-merthyr (accessed 1 September 2016).

Nicolescu, Basarab (2002), *Manifesto of Transdisciplinarity*, trans. Karen-Claire Voss, New York: State University of New York Press.

Palmer, Scott (2011) '3. Space. Introduction' in Jonathan Pitches and Sita Popat (eds.), *Performance Perspectives: A Critical Introduction*, Basingstoke: Palgrave Macmillan, 52–4.

Palmer, Scott and Louise Ann Wilson (2011), '3.2 Scenographic Space and Place. Louise Ann Wilson in Conversation with Scott Palmer' in Jonathan Pitches and Sita Popat (eds.), *Performance Perspectives: A Critical Introduction*, Basingstoke: Palgrave Macmillan, 63–74.

Pearson, Mike (2010), *Site-Specific Performance*, Basingstoke: Palgrave Macmillan.

Pipkin, John G. (1998), 'The Material Sublime of Women Romantic Poets', *Studies in English* Literature, *1500–1900*, 38: 597–619.

Pitches, Jonathan (2020), *Performing Mountains*, London: Palgrave Macmillan.

Pitches, Jonathan and Sita Popat (eds.) (2011), 'Scenographic Space and Place. Louise Ann Wilson in Conversation with Scott Palmer' in *Performance Perspectives: A Critical Introduction*, London: Palgrave Macmillan, 63–74.

Potash, Jordan (2020), 'Foreword' in Ali Coles and Helen Jury (eds.), *Art Therapy in Museums and Galleries: Reframing Practice*, London: Jessica Kingsley Publishers.

REFERENCES

Prague Quadrennial (2020), 'What is PQ?', Prague: PQ. Available online: https://www.pq.cz/what-is-pq/ (accessed 18 December 2020).
Probyn, Elspeth (1996), *Outside Belongings*, New York: Routledge.
Quarantine (2020a), 'About Us', *Quarantine*. Available online: https://qtine.com/about-us/ (accessed 1 June 2020).
Quarantine (2020b), 'Work: *Summer. Autumn. Winter. Spring*', *Quarantine*. Available online: https://qtine.com/work/summer-autumn-winter-spring/ (accessed 1 June 2020).
Radcliffe, Ann ([1795] 2014), *Observations during a Tour to the Lakes of Lancashire, Westmoreland, and Cumberland*, ed. Penny Bradshaw, Carlisle: Bookcase.
Radcliffe, Ann ([1797] 1981), *The Italian, or, The Confessional of the Black Penitents: A Romance*, ed. Fredrick Garber, intro. E. J. Clery, Oxford: Oxford University Press.
Roberts, Gwenant (2010), *Nantgwynant and Its Traditions*. Gwynedd: Gwenant Roberts.
Roff, Hermione (2014), 'Tracing the Ghost Harrier', (unpublished poem).
Sap Dance (2006), *The Saturated Moment*. Chor. Nigel Stewart, London: Royal Opera House.
Schechner, Richard (1968), '6 Axioms for Environmental Theatre', *Drama Review*, 12(3): 41–64.
Schechner, Richard (1971). On Environmental Design. *Educational Theatre Journal*, 23(4), 379–97.
Schechner, Richard (1973), *Environmental Theatre*, New York: Hawthorne Books, Inc.
Shaughnessy, Nicola (2012), *Applying Performance: Live Art, Socially Engaged Theatre and Effective Practice*, Basingstoke: Palgrave Macmillan.
Shearing, David (2019), 'Black Rock', *Performance Research*, 24(2): 36–44.
Shepherd, Nan (2011), *The Living Mountain*, Edinburgh: Canongate Books.
Small Acts (2021), 'About Us', *Small Acts*. Available online: https://small-acts.co.uk/small-acts/about/ (accessed 24 September 2021).
Smith, Rae (2021), 'Sketchbook', *Rae Smith*. Available online: http://www.raesmith.co.uk/sketchbook/ (accessed 11 January 2021).
Snyder, William C. (2001), 'Mother Nature's Other Natures: Landscape in Women's Writing, 1770–1830', *Women's Studies: An Inter-Disciplinary Journal*, 21: 143–62.
Solnit, Rebecca (2001), *Wanderlust: A History of Walking*, London: Verso.
Somewhere Nowhere (2014), '*Landkeepers*', *Somewhere Nowhere*. Available online: https://www.somewhere-nowhere.com/projects/landkeepers (accessed 1 December 2016).
Somewhere Nowhere (2016–17),'*Voices from the Land*', *Somewhere Nowhere*. Available online: https://www.somewhere-nowhere.com/projects/voices-from-the-land (accessed 1 December 2018).
Stewart, Michelle (1975), *Niagara Gorge Path Relocated*, Lewiston, NY: Artpark.
Stewart, Nigel (2015), 'Spectacle, World, Environment, Void: Understanding Nature through Rural Site-Specific Dance' in Victoria Hunter (ed.), *Moving Sites: Investigating Site-Specific Dance Performance*, London: Routledge, 364–84.
Stewart, Nigel and Louise Ann Wilson ([2008] 2009), *Still Life*, Morecambe Bay, Lancashire, UK.
Stewart, Nigel and Louise Ann Wilson (2010a), *Jack Scout*, Morecambe Bay, Lancashire, UK.
Stewart, Nigel and Louise Ann Wilson (2010b), 'Sap Dance and Louise Ann Wilson Company: Jack Scout', *Faculty of Arts and Social Science, Lancaster*

University. Available online: https://www.lancaster.ac.uk/fass/projects/jackscout/about.htm (accessed 27 September 2021).

Tate Gallery (2020a), 'Art Term: Socially Engaged Practice', *Tate Gallery*. Available online: https://www.tate.org.uk/art/art-terms/s/sociallyengaged-practice (accessed June 2020).

Tate Gallery (2020b), 'Art and Artists: Hamish Fulton', *Tate Gallery*. Available online: https://www.tate.org.uk/art/artists/hamish-fulton-1133 (accessed 1 January 2021).

Throsby, Karen (2004), *When IVF Fails: Feminism, Infertility and the Negotiation of Normality*, Basingstoke: Palgrave Macmillan.

Trimingham, Melissa (2017), 'Ecologies of Autism: Vibrant Spaces in Imagining Autism' in Joslin McKinney and Scott Palmer (eds.), *Scenography Expanded: Contemporary Perspectives and Performance Design*, London: Methuen Drama, 183–96.

Tuan, Yi-Fu (1977), *Space and Place: The Perspective of Experience*, Minneapolis, MA: University of Minnesota Press.

Turner, Cathy (2004), 'Palimpsest or Potential Space? Finding a Vocabulary for Site-Specific Performance', *New Theatre Quarterly*, 20: 373–90.

Turner, Edith (2012), *Communitas: The Anthropology of Collective Joy*, New York: Palgrave Macmillan.

Turner, Victor (1982), *From Ritual to Theatre: The Human Seriousness of Play*, New York: PAJ Books.

Usher, Graham B. (2012), *Places of Enchantment: Meeting God in Landscapes*, London: Society for Promoting Christian Knowledge.

van Gennep, Arnold (1960), *The Rites of Passage*, London: Routledge & Kegan Paul.

VARC (2005), 'Projects. *Gathering: Hill Farming, People, Animals and Landscape, 2004–2005*', *Visual Arts in Rural Communities (VARC)*. Available online: https://varc.org.uk/projects/gathering/ (accessed 1 September 2014).

Welfare State International (2006), 'About WSI', *Welfare State International*. Available online: https://www.welfare-state.org/pages/aboutwsi.htm (accessed 10 July 2019).

West, Thomas ([1778] 1802), *A Guide to the Lakes in Cumberland, Westmorland, and Lancashire*, 6th edition, London: W.J. & J. Richardson.

Willum Adrian, Stine (2019-ongoing), 'Technologies of Death and Dying at the Beginning of Life (Technodeath)', Aalborg: Aalborg University, Denmark. Available online: https://www.en.culture.aau.dk/research/projects/technodeath/ (accessed 21 September 2021).

Wilkie, Fiona (2002), 'Mapping the Terrain: A Survey of Site-Specific Performance in Britain', *New Theatre Quarterly*, 18: 140–60.

Wilkie, Fiona (2012), 'Site-Specific Performance and the Mobility Turn', *Contemporary Theatre Review*, 22: 203–212.

Wilkie, Fiona (2015), '"Three Miles an Hour": Pedestrian Travel' in *Performance, Transport and Mobility: Making Passage*, Basingstoke: Palgrave Macmillan, 18–45.

Wilson, Louise Ann (2011), *Fissure*, Ingleborough Fells, Yorkshire, England: Art Events.

Wilson, Louise Ann (2012), *Ghost Bird*, Langden Valley, Trough of Bowland, Lancashire: Green Close Studios, LAW Co, Lancaster Arts (formerly Live at LICA).

Wilson, Louise Ann (2014), *The Gathering / Yr Helfa*, Hafod y Llan Farm, Snowdonia, Wales: National Theatre Wales, Migrations and LAW Co.

REFERENCES

Wilson, Louise Ann (2015a), *Warnscale: A Land Mark Walk Reflecting on In/Fertility and Childlessness* (walking-performance: mapping- and launch-walks), Warnscale Fells, Cumbria: LAW Co.

Wilson, Louise Ann (2015b), *Warnscale: A Landmark Walk Reflecting on In/Fertility and Childlessness* (publication: walking guide/art book), Leeds: LAW Co.

Wilson, Louise Ann (2015c), '*Warnscale: A Landmark Walk Reflecting on In/fertility and Childlessness*', *Journal of Fertility Counselling*, 22(3): 24–8.

Wilson, Louise Ann (2016a), *Mulliontide* (unpublished performance script), Cornwall: Golden Tree Productions and LAW Co.

Wilson, Louise Ann (2016b), 'Creating Warnscale: Applying Dorothy Wordsworth's Mode of the Feminine Sublime to a Walking-Performance about In/Fertility and Childlessness', *Language, Landscape and the Sublime: A Two Day Symposium and Creative Gathering*, Schumacher College, Dartington, Devon (June 2016), art.earth. Available online: https://www.artdotearth.org/pdf/LLS/LA_Wilson.pdf (accessed 30 September 2020).

Wilson, Louise Ann (2016c), 'Emplacing, Re-Imaging and Transforming 'Missing' Life-Events: A Feminine Sublime Approach to the Creation of Socially-Engaged Scenography in Site-Specific Walking-Performance in Rural Landscapes', PhD thesis, Theatre Studies, Lancaster Institute for the Contemporary Arts, Lancaster University, UK.

Wilson, Louise Ann (2017), *Mulliontide: A Guide for Walkers* (publication), Leeds: LAW Co.

Wilson, Louise Ann (2018), *Dorothy's Room* (installation), Rydal Mount, Ambleside: LAW Co, Lancaster University and Wordsworth Grasmere.

Wilson, Louise Ann (2018–19), *Women's Walks to Remember: 'With memory I was there'*, Grasmere: LAW Co.

Wilson, Louise Ann (2019), 'Dorothy Wordsworth and her Female Contemporaries' Legacy: A Feminine "Material" Sublime Approach to the Creation of Walking-Performance in Mountainous Landscapes', *Performance Research*, 24(2): 109–11.

Wilson, Louise Ann (2020), *Walks to Remember During a Pandemic*, Lancaster: LAW Co.

Wilson, Louise Ann (2021), 'A Place that Stands Apart: Emplacing, re-imaging and transforming life-events through walking-performance in rural landscapes' in Silvia Batista (ed.), *The Performance of Sacred Places: Crossing, Breathing, Resisting*, Bristol: Intellect, 21–46.

Woof, Pamela (ed.) (1991), *The Grasmere and Alfoxden Journals*, Oxford: Oxford University Press.

Woof, Pamela (2015), 'Dorothy Wordsworth and Old Age', *The Wordsworth Circle* 46(3): 156–76.

Woolf, Virginia ([1972] 1978), 'Sketch of the Past' in *Moments of Being: Autobiographical Writings*, ed. Jeanne Schulkind, London: Triad/Panther, 71–159.

Wordsworth, Dorothy ([1824–35] 1978), 'Rydal Journals' (unpublished journals) in 'Dorothy Wordsworth's Rydal Journals, 1824–1835' (unpublished), ed. Carl H. Ketcham, *The Wordsworth Circle, Winter 1798* [1978 typographical error on the primary doc.], Jerwood Holdings: Journals. Ketcham's partial transcript: begins 1 December 1824.

Wordsworth, Dorothy (1824–35), *Rydal Journals*, Grasmere: The Jerwood Centre, Wordsworth Trust (Wordsworth Grasmere), DCMS 118.3. 12 February 1831–7

September 1833; DCMS 118.4. 6 February–3 October 1834; DCMS 118.5. 4 October 1834–4 November 1835.

Wordsworth, Dorothy ([1800–3] 1991), *The Grasmere and Alfoxden Journals*, ed. Pamela Woof, Oxford: Oxford University Press. First published 1897 by Ernest De Selincourt.

Wordsworth, William (1851), 'The Sparrow's Nest' in *The Complete Works*, Volume I, New York: Thomas Y. Crowall and Co.

Wrights & Sites (2001), 'Sketch for a Continuum of Site-Specific Performance' in 'Out of Place: The Politics of Site-Specific Performance in Contested Space (a performance presentation)', *Performance of Place Conference*, University of Birmingham (May), *Wrights & Sites*. Available online: http://www.mis-guide.com/ws/documents/politics.html (accessed 1 September 2016).

Wrights & Sites (2013), 'About', *Wrights & Sites*. Available online: http://www.mis-guide.com/ws/about.html (accessed 1 September 2016).

Index

Note: Productions and artworks are listed under the artist/maker or company. An italicised lower case '*n*' in a reference denotes a footnote, e.g. 5*n*33 refers to footnote 5 page 33. The letter '*f*' following locators refers to figures, e.g. 72*f* refers to a figure on page 72. The letter '*a*' denotes an appendix e.g. 208*a* refers to the appendix of page 208.

Abramovic, Marina
   The Lovers: The Great Wall Walk 4
alternative
   life-paths 41, 144, 149, 154, 157–8
   viewpoints and perspectives 5, 40, 42, 54, 66, 115, 116–18, 129, 132, 148, 151, 163–4, 179
   lying down 6–7, 42, 145, 148, 151, *see also* Haraway, Donna
   ways of seeing/thinking 41, 168
   See also close-up and observational looking; Scenographic Principles, Principles 6 and 7
applied scenography 1–2, 7–8, 11, 14, 20, 52, 101, 128–9, 135
   multiple applications 7, 181–3, 204
   See also scenography with purpose; socially engaged scenography
archive and family photos
   The Gathering 104, 111–12, 113–14, 118–19
   Women's Walks to Remember 194, 196, 197–8, 199–200
   See also objects (and photos), as scenographic tools
Aronson, Arnold 17, 19, 20, 22, 24–5
assemblage (scenographic) 106, 113–14, 150
   See also Bennett, Jane; storyboard
audience 2, 9, 11, 15, 18, 19, 21, 22, 24–5, 28, 40, 47, 83, 87, 98, 131, 133, 162, 194
   See also participant

autobiography, autobiographical scenography 2–3, 8, 13, 36, 37–8
   Fissure 45–6, 47–9, 50–1, 52–4, 55–9
   The Gathering 109–20
   Mulliontide 159–61, 164–5
   Warnscale 130, 132–5, 136, 138, 138*f*, 139–40, 139*f*, 140*f*
   See also Scenographic Principles, Principle 2; staying with the trouble
autotopography, autotopographical scenography 14, 37–8, 159–61, 165, 170
   See also objects; Scenographic Principles, Principle 2

Banham, Simon 23
   See also Quarantine
Barbauld, Anna Laetitia 35
Baseman, Jordan
   Cold Hand on a Cold Day, How to Manage Stillness, The Interval and the Instant 48
Baugh, Christopher 2, 3, 12, 13, 17–18, 20, 22, 164
Beer, Tanya (ecoscenography) 23
being located 34, 36–7, 108–9, 131–3
   See also feminine 'material' sublime; Scenographic Principles, Principle 1
Bellis, Kate and Matthews, Sally
   Gathering: Hill Farming, People, Animals and Landscape 107–9

INDEX

Bennett, Jane
   assemblage (agency of matter, vibrant matter) 114
   'thing-power' 105, 109–10
Berger, John 50, 67
Bowen, Keith 106, 109
Brada, Michael (neuro-oncologist) 46, 54–6, 5n56, 58, 58f, 6n58, 68–71
brain tumour (neurofunction and dysfunction) 45, 48, 51, 52–3, 56–8, 57f, 60–1, 67, 68–72, 72f, 75
   See also neuroscience/medicine
breast cancer 4, 50–1
Brotherus, Elena 5n33
   Annunciation series 116–17, 134–5
Burke, Edmund 34–5
Burns, Elizabeth, and *Fissure* 47–8, 53–5, 1n53, 3n56, 6n58, 60–1, 63, 69–73
Butterworth, Philip 18–19, 43–4, 83, 97
   See also McKinney, Joslin

CARE Fertility Group 138f, 140, 155
Carlson, Ann
   Picture Jasper Ridge Performance Hike 6
cave/caver
   Fissure 1, 46, 53, 54–5, 58f, 59–61, 67, 68, 69–70, 73–4
   Mulliontide 178–9, 178f
childlessness-by-circumstance (biological) 13, 109–10, 128, 130, 133–4, 142, 155, 156
   grief 133, 134–5, 139, 155
   See also involuntary childlessness; isolation/marginalization
choice of site and route *see* landscape/site; route
choir/singers 162
   Fissure 46, 52, 54, 59, 60–1, 63, 67, 69–70, 72–3
   The Gathering 104, 116, 119–21
   Mulliontide (The White Rose) 160, 169–70, 175–6, 180
   See also music and composition
choreography, movement and dance 5–7, 8, 20–1, 27, 27f, 37, 49, 52–3, 108–9, 164
   Fissure 52–3, 54, 67, 69–72, 72f, 74, 76
   Ghost Bird 80, 86, 90, 90f, 91, 94
   The Gathering 103–4, 106, 116, 118–21
   See also design, shepherds; site-specific dance; Stewart, Nigel
Clark, Chris (neurophysicist/imager) 46, 54, 56–8, 5n56, 57f, 58f, 69–70
Clarke, Gillian, and *The Gathering* 32, 105, 1n105, 119–21
close-up and observational looking 6–7, 38–9, 42–3, 50–1, 95, 109, 167–8, 185
   The Gathering 125–7
   Warnscale 130, 137, 138, 143, 145–6, 145f, 148, 151
   See also Scenographic Principles, Principles 6 and 7
co-creative 26, 28, 41, 101, 168, 183, 204
co-creation 194–200
Coleman, Simon 45, 62–3, 65–6, 74, 154
   See also Elsner, John
Collier, Tony and Green, Kate
   Mindwalks 4–5
Collins, Bridget and Jamie, Kathleen
   Frissures 50–1
Collins, Jane 21, 22, 28
   and Nisbett, Andrew 21, 28
communitas 4, 64–5, 76, 156, 179
   See also pilgrimage
composition (design) 6, 8, 21, 29, 37, 54, 67, 68–74, 85, 114, 139, 150
   composing the scene 39–40
   creating a scene 79, 81, 97
   design interventions 3, 54, 56, 68, 136
   orchestrating the landscape 66
   rules of 6, 40
   visual (non-verbal) 3, 6, 8, 21, 26, 37, 54, 85
   See also Scenographic Principles, Principle 4; silent (still) scenography; viewing
costume/clothes 9, 19, 21, 25, 26, 27, 27f, 68, 87, 107, 164
   The Gathering 106, 111–12, 118–21, 120f, 127
   Ghost Bird 90, 92–4, 92f, 93f
   Mulliontide 164, 168, 172, 172f, 177

INDEX

Cumming, Naomi
   'Grief Unconceived' 133–5
   quoted in *Warnscale* 148, 6n151
Curious 10
   Out of the Water 5–6
   Uproot 163
cynefin/heaf 109–13, 118, 122, 124, 148

defamiliarization (making strange) 32, 42–4, 95
   The Gathering 125–7
   See also moments of being; Scenographic Principles, Principle 7
Deiniolen Band 103–4, 113, 122–4, 162
democratization of process and performance 32, 161–3, 167–9
   See also site-specific performance
design process (creative methodology) 37, 106–7, 113–15, 150
   creative team 10, 36, 46, 51, 52, 56, 57f, 105
   collection of raw materials, field work (primary and secondary) 36–7, 51, 53, 55, 54–9, 57f, 58f, 83–5, 86, 96, 106, 109–12, 110f, 113, 123–8, 131–2, 137–9, 150–1, 184–5, 190
      comparable to Dorothy Wordsworth's (and contemporaries') journals 36, 37
      drawing/fieldnotes 37, 55–6, 86, 106, 110, 114, 137–9, 150–1, 183
      extended/in-depth research 9, 12, 21, 26, 46, 106–7, 107–9, 112–13, 114
      film, sound/voice recording 37, 54–8, 57f, 58f, 60, 68, 71, 72, 86, 106, 123–5, 126–7, 126f, 166, 185, 189–90
      photographing 37, 57f, 106, 114, 137f, 138f, 139f, 150–1, 183
   distillation of raw material 1, 37, 53–4, 59–61, 68, 86–7, 113–16, 123–8, 126f, 127–8, 131–3, 146, 151, 182–3, 187, 189–90, 194, 200
   See also archive and family photos; drawing; storyboards; transdisciplinary research, three strands
Di Benedetto, Stephen 8, 22
dialogue, dialogical process 10, 2n10, 163
Donald, Minty 23
Doughty, Karolina 4, 64–5
dramaturgy, scenographic (visual) 3, 8, 20–1, 26, 53–4, 59–62, 74, 97–8, 114
drawing (scenographic)
   as co-creative, participatory tool 101, 159, 195–6, 195f, 198–9, 198f, 202, 203
   as creative/thinking tool 3, 10, 16, 21, 101, 106–7, 183
   as design, communication tool 113, 114, 199–200
   as memory tool 198, 199–201
   attention 6, 31–2, 39, 63, 68, 80, 81, 96–7
   a walking-performance *out-of* and back *in-to* landscape 14, 39
   in a social science context 202–3
   in book pages, *Warnscale* 16, 147–8, 150–1, 156
   in or *with* the scene (scenography) 66, 67, 68–74, 114
   in the viewer/participant 151
   it out 106–7, 202–3
   looking, observational research tool 21, 37, 106–9, 150
   map-making 3, 113, 195–6, 198–9, 202–3
   See also composition; design process, storyboards; storyboard-memory card
   to capture raw material 37, 150
duration, distance (effort) 97–8, 144, 149, 179
   three days, *Fissure* 13, 45–6, 48, 54, 62–3, 75–7

Easter Trideum/Vigil 4
   Fissure 59–61, *see also* structure, structural elements (Days and Phases)

INDEX

effect/impact of scenography 15–16, 83, 114, 128
  empathetic, *Dorothy's Room* 192–3, *see also* empathy
  on community, *Mulliontide* 166
  on participants/social, *Warnscale* 49, 151, 152, 154–8, 7n155
  transformative, *Fissure* 46–7, 64, 65, 67, 74–7
  walking and immersion 4, 95, 96
  wellbeing, *Women's Walk to Remember* 183, 196–7
Elsner, John 45, 62–3, 65–6, 74, 154
  See also Coleman, Simon
embodied/multisensory scenography 3–4, 6–7, 8, 12, 29, 34, 46, 49, 52, 75, 82–3, 117, 135, 143–6, 170, 204
empathy, empathetic 19–20, 25, 53–4, 55, 95, 140, 165, 189–92
emplace, emplacing a life-event into a rural landscape 1–3, 37–8, 202–3
  meaning of term 54, 67
  Fissure 13, 37, 45, 53–5, 59, 65, 66–74, 72f
  The Gathering 113, 121–2
  Ghost Bird 86
  Warnscale 13, 146, 147–8, 7n155, 158–9
environmental forces as scenography (metaphoric use of) *see* landscape/site
environmental theatre/performance 24–5
ewes (and sheep), *The Gathering* 12, 103–5, 105–6, 107–11, 110f, 112, 114–15, 116, 118–19, 121–8, 126f
  wool/fleece 32, 110, 111, 112, 114, 118–20, 124–5, 127
  See also landscape/site, materials of/associated with; reproductive cycles
expanded scenography 1, 7, 11, 17–21, 22–3

farms, farming 11–12, 105, 106, 107–9, 163, 186–7, 200
  See also Hafod y Llan Farm
feedback/reflections 15–16
  non-verbal methods 99–101

feminine 'material' sublime 2, 11, 17, 33–6, 43
  scenographic, transformative qualities 2–3, 12
  See also Scenographic Principles; Wordsworth, Dorothy
Fertility Fest 155, 7n155
fertility treatment, IVF 116–17, 133–5, 167
  informing *The Gathering* 109–10
  in/forming *Warnscale* 130, 134–5, 136, 138, 138f, 140–1, 144, 148–9, 150–1, 155, 157–8
  See also Georgiades, Wanda; mapping-walks; transdisciplinary research, Strand 2
figure/s, human 5–6, 31
  naked 85, 93, 93f, 94, 95, 100
  See also solitary figure
film 4–5, 14, 37, 38, 48, 106, 107, 123–7, 185, 189–91, 192
frame/framing 12, 24–5, 31, 39–40, 116–18, 136, 147, 147f
  See also viewing/reviewing; viewing station and viewpoint
French and Mottershead 10
  Woodland (Afterlife Series) 7
Friedrich, Caspar David
  The Monk by the Sea 116
  Wanderer Above the Sea of Fog 40, 116
Fulton, Hamish 30
  Group Walk – Penzance Beach 6
Fusco, Maria
  Master Rock 5

Gateway Women 4n140, 153, 157
Gatrell, Antony 4, 65
  See also therapeutic landscapes and mobilities
Georgiades, Wanda (CARE Fertility Group) 140, 155
ghosting, ghost 28, 31, 71, 123–5, 127, 190–1
giving a voice (giving voice), centring people and place 26, 37, 161–3
  in *Mulliontide* 14, 159, 160–1, 163–5
  Mundy, Barry 173
  Pascoe, Jonny 164–5, 169, 173–4, 174f

INDEX

Ridley, Saul (palliative care nurse) 176–9, *see also* palliative care model/process
St Mellanus Singers 175–6, 175*f*, *see also* choir/singers
Whitehouse, Justin 165, 166, *see also* National Trust
Williamson, Wendy 159, 164, 172, 172*f*, 180
Women's Institute 170–1, *see also* Mulliontide flag
Golden Tree Productions
 Miss you Already 160, 166–7
Goldsworthy, Andy 7, 31
Gonzalez, Jennifer 14, 38, 159–60
Gough, Richard 3, 22–3, 81, 131
 See also Lotker, Sodja Zupanc
Grasmere Journals
 See also Wordsworth, Dorothy
grief (bereavement) and death 9, 37–8, 48–9, 202–3
 Fissure 9, 13, 45–6, 47–9, 50–1, 52–4, 55, 59–62, 73, 74, 76–7
 See also childlessness-by-circumstance; emplacing; staying with the trouble
guide/guiding 87, 95, 107, 142
 mountain guide 103
 Pointing People, *Ghost Bird* 84–5, 86, 87–8, 89, 90, 92–3, 92*f*, 93, 94
 self-guiding, *Mulliontide: A Guide for Walkers* 14, 161, 180
 signs, *Ghost Bird* 80, 86, 87–90, 91, 92, 94, 95, 96–8
 walking guide/art book, *Warnscale* 1, 13, 129–32, 131*f*, 150, 151–3

Haedicke, Susan 11–12
Hafod y Llan Farm 103–13, 110*f*, 115*f*, 120*f*, 118–22, 126*f*, 136, 162
Hann, Rachel 20–1
Haraway, Donna
 being located 36
 situated/embodied knowledge 132
 staying with the trouble 37, 49
Harrison, Ellie
 The Grief Series 48–9
Heddon, Deirdre 32–3, 38, 47, 59, 159–60
 and Turner, Cathy 4

hen harrier 80–4, 1*n*80, 87–92, 94–7
Holt, Nancy 7, 5*n*33
 Sun Tunnels 31
Howard, Pamela 21, 43–4, 114

Illingworth, Shona
 Lesions in the Landscape 5
immersion, immersive 3, 4–7, 9, 11, 14, 15, 16, 19, 28–9, 35, 41, 109, 161
 Dorothy's Room 181–2, 189–92
 Fissure 45–6, 62, 63, 64–5
 The Gathering 106–9
 Ghost Bird 87, 89, 95
 Warnscale 142–3, 143–5, 151
immobility, immobilization 4, 14, 182, 187–9, 197, 200
intergenerational performance 163–6
invisible scenography 131
involuntary childlessness 13, 130–1, 133–4, 136, 138–9, 141, 151, 155
 See also childlessness-by-circumstance
isolation/marginalization 1, 5, 14, 36, 201
 recognition and transformation, *Warnscale* 130–1, 133–5, 138, 140–3, 145–5, 149–50, 155–7
 See also childlessness-by-circumstance; 'missing' life-event

Jamie, Kathleen 5*n*33
 Frissures (with Collins, Bridget) 50–1
 'Pathologies' 50–1
Jones, Ffion
 The Only Place We Ever Knew 108–9
juxtaposition 32, 46, 63, 67, 74, 90, 97, 147, 149, 150

Kelly, Mike (geophysicist) 86, 137
 Fissure 46, 54, 55, 2*n*55, 3*n*55, 58, 58*f*, 70
Kenyon, Simone 5*n*33
 Into The Mountain 6–7
Knight, Paula
 'Heredity', *X Utero: A Cluster of Comics* 135

Laine, Jude (RSPB) 80, 83–5, 93, 96
Lancashire 'Pendle' Witches 13, 80–3, 81, 85, 88–91, 93–7
land art/environmental art 7, 17, 23, 30–2, 67, 80, 108, 127–8
  See also landscape/site, materials of/associated with
landmarks in the landscape 188
Landmarks/Stations, *Warnscale see* viewing station and viewpoint
landscape/site, choice of 45–6, 54–5, 67, 77, 80, 82, 85–6, 105–6, 118–21, 136, 137, 146, 167–9
landscape/site, environmental forces
  duration, distance (effort) 97–8, 144, 149, 179
  three days, *Fissure* 13, 45–6, 48, 54, 62–3, 75–7
  metaphorical use of landscape and environmental forces 5, 32, 34, 36, 38–9, 40–1, 42
    Fissure 47–8, 54, 59, 60–2, 67–9, 71, 72–3, 72f, 75, 76, 76f
    The Gathering 13, 103, 104, 106, 109–10, 118, 123, 127–8
    Ghost Bird 13, 79–80, 82–3, 85, 91, 95, 97–8
    Mulliontide 160–1, 167, 175–6, 175f, 177–9
    Warnscale 136, 137, 139, 143, 144, 147, 149–50, 158, 182
  See also Scenographic Principles, Principles 3, 4, 6; walking; weather as scenography
landscape/site, materials of/associated with 5, 6, 7, 9, 30–2, 38–40, 42–3
  Fissure 55, 59–60, 68
  The Gathering 103–5, 114, 111, 113–14, 118–21, 120f, 128, *see also* ewes, wool
  Ghost Bird 79–80, 83–6
  Mulliontide 179
  Warnscale 131–2, 150–1, 156
  See also objects; transdisciplinary research, Strand 1
Langden Castle 85, 86, 89–91, 90f
Langden Valley 80, 1n80, 82, 83, 85, 86, 88–9, 92f, 93f

Lavery, Carl
  Mourning Walk 4
Lee, Rosemary
  Passage for Par 5–6
legacy, lasting
  Mulliontide 159, 164–6, 180
  Warnscale 153
Lehmann, Hans-Thies 81, 97
life-event 1–2, 3, 4, 7–8, 10, 13–14, 32, 36–42, 204
  facing, transforming 13, 36, 59, 130
  Fissure 13, 46, 47, 49, 55–9
  The Gathering 109–10, 118, 125
  'missing', *Warnscale* 128, 129–32, 138, 139, 141, 150, 153
  real-world situations and outcomes 1–2, 3, 7, 36
  See also autobiography; staying with the trouble; transdisciplinary research, Strand 2
Lotker, Sodja Zupanc 3, 22–3, 81, 131
  See also Gough, Richard

MacFarlane, Robert 142, 186
Machon, Josephine 11, 3n11
mapping-walks, *Warnscale* 13, 129, 139–40, 151, 154, 157, 183
  callout and participants 133, 139f, 139–41
  framing (*Grasmere Journals*) 143–5
  process 140f, 142–6
  See also transdisciplinary research, Strand 3
Marranca, Bonnie, 'theatre of images' 79
masculine 'transcendent' sublime 34–6, 49
  gendering of, and exclusion of women 34–5
McCracken, David
  Farm Walk 108–9
McEvoy, Andy (neurosurgeon) 46, 54, 56–8, 57f
McKinney, Joslin 75, 81, 98
  and Butterworth, Philip 18–19, 43–4, 83, 97
  and Iball, Helen 8
  and Palmer, Scott 19, 22, 29, 97

INDEX

McLucas, Cliff 28
meaning, making meaning (unique/personal to participant) 27, 27f, 59, 74–7, 96–8, 99–100, 146
   co-construction 74, 81, 89, 91, 94–5, 114, 128
      scenographic exchange 97–8
   cumulative effect 67, 98, 116
   multiple 27–8, 47, 70, 97–8, 103, 117, 127–8, 155, 199, *see also* polysemous
memory-mapping 182–3, 194–9, 201
   memory-maps 182, 194, 195f, 198f, 199
   multiple applications 200–3, 204
   storyboard/memory card 182–3, 187, 194, 199–200
   See also Potter, Harold; surrogate walk/ing
memory-walk/walking 14, 193–4
memory-walker/mapper, *Women's Walks to Remember* 182, 183, 193–5
   Crayston, Margaret 195–7, 195f, 199–200
   Fraser, Harriet 197–8, 199–200
   Heim, Wallace 192, 197, 199–200
   McLaren, Joanna 192, 197, 199–200
   Peel, Jill 193–94, 198–9, 198f
   Walks to Remember During a Pandemic 201
   See also Wordsworth, Dorothy, *Rydal Journals*
Mendieta, Ana 7, 5n33
   Silueta (*Silhouette*) 31
metaphor, metaphorical *see* landscape/site, environmental forces
metaphor, metaphorical 5, 32, 34, 36, 38–9, 40–1, 42
methodology *see* transdisciplinary research
moments of being 42–3, 143, 187
   See also Scenographic Principles, Principle 7
Moses, Tabitha
   Investment 134–5
   Island of Blood and Longing 134

mountain (fell) 5, 6–7, 12
   association with transformation 136
   in performance/art 1, 4–7, 10–12, 13, 14, 66, 75–7, 76f, 136
Mullion Cove/Mullion, Cornwall, UK 14, 160, 164–6, 166–9
multimedia installation 5
   Dorothy's Room 14, 181–2, 189–92
   The Gathering 104, 106, 124–7, 126f
multimodal scenography 46, 49, 59, 67, 75–6
music and composition 6, 37, 39, 49, 54, 59, 67, 73–4, 76, 104, 105, 123–4
   See also poetry, sung poetry; sound

National Theatre Wales
   The Gathering 103, 105, 162
   The Passion of Port Talbot, *Big Democracy* Project, *People's Platform: Merthyr* 161–2
National Trust 10, 106
   Mulliontide 160, 165, 166–7, 173
neuroscience/medicine, neurology 46, 51, 53, 54–8, 5n56, 57f, 58f, 60–1, 67–8, 69–74
   See also Brada, Mike; brain tumour; Clark, Chris; McEvoy, Andy; structure, structural elements, *Fissure*
NVA
   The Storr: Unfolding Landscapes 5

objects (and photos), as scenographic tools 4, 5, 14, 38–40, 43–4, 130, 204
   Dorothy's Room 190–2
   Fissure 49, 52, 54, 55, 60–1, 65–6, 68
   The Gathering 104, 105, 111–12, 113–14, 116, 118–21, 123–8, *see also* 'thing-power'
   Ghost Bird 84–5, 86, 90–4
   Mulliontide 159–61, 164, 168, 170–1, 172–6, *see also* autotopography

Women's Walks to Remember 183, 187, 194, 195–200, 195f
   See also archive and family photos; landscape/site, materials
other-than-human 6, 13, 23, 43, 52, 67, 106, 189–90
outside belonging 37, 130–1
   See also Probyn, Elspeth

palliative care model/process 46, 170, 176–9
palliative curation 167
Palmer, Scott 8, 11, 17, 66, 114
   and McKinney, Joslin 19, 22, 29, 97
   and Wilson, Louise Ann 26
participant/s 3, 11, 14, 15, 22
   active, engaged 23, 25–6, 28–30, 32
   co-creative 26, 27–8, 97–8, 101, 168, 183, 194, 204
   as collaborator (contributor/performer) 159, 161, *see also* giving a voice
      mapping-walk 133, 139–41, 139f, 140f
   participant rather than audience 15
   performing actions 4, 7, 42, 143, 145, 145f, 146–7, 148–9, 151, 156, 160, 168, 170, 178
   as pilgrim 62–6, 74–7, 173
      as agent of change 154
   in site-specific performance 11, 28–30, 30f, 32
   subject-specific 2, 37, 39–42, 128, 139–40
   as temporary community 10, 62–3, 64, 163, 204
   in walking-performance 39–42, 45, 74–7, 76f, 79–80, 96
Pearson, Mike 27–8, 3n28
performance/theatre *see* environmental theatre; site-specific performance
performer/performers
   city as performer (incidental) 29
   people (and animals) of the place 14, 23, 46, 103–4, 108–9, 115, 122–7, 159, 160–1, 161–3, 165, 168–9, 171, 180, *see also* giving a voice

   professional (dancers, singers, actors) 4–6, 29, 30f, 46, 59, 67, 86, 103–4, 162
   life models 86
   self-performed *Warnscale* 1, 13, 129–32, 131f, 150, 151–3
   Mulliontide: A Guide for Walkers 161, 180
   subject/place-specific experts 46, 54, 67, 103, 119, 122–3, 2n123, 162, 164, *see also* neuroscience/medicine; shepherds
pilgrim/pilgrimage 4, 13, 62–6, 154
Pitches, Jonathan 12
   and Popat, Sita 11
poetry, poetic text 5, 37, 108, 135
   sung poetry 104
      factual-poetic text 105, 122, 123, 2n123, 124
      Fissure 46, 47–8, 49, 53–5, 5n56, 6n58, 60–1, 63, 69–73, *see also* Burns, Elizabeth
      The Gathering 104–5, 116, 118–21, 122, *see also* Clarke, Gillian
      Women's Walks to Remember 187, 194, 200
Poldhu Care Home 14, 165, 171, 181, 184–6, 189
polysemous, polysemiotic 97, 103
Pook, Jocelyn, and *Fissure* 55, 59
Potter, Harold (memory walker) 181, 184–7, 184f, 185f, 189
   See also Skype exchange
practice-led research 8, 19, 20, 207a, 208a
   See also scenographer-researcher
Prague Quadrennial 18, 1n18
Principle *see* Scenographic Principles
Probyn, Elspeth 37, 130–1
processional walk/ing 3, 160, 170–1

Quarantine 10
   Summer. Autumn. Winter. Spring 23

Radcliffe, Ann 3, 5n33, 36, 37–8, 40, 117–18
reproductive cycles (animal and human) 13, 103, 104–5, 106, 110, 110f, 125, 137

INDEX

See also ewes
research (creative) *see* design process; transdisciplinary research
rite of passage 13, 45, 64, 130–1, 163
   absence of 130
   ritual phases (separation, transition, incorporation), *Fissure* 46, 62–6
   transition places 1, 142–3, 146, 147
ritual 13, 46, 52, 62–6, 129, 141, 153, 163
   social, lack of 48–9
Roberts, Celia (social scientist) 129
Roff, Hermione
   'Tracing the Ghost Harrier' 99–101
Romanticism, early 17, 34, 40
route, choice of 54–5, 67, 73, 75–6, 103–4, 106, 114–15, 127, 132, 136, 137, 142–3, 146, 160, 168, 169–70
RSPB 10, 80, 1*n*80, 83
   See also Laine, Jude
Rydal Journals see Wordsworth, Dorothy
Rydal Mount, Lake District, Cumbria, UK 182, 187–90, 192

Santana, Fabiola
   Home for Grief 49
Sap Dance 6, 52–3
scenic/scenographic interventions 24, 28, 54, 67, 85
scenographer 7–9, 19–23
   adoption of term 20
   skills 8
scenographer-researcher 5, 10–12, 19–23
   See also practice-led research
scenographic language 6, 12, 25, 33–4, 46, 49, 52–3, 79, 83, 84, 204
   suitably for transforming life-events (transcend limitation of language) 32, 46, 48, 49–50, 52, 83, 201, 202–3, 204
   See also composition; embodied/multisensory scenography;

multimodal scenography; silent (still) scenography
Scenographic Principles 2–3, 12, 17, 19, 32–44
   Principle 1 36–7
   Principle 2 37–8
   Principle 3 38–9
   Principle 4 39–40
   Principle 5 40–1
   Principle 6 42
   Principle 7 42–4
scenographic walkscape 2, 65
scenography 1–3, 7–9, 17–25, 27
   definitions of 17, 66
   See also applied scenography; socially engaged scenography; scenographic language
scenography expanded 1, 7, 11, 17–20, 22
scenography with purpose 2, 3, 12, 13, 17–19, 44, 81, 158
   See also Baugh, Christopher
Schechner, Richard 24–5
Shaughnessy, Nicola 163, 165
   Imagining Autism 19–20
Shearing, David 22
   Black Rock 5
sheep
   informing design and writing 111, 118–19
   as performers (live and mediated) 115, 122–7
   See also ewes; landscape/site, materials (and object); objects
Shepherd, Nan 5*n*33
   The Living Mountain 6
shepherds, *The Gathering*
   informing design and choreography 105, 107–10, 111–12, 114–15, 115*f*, 118, 121, 124
   as performers 103, 119, 122–3, 2*n*123, 162
Shklovskii, Viktor 43
silent (still) scenography, performance 7, 13, 79, 80, 87–9, 96
   stillness 6, 25, 27, 27*f*, 66, 79, 81, 84–5, 91, 92, 96, 107, 119, 148, 151, 179
   stripping out word, text and narrative 79, 80, 87–94, 96–7, 98

INDEX

tableaux vivant (living pictures) 5–6, 10, 27, 27f, 81
'theatre of images' 79–81
site of transformation 1–3, 8, 12–13, 45, 133, 135, 136, 158, 179
site-specific dance performance 5–6, 10, 27, 27f, 87
site-specific performance 9, 10–12, 23–31, 27f, 32, 67, 87, 161–3, 167–9
   born out of the landscape/site 26, 54, 67
   evolution of term 23–8, 30–1
   mobilization of performance and participants 28–30, 30f
   models of practice
      archaeological (stratigraphy) 27–8
      excavatory process 26
      host, ghost, witness 28
      palimpsest 27
      place and work co-creative 26
   See also land art/environmental art; walking-performance
site-specific performance-installation (live art)
   The Gathering, Tramway Walker 105, 113, 115, 127–8
   Ghost Bird 79–80, 90–4, 90f, 92f, 93f, 95, 97–8
site/landscape *see* landscape/site
situated/embodied knowledge 131–2, 137–9
   See also being located; Haraway, Donna; Scenographic Principles, Principle 2
Skype exchange 185–7, 185f, 200–1, 203
Small Acts 10
   Future Feast 163
   Public House 163
Smith, Charlotte 2, 5n33, 36, 37–8, 40, 42
Smith, Rae 107
Smithson, Robert 31
Snowdon (Mount), Wales, UK, *The Gathering* 106, 119, 122, 124
   See also Hafod y Llan Farm
social engagement 10, 44, 135, 163, 191–2

socially engaged performance 10, 23, 26, 161–3
socially engaged scenography 1–2, 7, 8, 11, 14, 18, 20, 23, 101, 128, 204
   Mulliontide 163–6
   See also applied scenography
solitary figure/s (in the landscape) 6, 12, 39, 84–5, 93–4, 95, 105, 116, 151
   Pointing People, *Ghost Bird* 86, 89–90, 92–3, 92f, 94
   female 3, 27, 27f, 31, 36, 37–8, 40, 42, 116–18, 134–5
      The Gathering 104–5, 112, 116, 118–21, 120f, 127–8
      Ghost Bird 84–5, 90, 93f
      Warnscale 151, 152f
   male 40, 92f, 116
   See also figure/s, human
solitary plant/flower 31, 39, 144, 149–50
Solnit, Rebecca 3, 40–1
Somewhere Nowhere 7
   Landkeepers and *Voices from the Land* 108–9
   Yellow at the Wasdale Oak 31–2
sound, soundscape 2, 6, 7, 8, 14, 19, 25, 39, 123
   environmental (live) 6, 66, 69
   ghosting 123–4, 127
   installations 54, 55, 60, 67, 68, 71, 72–3, 91, 104, 106, 124–5, 126–7, 190, 191
   See also collection, recording of raw materials
Spivak, Gayatri Chakravorty 156
spots of time 187
   See also Wordsworth, William
Stations *see* viewing station and viewpoint
stations of the cross 171
staying with the trouble 13, 37–8, 49–51
   See also Haraway, Donna; Scenographic Principles, Principle 2
Stewart, Michelle 7, 5n33
   Niagara Gorge Path Relocated 31
Stewart, Nigel
   Fissure 52–3, 69–72, 72f, 74

INDEX

The Gathering 103–4, 105, 106, 116, 118–21
Ghost Bird 86, 90, 90f, 91, 94
Jack Scout (with Wilson, Louise Ann) 6, 10, 2n10, 32, 87, 99
Saturated Moment 52–3
Still Life (with Wilson, Louise Ann) 6, 10, 27, 27f, 87
See also Sap Dance
stitching, embroidery
  Dorothy's Room, 190–2
  Mulliontide flag 159, 160, 170–1, 192
storyboard/memory card *see* memory-mapping
storyboards, storyboarding 3, 8–9, 12, 14
  assemblage 106, 114, 150, *see also* Bennet, Jane
  palimpsest 113, 199
  in book pages, *Warnscale* 150–1
  collage/montage 114, 150, 151, 199
  The Gathering 113–15, 115f
  as scenographic, design/ communication tool 8–9, 14, 21, 107, 113–15
  strategic essentialism 157
structure, structural elements 3–4, 9, 11
  Fissure (Days and Phases) 13, 53–4, 56, 59–62, 64–6
  Mulliontide (Stations) 160, 169–79, *see also* choir/singers
  palliative care model stations
  Warnscale (Phases and Landmarks/Station) 132, 146–50
sublime 11–12, 34–5, 40
  See also feminine 'material' sublime; masculine 'transcendent' sublime
surrogate walk/ing 14, 41, 181–2, 183, 184–6, 184f, 193–200

Tanning, Dorothea
  Self-Portrait 116
theatre and performance design/er 7–10, 18, 1n18, 19, 21–2, 23, 24–5, *see also* scenographer

therapeutic landscapes and mobilities 4, 64–5
therapeutic scenography 1, 4, 41, 64–5, 101, 181
  See also transformation, transformative
thing-power 105, 109–10
  See also Bennett, Jane
topophilia 169
transdisciplinary, methodology 2, 3, 7–8, 13, 36–7, 51–2
  Fissure 13, 46, 51–2, 54–9, 57f, 58f
  for socially engaged and applied scenography
  three strands of research 2, 36–7, 54, 106, 113, 131–3, 137
    Strand 1, site/landscape-specific 2, 36, 54–5, 58–9, 137, 137f
    Strand 2, life-event/subject-specific 2, 37, 54–9, 138, 138f
    Strand 3, people/participant-specific 2, 38, 139, 139f
  Warnscale 131–3, 137–9, 137f, 138f, 139f, 140–1, 140f, 150, 155
  See also Scenographic Principles, Principle 1
transformation 45, 46, 51, 65, 133, 136, 144–5, 149, 204
transformative (revelatory/ therapeutic) effect 1, 2, 4, 6–7, 12, 19–20, 43, 41, 43, 45, 64–5, 75, 100, 128, 129, 144–5, 181, 182, 183, 192
  See also site of transformation
Trimingham, Melissa 22
  Imagining Autism 19–20
triptych 90, 124, 125–7, 126f, 173
Trough of Bowland, Lancashire, UK 80, 85, 89
  See also Langden Valley
Turner, Cathy 26, 27, 28
  and Heddon, Deirdre 4
Turner, Edith 64
Turner, Victor 64
Tuulikki, Hanna
  Away with the Birds, Women of the Hill 5

van Gennep, Arnold 13, 62, 154
    See also rite of passage, ritual phases, Fissure
view/s from somewhere 36, 132
    See also being located
viewing devices
    geology eye glass/lens 130, 137, 143, 145–6, 146f, 148, 151
    microscope/microscopic 50–1, 138, 146, 148
    See also close-up and observational looking
viewing station and viewpoint 12, 39–40, 146
    The Gathering 114–15
    Landmark/Stations, Warnscale 137, 137f, 139f, 146, 147–50, 147f, 151, 152f, 157, 180–90
    picturesque 12, 39–40
    Stations, Mulliontide 160, 166, 169–70, 171–5, 172f, 174f, 175f, 177–9, 178f
    See also frame/framing
viewing/reviewing 40, 118, 147, 147f
    window 39, 40, 117–18, 136, 147, 147f, 188, 190
visual (non-verbal) scenography see composition; scenographic language; silent (still) scenography

walking guide/art book, Warnscale 129–31, 131f, 132, 133, 146, 147–50, 151–3, 151f
    as memory/revisiting tool 158, 182
    as scenographic tool 14, 150–2, 153
    self-guided and performed 1, 13, 129–32, 131f, 150, 151–3
    storyboard, multi-layered 155–6, 157
    as tool for conversation, understanding and change 153–5
walking women 2–3, 4–5, 6–7, 14, 32–4, 5n33, 35–6, 40–1, 42–3, 142–3, 187–90, 193–4, 195–9
    See also Wordsworth, Dorothy
walking-performance, site-specific 1–2, 3–6, 7, 8–12, 13–14, 17, 30, 35, 37, 39, 40–1, 54, 67

Fissure 13, 45, 52, 54
The Gathering 13, 103, 128
Ghost Bird 13, 79–80, 86
Mulliontide 14, 159–60, 166, 181–2
scenographic landscape, moving through the scene 39–40
walkscape 2, 65
site-, subject- and person-specific 20
Warnscale 13, 129–30, 133, 136, 139
walking, practices 3–4, 7–8, 30, 65–6
    beyond knowledge 40–1
    as metaphor 40–1, 179
    See also Scenographic Principles, Principle 5
Warnscale Fells, Lake District, UK 131f, 137, 137f, 139f, 145f, 147f, 158
weather as scenography 6, 13, 71, 76, 84, 93–5, 142–5, 148, 151
Welfare State International 162–3
Wilkie, Fiona 26, 29
Willum Adrian, Stine 202–3
Wilson, Louise Ann
    background, training, theatre designer/scenographer 8–10
    Dorothy's Room 5, 14, 181–3, 189–93
    Fissure 9–10, 11, 13, 37, 45–77, 57f, 58f, 72f, 76f
    Ghost Bird 13, 16, 79–101, 90f, 92f, 93f
    The Gathering 12, 13, 32, 87, 103–7, 109–28, 110f, 115f, 120f, 126f
    Harold Potter's 'Walk to Remember' 184–7, 184f, 185f, 189
    Jack Scout (with Stewart, Nigel, Sap Dance) 6, 10, 2n10, 32, 87, 99
    Mulliontide 14, 46, 159–61, 163–80, 172f, 174f, 175f, 178f, 184
    Mulliontide: A Guide for Walkers 14, 161, 180
    scenographer-researcher 10–13, 20
    Still Life (with Stewart, Nigel, Sap Dance) 6, 10, 27, 27f, 87
    Walks to Remember During a Pandemic 201

Warnscale 1, 12, 16, 35, 101, 128, 129–58, 131*f*, 137*f*, 138*f*, 139*f*, 140*f*, 145*f*, 147*f*, 152*f*, 182, 183, 202
Women's Walks to Remember: 'With memory I was there' 5, 14, 16, 101, 181–3, 192–200, 195*f*, 198*f*
See also Scenographic Principles; wilson+wilson company
Wilson, Wils 9
See also wilson+wilson company
wilson+wilson company 9, 11, 23–4, 26, 28–30, 30*f*, 32, 87, 99
House 9, 26, 29, 32
Mapping the Edge (city as stage) 9, 26, 29–30, 30*f*
Mulgrave 9, 29, 32
News from the Seventh Floor 9, 29
See also site-specific performance, models of practice
Wollstonecraft, Mary 35
wonderment 42–4, 104, 107, 125–7, 179
See also defamiliarization; Scenographic Principles, Principle 7
Woolf, Virginia 42–4, 143, 187
Wordsworth, Dorothy 17, 33, 182
feminine 'material' sublime 34–5, 36, 43
Grasmere Journals 32, 35–6
in/forming, framing *Warnscale* 143–5, 147–50, 151, 182
influence on landscape aesthetics 5n33
informing Scenographic Principles 2, 12, 17, 36–43
Rydal Journals 14, 181, 183, 187–9
in/forming *Dorothy's Room* 189–92
Scafell Pike Account 32–4, 5n33
scenographic qualities 2–3, 12, 33–4
sound 33–4, 35, 41, 42, 43, 188–90
visuality 35, 37, 41, 148, 188–90
therapeutic 2, 12, 14, 19–20, 33, 188, 193, 200–1
See also Radcliffe, Ann; Smith, Charlotte
Wordsworth, William 5n33, 35, 37, 41, 188
'spots of time' 187
Wrights & Sites 10, 23–4

Yorkshire Dales, UK 108
Fissure 45, 54, 58*f*, 62, 62–6, 68, 72*f*, 76*f*
See also landscape/site, choice of

www.ingramcontent.com/pod-product-compliance
Lightning Source LLC
Chambersburg PA
CBHW062144300426
44115CB00012BA/2031